UNPACKING IKEA

This book represents the first anthropological ethnography of Ikea consumption and goes to the heart of understanding the unique and at times frantic popularity of this iconic transnational store. Based on a year of participant observation in Stockholm's Kungens Kurva store – the largest in the world – this book places the retailer squarely within the realm of the homebuilding efforts of individuals in Stockholm and to a lesser degree in Dublin. Ikea, the world's largest retailer, is the focus of intense popular fascination internationally, yet is rarely subject to in-depth anthropological inquiry. In *Unpacking IKEA*, Garvey explores why Ikea is never 'just a brand' for her respondents, and questions why it is described in terms of a cultural package, as everyday and classless. Using in-depth interviews with householders over several years, this ethnographic study follows the furniture from the Ikea store outwards to probe what people actually take home with them.

Pauline Garvey is senior lecturer in the Department of Anthropology at Maynooth University, Maynooth, County Kildare, Ireland.

Culture, Economy and the Social
A new series from CRESC – the ESRC Centre for Research on Socio-cultural Change

Editors
Professor Tony Bennett, Social and Cultural Theory, University of Western Sydney; Professor Penny Harvey, Anthropology, Manchester University; Professor Kevin Hetherington, Geography, Open University

Editorial Advisory Board
Andrew Barry, University of Oxford; Michel Callon, Ecole des Mines de Paris; Dipesh Chakrabarty, The University of Chicago; Mike Crang, University of Durham; Tim Dant, Lancaster University; Jean-Louis Fabiani, Ecoles de Hautes Etudes en Sciences Sociales; Antoine Hennion, Paris Institute of Technology; Eric Hirsch, Brunel University; John Law, The Open University; Randy Martin, New York University; Timothy Mitchell, Columbia University; Rolland Munro, Keele University; Andrew Pickering, University of Exeter; Mary Poovey, New York University; Hugh Willmott, University of Cardiff; Sharon Zukin, Brooklyn College City University New York / Graduate School, City University of New York

The *Culture, Economy and the Social* series is committed to innovative contemporary, comparative and historical work on the relations between social, cultural and economic change. It publishes empirically-based research that is theoretically informed, that critically examines the ways in which social, cultural and economic change is framed and made visible, and that is attentive to perspectives that tend to be ignored or side-lined by grand theorising or epochal accounts of social change. The series addresses the diverse manifestations of contemporary capitalism, and considers the various ways in which the 'social', 'the cultural' and 'the economic' are apprehended as tangible sites of value and practice. It is explicitly comparative, publishing books that work across disciplinary perspectives, cross-culturally, or across different historical periods.

The series is actively engaged in the analysis of the different theoretical traditions that have contributed to the development of the `cultural turn' with a view to clarifying where these approaches converge and where they diverge on a particular issue. It is equally concerned to explore the new critical agendas emerging from current critiques of the cultural turn: those associated with the descriptive turn for example. Our commitment to interdisciplinarity thus aims at enriching theoretical and methodological discussion, building awareness of the common ground that has emerged in the past decade, and thinking through what is at stake in those approaches that resist integration to a common analytical model.

Other series titles include:

Markets and the Arts of Attachment
Edited by Franck Cochoy, Joe Deville and Liz McFall

The Known Economy
Romantics, Rationalists, and the Making of a World Scale
Colin Danby

UNPACKING IKEA

Swedish Design for the Purchasing Masses

Pauline Garvey

E·S·R·C
ECONOMIC
& SOCIAL
RESEARCH
COUNCIL

First published 2018
by Routledge
2 Park Square, Milton Park, Abingdon, Oxon OX14 4RN

and by Routledge
711 Third Avenue, New York, NY 10017

Routledge is an imprint of the Taylor & Francis Group, an informa business

© 2018 Pauline Garvey

The right of Pauline Garvey to be identified as author of this work has been asserted by her in accordance with sections 77 and 78 of the Copyright, Designs and Patents Act 1988.

All rights reserved. No part of this book may be reprinted or reproduced or utilised in any form or by any electronic, mechanical, or other means, now known or hereafter invented, including photocopying and recording, or in any information storage or retrieval system, without permission in writing from the publishers.

Trademark notice: Product or corporate names may be trademarks or registered trademarks, and are used only for identification and explanation without intent to infringe.

British Library Cataloguing-in-Publication Data
A catalogue record for this book is available from the British Library

Library of Congress Cataloging-in-Publication Data
Names: Garvey, Pauline, 1971– author.
Title: Unpacking IKEA : Swedish design for the purchasing masses / Pauline Garvey.
Description: 1 Edition. | New York : Routledge, 2018. | Includes bibliographical references and index.
Identifiers: LCCN 2017029615 | ISBN 9781138793965 (hardback) | ISBN 9781315760704 (e-book)
Subjects: LCSH: Ikea (Firm)—History. | Furniture design—Sweden. | Industrial design—Sweden. | Product differentiation—Sweden.
Classification: LCC NK2595 .G37 2018 | DDC 749.09485—dc23
LC record available at https://lccn.loc.gov/2017029615

ISBN: 978-1-138-79396-5 (hbk)
ISBN: 978-0-8153-9395-5 (pbk)
ISBN: 978-1-315-76070-4 (ebk)

Typeset in Bembo
by Apex CoVantage, LLC

For Hugh

CONTENTS

List of figures ix
Acknowledgements xi

1 Unpacking Ikea   1
   Introduction 1
   Extraordinary claims for ordinary things 4
   *Ikea at large: exhibition spaces, media discourse, popular
       perceptions 5*
   Ikea-in-the-abstract: retailer and brand 9
   Brand as material culture 11
   This book 12
   Setting the scene: visiting Ikea in Kungens Kurva 16
   Inside the Ikea store 17

2 Benign intervention: Ikea showrooms as tableaux vivant   27
   'Now Ikea is into design!' 30
   *Setting up the showrooms: international modernism, traditional,
       Scandinavian modernism and young 32*
   Inspiration 37
   Design and agency 38
   Showrooms as traps 39
   'It is like a designer is in my home' 43
   Tableaux vivant 46

3   Home staging, housing theatre: design, domesticity and the
    People's Home   51
    Placing the home centre stage 53
    Skansen and spatial effigies 54
    The home and social reform 56
    The material culture of social democracy 59
    Revolution from below 63
    Home staging 68
    Design legacies 69

4   Standardisation, democracy and equality: design for the
    many people   76
    Democracy and consensus 78
    Democratic design 79
    Everyday design 81
    The launch of diversity 83
    Post-standardisation 88
    The impact of ubiquity 91
    Managing ubiquity: Anders and Mia 92
    Standardisation and equality: Ikea as aggregate practice 94
    Fashion as investiture 97

5   Storage solutions: Clutter and Containment   103
    Storage solutions 106
    The suppression of clutter 107
    Good housing 109
    The material minutiae of storage practices 110
    *Home staging/the home as stage: 'We want to enjoy the
        emptiness!' 116*
    *Emotional economies, colourful environments, animated
        surfaces 119*
    What does Swedish style make possible? 123

6   Still life?: circulation, emotion and mobility   130
    Circular Ikea and informal markets 131
    Flea markets, mixing and matching 133
    Shopping for inspiration 136
    Thrift, inspiration and gender 137
    Social isolation and loneliness 140
    The domestic nexus 144

Epilogue   149
Index   154

FIGURES

1.1	The arrivals atrium in Ikea Kungens Kurva.	15
1.2	Interior of Ikea Kungens Kurva, illustrating the corkscrew plan partly inspired by the Guggenheim Museum in New York.	18
2.1	Children's drawings hanging in one of the 'houses' in Ikea Kungens Kurva.	35
2.2	Photographs of fictional family members in showrooms in Ikea Kungens Kurva.	35
2.3	Knitting needles and wool on a shelf in a showroom in Ikea Kungens Kurva.	36
2.4	Shoppers trying out furniture in Ikea Kungens Kurva.	36
2.5	Shoppers trying out furniture in Ikea Dublin.	44
2.6	Beds in the Ikea showroom in Dublin with a sign encouraging shoppers to try them out.	45
3.1	A Carl Larsson painting used by the National Museum of Stockholm in an advertising campaign in 2008. The pairing of the painting with an icon of modern design (Jonas Bohlin's concrete chair) signifies a bridge from past to present.	57
3.2	A bedroom from the Accept exhibition.	61
3.3	Research into efficient kitchen practices.	64
3.4	Research into efficient kitchen practices.	65
3.5	Konsumentverket (the Consumer Agency). Two people in the test kitchen, seen from above. 1971, Studio Granath.	66
3.6	Kitchen in the 1957 Without Borders exhibition. Lennart Holm (no. 7 on Plate 2.1.4).	67
4.1	'We call it democratic design' from the *Ikea Family* magazine.	79

4.2	Advertisements for Ikea's 'Long Live Diversity' campaign posted in Stockholm train stations during 2008.	82
4.3	Advertisements for Ikea's 'Long Live Diversity' campaign posted in public places in Stockholm.	87
5.1	Hooks are commonly used in the living spaces of my respondents. The ones pictured are secured to the underside of shelves to hang keys.	110
5.2	Light and airy homes are created through storage practices.	111
5.3	Storage cages in the basement of some apartment blocks.	112
5.4	Storage cupboards are common in apartment hallways.	113
5.5	Displays of Scandinavian design in the National Museum in Stockholm.	122
5.6	An Ikea product as index of Swedish design in the National Museum in Stockholm. The red table is an Ikea Lack table.	123

ACKNOWLEDGEMENTS

Ethnographic research for this book was a genuinely enjoyable experience, and thanks are due to many people who helped me along the way. Ethnographic research is always dependent on the generosity of strangers, and I would like to acknowledge the exceptionally kind people who made my experience of Stockholm so rich and who allowed me to spend afternoons and evenings in their homes. I owe a debt of gratitude to Helena Wulff for tirelessly assisting me in getting established in Stockholm and encouraging me in pursuing this project. I am also deeply grateful to Christina Garsten for unstinting encouragement and generous advice during and after my time in Sweden. Likewise, I am grateful to various members of the Ikea management teams in Stockholm and Dublin who met with me and allowed me to establish a base in the Kungens Kurva arrivals atrium for some months.

I would like to thank Daniel Miller, Kevin Hetherington, Adam Drazin, Johan Nilsson and Lawrence Taylor for reading and commenting on drafts of my work and Christina Garsten, Brian Moeran and Alison Clarke for commenting on the chapters that are in print elsewhere. I have benefited from questions and comments made by the staff and students who attended department seminars in the anthropology department in Stockholm University, Queen's University Belfast, University College London and Maynooth University. I was grateful for the invitation to participate in Johan Lindqvist and John Freyer's *Billy Bookcase* project held in Konstfack (University College of Arts, Craft and Design), Stockholm, which was both fun and informative. Helena Jönsson was a terrific ally during fieldwork, and Felicia Garcia and Michelle Alm Engvall helped with language skills and noticed small errors that I missed. I owe Alison Clarke and Victor Buchli a word of thanks for scholarly inspiration and selfless collegiality, and lastly, Judy Attfield for originally suggesting this project to me. I learned a lot from all these people and from the comments of anonymous reviews, but of course, any weaknesses in my writing are entirely my own.

This research was funded by the Irish Research Council, and by the Swedish Institute. I wish to thank the individuals working in these institutions, particularly those in the Irish Research Council who allowed me to postpone my project due to the birth of my twin children. Sections of Chapter 2 and Chapter 6 are published in the *Journal of Business Anthropology* (2013) and *Design Anthropology* (2010), the second edition of which is forthcoming.

In my home institution, I would like to thanks members of the anthropology department in Maynooth: Mark Maguire, Abdullahi El-Tom, Thomas Strong and Steve Coleman. Chandana Mathur, Jamie Saris, Seamas O'Siochain, Elzbieta Drazkiewicz-Grodzicka, Denise Erdman, Jacqui Mullally and Patty Gray, who is a dear friend and was a valuable colleague for many years. Both my colleagues and my PhD students Amiee Curran and Tara McAssey were supportive, kind and patient during a period of personal illness. Adam Drazin, Fionn Garvey Drazin and Leah Garvey Drazin were cheerleaders from the sidelines and constantly remind me of what matters. I also wish to thank Anne, Damien, David, Brian, Claudia and Aideen for laughs and Ruth for a sympathetic ear. I wish to remember Padraic, who died during writing, as did Hugh. Both enriched to my life immeasurably. I think of them every day.

1
UNPACKING IKEA

Introduction

There is a museum in the town of Älmhult in southern Sweden that is somewhat unusual.[1] Located in the same building as the first ever Ikea store (established in 1958), it is called the IKEA Museum, and it opened to the public on June 30, 2016. Under the themes of 'Our Roots', 'Our Story' and 'Your Stories', the exhibit presents a potted history of the Swedish furnishing company in the context of post-war domestic interiors, complete with typically furnished rooms.[2] The museum replaces an earlier, smaller exhibition of twenty room sets (800 m2) that was located in the Tillsammans building (trans: Together) and was noteworthy only because it was available for the training of staff, a showcase of corporate 'culture' for select visitors.[3] The IKEA Museum by contrast is altogether more ambitious. It caters, for a start, to a general public and has been significantly revamped: the facade of the building was restored to recreate its original Ikea store appearance, and the exhibition space has been enlarged to cover an impressive 3,500 m2. With interactive areas, products on plinths and glassed-off exhibits, it carries off a museological format in which the visitor is educated while moving through the exhibition space. Through progressive stages and temporal milestones, the corporation is accreted into a broader social and historical weave. What is remarkable, however, is that nearby Ikea showrooms play on a similar series of museological themes but do so in a way that deliberately brings together standard exhibition and commercial practices. Specifically, Ikea showrooms typify a form of display that transmogrifies the housing exhibit into a high-performing commercial enterprise. Whereas the Ikea Museum adopts a somewhat conventional museological format, standard Ikea showrooms are singular in overturning it.

In this book, I trace how designed objects and environments conflate Ikea products with normative domesticity to the extent that such goods become a material shorthand for aggregate behaviour.[4] In other words, I look at the ways in which Ikea is dispersed (cf. Garvey and Drazin 2016).[5] During fieldwork, it was striking how often Ikea warehouses, designers, personnel and goods were indiscriminately subsumed under the term 'Ikea'. Lacking a clear centre respondents tended to focus on the corporation as an abstract global brand that hovers over routinised daily life, or alternatively, they would hone in on the very ordinary objects that provide the scaffold for this same household activity. Beyond this introduction, then, this is not a book dedicated to brand narrative, organisational management or the machinations of corporate strategy. To be sure, during fieldwork in Sweden in 2008 and again in 2010, I duly visited the stores, I spoke to store managers and I interviewed marketing managers, range strategists and designers in 'service offices' in Helsingborg and Älmhult. I read volumes dedicated to Swedish design and perused the catalogues, web pages and business literature that expounded on the Ikea corporation's many successes, challenges and failures. But in addition to the remarkably homogenous and successful brand narrative that emerged, it was clear to me that myriad contradictions – or at least polarisations – characterise Ikea consumption.

As a global corporation that is both dispersed and disembedded (Foster 2010; Giddens 1990), it is not surprising perhaps that the Ikea 'vision' advanced by the marketing arm of the corporation is experienced in contradictory ways for the consumer. Research respondents witness a disconnect between a brand proffering Scandinavian lifestyles, a modern Swedish aesthetic and mass accessibility on the one hand and unsustainable mass production and market rationalisation on the other. There are the inconsistencies of flat-pack rationalization, lengthy queues, maze-like stores and frustrating reassembly all subsumed under the naturalising imperative that 'Home is the most important place in the world'.[6] Then again, the renowned thriftiness of Ikea's founder (Ingvar Kamprad) can be contrasted with the reputed spendthrift reputation of the store's many shoppers. The design is self-consciously Swedish, yet the corporation stands as a potential meta-symbol of cultural homogenisation on a global scale (see Miller 1998). Moreover, the idiom of democratic design or design for the many, as Ikea's design philosophy, is pitched as an egalitarian solution for the purchasing masses, irrespective of income, but simultaneously alternates as a byword for common, everyday, pedestrian purchases lacking individual expression. Affordable versions of high-end goods found in Ikea stores seem to undercut the last bastion of elitist expression – art and design, and yet it is equally clear that individuals struggle to capture something that is at once so abstract and so concrete, where far-reaching claims pivot on ordinary things.

During anthropological fieldwork, it was striking how often respondents adopted a dual register to discursively move from the store as an abstract entity, as a Scandinavian aesthetic and as an international brand to the brute materiality of more immediate and proximate concerns: 'I put Ikea blinds in the boys' bedroom because they are going to get thrashed anyhow', said Johanna, a thirty-seven-year-old mother of two. At first, I judged the consequent ambiguity as an outcome of an ineffective interview technique, but later I realised that the seemingly incommensurate regimes of Ikea as a global retailer, and 'the blinds in the boys' bedroom' are captured through a register that moves from the abstract level of global corporate retail to specific home-based goods. This dualism is significant in understanding how individual householders negotiate a tension between Ikea as both distant and proximate, predicated on rationalised productivity but also integral to domestic, family-oriented cares. Appreciating the complexity of this double helix is central to this book.

Recently, anthropologists have focused on 'corporate oxymorons', meaning that marketing strategies dominate the popular vocabulary and ways of thinking about products in order to minimise their harmful effects (Benson and Kirsch 2010; Foster 2010). But here, instead of the percolations distilled from a corporate source, I focus on the multidimensional translations that operate amongst a nexus of households, public spaces and commercial outlets. One of the aims for this work, therefore, is to understand how design, understood by my respondents as a kind of benign intervention, represents the bridging point between a diverse range of specialisms on the one hand and something that makes sense on a domestic level on the other. In looking at Ikea showrooms and Ikea design, I am drawn into considering how perceptions of design entail ideas of intercession for the good, how aggregate practices inform values of equality or its inverse and how extra-domestic activities contribute to the traversal of public and private distinctions, rendering the home a public object as well as a private one. So although Ikea as the world's largest furniture retailer may be an apposite example of the uneven production, distribution and circulation of corporate goods, neoliberal policies and uneven life chances in a global perspective, my interest in this work is very specifically focussed on the role of one particular corporation as a structural component of domesticity in Stockholm.

In the chapters that follow, I explore some of the dualities underpinning Ikea consumption, which are pretty unexceptional for my research respondents. Inconsistencies amongst the workings, the stakeholders and the publics of transnational corporations are common, not least in the world's largest furniture retailer. I scrutinise the Ikea brand in this chapter, but thereafter, I shift focus from Ikea as a legal or financial enterprise – which is well represented in business literature (eg. Jonsson and Foss 2011; Tarnovskaya and de Chernatony 2011) – to explore one Ikea store and its role within quotidian life in Stockholm. In so doing, I suggest the boundaries of 'Ikea' as a commercial entity are perceived as blurred. This anthropological perspective opposes, then, discursive clusters found in the media and business-oriented publications that present the Ikea brand as distinct from everyday life, in stark contrast to actual manifestations of it in very ordinary things.[7] During fieldwork, I suspended assumptions about where the corporation begins or ends and adopted a perspective that explored how Ikea products circulate in various corporate (Ikea designers, retail centres, service offices); institutional and cultural (community creches, museum exhibits, broadsheet and satellite-based media); and popular and everyday settings (second-hand websites, local buy-and-sell markets, office and hotel lobbies, the Ikea catalogue, individual households). Far from being an immutable juggernaut, Ikea represents a material reality, a financial entity and a social relation that captures a social kaleidoscope of people, practices and places that actively constitute (rather than merely feature in) these diverse corporate, state, cultural and popular fora.

While sitting in Stockholm living rooms during fieldwork, householders did not concern themselves unduly with brand but quickly focussed on the scented tea lights, cups and bookcases around them. And although individuals were familiar with the brand narrative – the establishment of the company and tales surrounding its founder – beyond that, it was simply inconsequential to their concerns. Aligned more with their priorities were the fiscal resources required to buy or rent a home and the myriad activities dedicated to home maintenance, which, despite the diverse forms this practice took, was lauded by all my respondents as a 'good thing'. Research participants describe their homes in highly emotive terms, the backdrop for the essentials of everyday life; the source for ambivalence regarding reconfigurations in domestic planning and the housing market; the bulwark against extra-domestic stresses; and the platform for the traditional state-citizen contract. In this spirit, most of this book adopts the more expansive meaning of the term *corporate* and focuses anthropologically on the cross-cutting influences that draw household groups into broader collectivities. For my respondents, I suggest, the sheer volume of circulating narratives about Ikea and the frequency with which they are encountered on an everyday level work to perpetuate an experience of Ikea as ubiquitous and largely associated with mainstream, aggregate householding practices. In other words, the most ordinary of goods becomes the channel for the most extraordinary of claims.

Extraordinary claims for ordinary things

Deriving its name from an acronym consisting of the initials of founder Ingvar Kamprad, Elmtaryd (the farm where he grew up) and Agunnaryd (his hometown in Småland, southern Sweden), Ikea was founded in 1943 by the seventeen-year-old Ingvar Kamprad. From humble beginnings, it is now a global concern and represents the world's largest furniture retailer. Ikea has been described as a new creeping avatar of the twentieth-century modernist international style, responsible for homogenous domestic environments on a global scale – a 'monolithic tyranny of aesthetics' (Hartman 2007: 492). Research respondents readily subscribe to this view, comparing Ikea Malaysia to its equivalent in Moscow without pausing for breath. Yet, on the whole, as popular perceptions of global corporations go, Ikea is largely atypical. Although subject to occasional and prominent critique (Stenebo 2012), the store avoids the stigma of extreme corporate greed levelled at corporations such as Nike, for example (Cronin 2004; Klein 2000; Lury 2004; Stolle and Micheletti 2013). In academic literature, one does not read of Ikeaization to the same degree as Coca Globalization (Foster 2008b) or McDonalisation (Smart 1999; Ritzer 2011), and outside the academy, Ikea has largely avoided the concerted and intensive negative attention formed through sustained media critique, consumer boycotts or buycotts to which other companies have been subject. Such critiques do exist (Hartman 2007; Lindqvist 2009; Roberts 2012), but they are more muted, less profiled and accrue less momentum than the popular activism that surrounds other, typically American-sourced products. Instead, Ikea exports a cultural package made up of tantalising images of Swedish domesticity that are pitched as essentially benign, self-styled as quirky, the darling of lifestyle pages of global popular press. Clearly, this breed of Scandinavian style is not popularly identified as cultural or economic imperialism (cf. Bengtsson 2010, Cieraad 2014).[8]

The store has a staggering international following. In 2016, the Inter IKEA Systems BV web page stated there are now 389 stores worldwide visited by 915 million people, while 2.1 billion visited its web page.[9] By now, the stampede on Ikea in Edmonton, London, in 2005, in which 'people grew agitated and charged the doors' is infamous and a common idiom for the extremes of Ikea fascination. On that occasion, the south London store remained open for a mere thirty minutes as overwhelmed staff battled to hold back the surge of four thousand who stormed in, anxious to acquire the touted bargains on offer.[10] It is events such as this that leave people scratching their heads at the phenomenal, and at times frantic, attraction of Ikea stores. As a singularly disadvantaged constituency whose population was offered one-off bargains, Edmonton reminds us of the desperation that variously accompanies deprivation and the role of global commerce in contributing to a social cartography of feast or famine. On this occasion, fascination erupted into frenzy, a situation that could, in theory, happen anywhere but particularly so where opportunities to furnish one's home inexpensively are somewhat rare. In global Ikea showrooms, posters attempt to promote a feeling of wild excitement with frequent references to 'being crazy about' design or cheap prices, underlining the perceived alignment of the Ikea brand with youth, vitality, thrift and, above all, Sweden.

Ikea at large: exhibition spaces, media discourse, popular perceptions

Rippling from a source that is symbolically located in Sweden but actually based in several countries, Ikea is iconic of transnational corporate structures that reach into myriad sites of popular culture and cultural production. Ikea's corporate and cultural influence emerges in popular forms and institutional circles, such as an exhibition in the contemporary art museum Liljevalch Konsthall in Stockholm dedicated to Ikea (2009), to displays of Ikea design in Stockholm's National Museum and Moderna Museet, New York's Museum of Modern Art (2016),[11] the Pinakothek der Moderne in Munich (2009)[12] and Vienna's Imperial Furniture Collection (2010).[13] Not forgetting too the countless international media publications dedicated to Ikea stories that make repetitive reference to its Swedish design pedigree, such as the *New Yorker* (Collins 2011) and the *Guardian* (Burkeman 2004).

As part of its international appeal, these exhibition spaces and discursive practices can be viewed as part of Ikea's 'symbolic production' in which images, descriptions, critiques, exposés, exhibits and goods proliferate in institutions or amongst agents of 'cultural consecration' thereby claiming broad cultural authority (Bourdieu and

Johnson 1993: 121). Indeed, the circulating stories based on Ikea stores and products that feature in international media and on the Internet could be described as relentless. Through global satellite-based forms of mediation, one finds Ikea stories polarising along two fairly standard routes, the first typified by the movie *Fight Club*. The film starts with a description of a middle-aged man played by actor Edward Norton, living a bland pedestrian life in an American city in which his most pressing concern is to have a house kitted out with the latest Ikea furniture. The character is clearly meant to represent the perceived petty frustrations of a broad normative lower-middle class, unwilling or unable to see the broader questions that concern life and death. Through subsumption to an Ikea lifestyle, the movie suggests that this figure had in fact stopped living beyond mere functioning and was so dispirited by contemporary consumer culture that it took devastation – losing his apartment in an apparent bomb blast – to catapult him out of his stupor. Ikea furniture, in this movie, metaphorically signals the perceived dullness that is induced by consumer culture, prompted and pushed by the machinations of large, aggressive corporations that exacerbate the public's voracious desire for goods. Our goods own us, Edward Norton's fictional character is told; we don't own them.

On the other hand, there is another tale, equally popular in Hollywood blockbusters, TV drama and global satellite-based media that focuses not on the Ikea corporation as representative of global commerce but on visits to the store as iconic of contemporary romance. Here the stage-like tableaux of Ikea showrooms provide the context for romantic imagination, and visiting the store together notches up 'the next level' of a budding relationship. Coupledom, thus, is not only marked but measured through the joint kitting out of a home, and showrooms provide the first step in this direction. In one such movie, *500 Days of Summer*, the young couple literally skip through Ikea showrooms, the staged kitchens and bedrooms providing the mise-en-scène for this blossoming romance. Replicated in international popular media, the trip to Ikea provides the imaginary landscape for romantic couples to envisage life together while others visit Ikea to assuage loneliness or to furnish a home in the face of transition, such as acquiring a new place or marriage breakdown.

Stepping back from the content of such media attention for one moment, one quickly recognizes the effect of this constant reiteration; the sheer staggering scale of it reminds us of the efficacy of the overall message. Endemic to the Ikea brand is the endless repetitive anecdotes that detail just how ubiquitous Ikea merchandise is. Mass production assumes breathtaking, vertiginous proportions when describing Ikea's reach. Broadsheet media and Internet sources alike make the same allusions to Ikea beds being party to the conception of one in every ten Europeans (eg. Collins 2011), as well as to the mind-boggling numbers of Billy bookcases and catalogues, all implying that Ikea goods reveal an instant snapshot of broad, normative domesticity. Reminding us, in other words, of the political scientist Benedict Anderson's observation that the first 'modern-style mass-produced industrial commodity', (the printed newspaper) occupied a key role for collective ceremony, while simultaneously heralding the obsolescence of the modern age (1983: 34).

Each communicant, he tells us, is well aware that the ceremony he (*sic*) performs is being replicated simultaneously by thousands or millions of others of whose existence he is confident yet of whose identity he has not the slightest notion. Striking too, Anderson notes, is that these actions replace the morning prayers of previous ages, and although following a market logic, they are performed in private, intimate ways. The incessantly repeated ceremony that foreshadows the imagined world is thereby visibly rooted in everyday life, rendering a remarkable 'confidence of community' (Anderson 1983: 35–36). Mass production and distribution is not merely preeminent in the effective realization and expression of identity, but the inconspicuous and the intimate demonstrably prefigure the realisation of national modernity.

Ikea occupies a particular place on the national stage in Sweden. Big corporate players like Ikea (and Tetra Laval) are admired by many Swedes because it aggressively avoided going public, preferring to keep full and private control of the business. Amongst Ikea managers and members of the public I spoke to, individuals often commented first and favourably on the fact that Ikea was not launched on the stock market. Without avaricious shareholders demanding profit at every turn, Ikea can make long-term projections and invest in strategy, I was told. Such depictions, coupled with the intertwining of Ingvar Kamprad's personal story with that of the store, set Ikea apart as a bulwark against the unrelenting demands of global capital that force business to capitulate to immediate gains over long-term planning and ultimate stability. Kamprad is closely associated with thrift in circulating anecdotes that inflate his proclivity for parsimoniousness (reputedly using the same teabag twice, flying economy class). Thrift is localised in tales of the doggedness of Älmhult, or Småland residents (where Ikea was founded), and then further distilled into the person of Kamprad himself. On several occasions, individuals outlined how sacrifices on his part – with Kamprad as coeval with the corporation – translated into benefits for the consumer. One woman, Linda, told me she admires Kamprad because he 'only charges five SEK for hotdogs at the checkout tills, but he could charge ten SEK'. The parsimoniousness of Ikea's founder is thus presented as evidence of the cost-cutting ethos of the store, Kamprad championed as an advocate of thrifty living, relentlessly advancing the interests of Ikea shoppers. More than a champion of household thrift, Ikea's founder thus becomes an embodiment of it in which the person of Kamprad assumes the effect of sacrifice to the direct benefit of Ikea consumers. As a result, respondents spoke of what they saved on shopping trips instead of what they spent in Ikea. Acknowledging this tendency, one woman commented that 'people are spending like crazy'.

Therefore although Ikea is unquestionably global in scale and reach, it is accorded a unique and largely trusted presence on the national stage. Ikea consistently achieves the status of one of the most trusted brands in Sweden, occasionally outranking the media, politicians or religious orders. An annual trust barometer compiled by academics within the University of Gothenburg charts public trust in national institutions, political parties, the mass media and companies.[14] During fieldwork, in 2008, Ikea retained a position of 78 per cent, indicating a lot/quite a lot of trust in Ingvar Kamprad, the founder and public face of the furniture giant. Ikea ranked top that year as the most trusted institution in Sweden, far surpassing the government, but came in second place in 2009 after Swedish radio. In 2012, Ikea was named the third most sustainable retail brand in Sweden by one of Scandinavia's largest insight and analysis firms, Sustainable Brand Insights (Bertilsson 2014: 128). While visiting the Ikea marketing service office in Helsingborg in 2008, then-marketing manager Nils Larsson told me that approximately 80 per cent of Swedes visit the store at least once a year. Respondents meanwhile describe Ikea merchandise as ubiquitous and pervasive, part of an aphorism that 'everyone should be able to have a nice home'.

Design historian Sara Kristoffersson charts the Ikea brand since the company's registration in 1943. The Ikea brand, she argues, can be viewed as the product of stories or discourses that have evolved around it through the work of diverse authors: companies, cultural industries, intermediaries such as salespersons and consumers. National narratives are interpolated into the brand such that Sweden and Ikea are 'co-branded', she argues, meaning the image of one supports and feeds into the international perception of the other (Kristoffersson 2014: 84). From the blue-and-yellow exteriors to imported Swedish meatballs in cross-global cafes, the marketing image of the store links common icons of 'Swedishness' with a non-hierarchical, non-elitist modern solution for the purchasing masses. Since the turn of the millennium, such branding has gathered momentum, driven in part by the Swedish Institute, a state agency tasked with promoting Sweden abroad. The institute puts baldly the entanglement of national profile and corporate brand: 'To visit IKEA is to visit Sweden: IKEA fits very well onto the official brand platform of Sweden . . . The brand of the company could very well be described in the same terms as the platform for Sweden' (quoted in Kristoffersson 2014: 84). Furthermore, a government report from 2004 notes the benefits from 'piggybacking', meaning co-branding, on the mutually beneficial branding opportunities that arise when major Swedish corporations such as Ikea open a new store, creating a 'natural opportunity for linking up with an activity that promotes Sweden' (Kristoffersson 2014: 85). State-sponsored initiatives such as this illustrate a branding policy that shores up the positive associations that accrue to both Sweden and Ikea, pulling financial opportunities and symbolic resources into the orbit of both, illustrating that in addition to a cultural package propagated by the superstore, we find it perpetuated elsewhere, often defying boundaries of commerce or politics. An identifiable national imaginary is thus constituted by these means as much as recorded.

Concomitant with local claims are global processes and stretching beyond any single national border are the transnational networks, flows, objects and people that form the bedrock of sociality on a day-to-day and seemingly local level (Appadurai 1990). As is common with corporations of this size, Ikea is Janus-faced in occupying the role of vast global corporation and the go-to place for familiar design and household goods. Daily life is shot through with 'worldly things' in which flows of capital and material goods represent not only an increasing presence of particular companies but also different kinds of social and hegemonic relationships

(Foster 2008b: 17). Global connections are marked by a variety of diverse modalities, from structural and institutional, including the movement of goods and people, to the proliferation of electronic communication systems at the household level (Tomlinson 1999: 2). Hannerz (1996) emphasises social networks and the subjective and objective dimensions through which global forms and forces operate. In these processes, market relations contribute to the organization of people, ideas and commodities so that diversity finds local expression, allowing vastly separated populations to feel connected. Ikea products participate in all these modalities but often in indefinable, difficult-to-grasp ways. This elusiveness is evident in consumer allusions to analogous circulating forms of communication such as found on the Internet. Indeed, because of its frequent appearance on satellite-based media, Ikea appears to transcend and obliterate national boundaries and cultural differences as yet another expression of ubiquitous consumer culture. Linkages to the Internet can be viewed as an expression of virtuality, as informants refer to Ikea in Saudi Arabia to Milan without pause so that, during my research, it was common to be swiftly drawn to my interlocutors' last Internet surf where some example of Ikea furniture was either reported on or creatively used in an artist's installation. Alliances between Ikea and the Internet are idiomatic of a vision of contemporary commerce as abstract, virtual and homogenous over vast geopolitical and social tracts. I call this macro-level Ikea-in-the-abstract.[15]

Ikea-in-the-abstract: retailer and brand

Ikea's success, we are told, lies not only in its low-cost sales pitch but on its insistence on centralised control, product standardisation and homogeneous Scandinavian corporate culture, pushing Scandinavian concepts overseas without adoption to local preferences. Ikea is undoubtedly global yet conforms to the 'curious reality' of a chain store that is present in the physical sense but is substantively composed of relations that are elsewhere (Cassell 1993: 28).[16] Ikea's financial organisation is critiqued as being so distributed across international territories that an actual centre is evasive. The Ikea brand and concept is owned by Inter IKEA Systems BV, a Dutch company, while Ingka Holding, which is registered in Luxembourg, is parent of the IKEA Group, controlling 284 stores in 26 countries (Kollewe 2011).[17] The IKEA Group is the largest franchisee, but other franchises run the remaining stores and pay royalties to Inter IKEA Systems. A Swedish documentary aired in 2011 uncovered that these profits were paid to Interogo, a Liechtenstein foundation controlled by the Kamprad family.[18]

Ikea is similarly dispersed in ways beyond the financial. Looking at its production and supply base, Ikea has over two thousand suppliers in more than fifty countries globally. It has been pointed out that the reach of Ikea's commercial presence represents a cartography of affluent countries (Hartman 2007). In the past, this distinction was more marked, as Ikea suppliers were often found in Soviet and later post-Soviet countries, underlying an axis separating Eastern European producers from Western capitalist consumers. Russian suppliers were first approached in the

1980s, while Poland was home to Ikea's first suppliers outside of Sweden as early as 1961. Amongst the top five countries from which Ikea purchases goods include China, Poland and Sweden.[19]

Corporations thus are difficult to pin down. As linchpins of the 'almost but not-quite-there-globality', they are evasive and resistant objects for anthropologists to study (Tsing 2000: 332; see also Garsten et al 2015; Garsten and Nyqvist 2013; Krause Jensen 2010; Lien 1997; Moeran and Garsten 2012; Rajak 2011; Urban and Koh 2013).[20] Although legal and financial boundaries appear fixed, enduring and stable, we encounter the corporation in diverse forms, including in product design, online encounters or everyday situations and work practices. Studies of branding, as virtually synonymous with global capitalism, encompass one example of divergent economies of scale, and anthropologists have attempted to understand some of the ways human experience is enmeshed in corporate strategy (Foster 2007, 2008a, 2008b; Rajak 2011). Scholars have shown a particular interest in how corporate brands acquire or transmit intense cultural and political values, described as brand icons (Holt 2004; see also Coombe 1996; Klein 2000). Brands are 'material semiotic forms whose circulation defines a broader social imaginary' (Manning and Uplisashvili 2007: 628; see also Lee and Li Puma 2002), and these imaginaries may consist of the market or the nation or other interpretative groups that congregate around them. Brands thus refer to more than commercial enterprises and anthropologists have studied the processes by which individuals associate state institutions and agents with goods and services on offer (Fehérváry 2009; Kravets and Örge 2010). The brand may serve a symbolic function, signalling certain values or social, political or economic circumstances – Coca-Cola as a 'metasymbol' of Western capitalism or globalization, for example (Miller 1998). Douglas Holt argues that successful iconic brands provide imaginative platforms to address social contradictions. Ideologically, brands distill these tensions into new aspirations or insights, particularly when traditional cultural symbols become problematic. Brands create myths through the confluence of actors, including commercial interests and agents, consumers and forms of popular culture (Kravets and Örge 2010: 208). They reinforce a sense of belonging, unity and continuity in the face of shifting local and global contexts (Holt 2004: 6). The co-option of consumer action into brands moreover, has been identified as the singular site for the development of loyalty between consumers and corporations. The bilateral relationships that follow are frequently long-standing but do not necessarily - or even usually - operate on equal terms (Foster 2008a). As part of this literature the intangible meanings of brand have come under scrutiny in interrogations of how capital is displaced from a product to the sign that represents it, heralding a unique elevation of the brand as a measure of value and site of fetishism (Arvidsson 2006; Coombe 1996; Manning 2010; Manning and Uplisashvili 2007; Meneley 2004; Moore 2003). As an omnipresence that encompasses all products and practices into one giant managerial web, brand as sign potentially signals the trumping of 'meaning' over 'matter', relatively abstracted from the vagaries of actual life.

Brand as material culture

As an ontological exercise, the conceptual framework that privileges the immaterial brand over actual product is persuasive, but becomes problematic when situated within domestic practice when acquiring, assembling, cleaning, maintaining and storing goods brings their burdensome materiality into sharp focus. Consequently, I find instructive anthropologist Webb Keane's argument that even the most abstract form of value successfully operates as abstract only because of the very material forms from which it is seen to deviate (Keane 2003, 2008: 38; see also Gilbert 2005; Maurer 2006).[21] Treating objects as merely a sign of something else, of something other than themselves, obscures their consequences and intercessions in a world of causality (Keane 2005: 8; see also Garvey 2013). The sensual qualities of any thing – its colour, its material, its form– can be considered unrealised potential because often one material quality will be foregrounded over others.[22] The social significance of any sign, therefore, is open to the vagaries of convention, challenge or change. This argument destabilises any separation of signs as meaningful without equal attention to their material manifestation.

In tracing the place of Ikea and Swedish design in the formation of architecture, domestic material culture and household subjectivities in Stockholm, I follow anthropological arguments that seek to overcome a dualism inherent in subject and object positions, whereby the latter is the inert instrument, playing to the tune of the social actor. Material forms – our physical world in all its splendid complexity – generate thought and action in historically contingent ways. Cultural identity is part and parcel of our material environment as much as it is a value that is rationalised or felt (Tilley et al 2006). One way this has been expounded in studies of consumption has been through Daniel Miller's theory regarding the dual processes of objectification and appropriation (1987). Through deliberate acts of appropriation of commodities – often alienable, distant and estranged – consumers engage in a process of self-fashioning, thereby converting something vast and estranged into something inalienable, singular and intelligible. This perspective emphasises recursive relationships between people and things, in which both are mutually constituted through their interactions rather than engaging from immutable, fixed states (Miller 1987, 2005, Tilley et al 2006). Far from being inert matter or the backdrop to the stuff of life, artefacts – no matter how seemingly unimportant, overlooked or invisible – are formative of social action.

This perspective does not assume an even playing field in interactions between global commerce and individual actors (Foster 2008b), but nor does it ignore that corporations produce unintended effects in the social landscape in addition to their wares. Despite being a vast commercial enterprise, Ikea-in-the-abstract percolates into actual life in myriad unforeseen ways, rendering the distinction amongst the dualities of local and global, material and immaterial problematic (Carrier and Miller 1998; Keane 2008; Miller 2005; see also Buchli 2013). Rather than privilege one over the other, there is a striking disparity amongst the world's largest furniture retailer, the larger-than-life media savvy corporation, the globally recognized brand and the contexts of its materialisation. Considering the scale of a corporation of this size, it is easy to lose sight of the banality of goods sourced there – kitchen utensils, toilet brushes and tea-light candles as much as sofas and shelving units. Although the resonances of the Ikea label linger in my research participants' homes, things become part of this extensive domestic composite and are thereby entangled with more biographies, more abstract qualities and material manifestations, with broader domestic routines and the symbolic densities of other objects (Weiner 1992). During discussions, generalities regarding Ikea as an abstract entity immediately evolve into a palimpsest of associations when one moves to specific items in individual households. Ikea-in-the-abstract therefore becomes more difficult to follow over time as individuals make purchases and interact with these purchases – use them, store them, clean them, recycle or dispose of them on a daily basis. Keane's framework of an ideological nexus is helpful because it allows for more contingency, diversity and complexity in understanding the cultural claims of the Ikea corporation as distinct from Ikea goods as parts and participants in domestic environments and its manifold social actions (Keane 2008: 38). This framework thus includes inter alia the ideas and uses, moralities and discourses, stakes and claims, and actual material forms that are mutually entangled, and offers an appropriate pathway to consider a global corporation the size and scale as Ikea, particularly when the claims are many and of obscure origin, the size of production vertiginous, the goods diversely appropriated and yet a common everyday presence. Emphasis on products alone obscures the fact that Ikea represents a nexus for myriad intersecting agents and practices.

There is something to be learned from the ambiguity that surrounds the boundaries of the Ikea corporation. Beyond identifying the local store, individuals are often at a loss to identify not only a fixed geographical centre of gravity but also where a corporation of this magnitude begins and ends. 'Ikea', quite simply, can refer to either products, places or people. There is a seeming dialectic between the corporation as vaguely understood and distant versus the products that are easily accessible, manifestly common and proximate. To combat this ambiguity, I put to one side questions of the material or immateriality of brand and attend instead to the processes by which 'social materialisation' occurs (Slater 2003). What this implies is that things not only have a physical materiality but a social presence that ascribes them worth and coherence. Designed things are thus labelled in order to distinguish and elevate them from the jetsam of ordinary stuff.[23] At issue is not the ramping up of more signs but the destabilisation of agents and processes, structures and things that hold a physical entity and its meaning secure.

This book

In what follows, we move between the dual realities of the everyday on the one hand and structural contingencies on the other. We look at the actions and agencies that 'conspire to script experience' and shape the production and consumption of the material world while paying close attention to how these scripted experiences make sense on a household level (cf. Julier 2013: XIII). There is a history of alignment between design practice and perceptions of social betterment in Sweden, and understanding this history requires exploring beyond the designer's frame to 'the cultural imaginaries and micro-politics that delineate design's promises and practices' (Suchman 2011: 3; see also Garvey and Drazin 2016; Murphy 2015). In Chapter 2, we consider the 'Ikea experience' and look at design as a kind of benign intervention, whereby an object manifests the positive intentions of its creator. Through an examination of the showrooms, we explore the interpellation of inspiration and material culture through showroom exhibition techniques. Ikea showrooms actively orchestrate a holistic experience, encouraging shopper engagement with the items on display and providing a tightly choreographed experience based on sensorial engagement. This sensorial quality serves to enhance and enliven the showrooms and to heighten the presence and activities of others. Chapter 2 is the only part of the book that I explicitly compare Ikea showrooms in Dublin with those in Stockholm. Ikea stores carry a reputation of homogeneity across all their stores, and through examining the establishment of showrooms as part of an entry to a new (Irish) market, I show how Dublin's store managers were occupied with navigating a middle path between conforming to the Ikea range strategy as dictated by the relevant offices in Sweden and the United Kingdom and catering to the trends of the local market.

Distinguishable from edicts issued from head offices, there is also a long history in Sweden of staging 'the vernacular home with its everyday objects and domestic scenery into a *public* object' (Arrhenius 2010: 138, emphasis in original). In Chapter 3, I draw comparisons between 'housing theatre' as found in home exhibitions and folk-housing displays promoted during the development of the Swedish model of the Social Democratic state (Habel 2010) and consider the ways in which Ikea tableaux participate in widespread contemporary practices of 'housing theatre' or 'home staging'. In modelling the modern, design in Sweden was formative in the production of domestic architecture and objects, linked to political advancement and the betterment of everyday life. Internationally, Swedish design implies the Scandinavian modern, the style that dominated the European post-war furniture market and that Ikea actively perpetuates. Twentieth-century modernist movements were both global and revolutionary in ambition but were territorialized in different ways across Europe. The coupling of a specific geopolitical cadence of Scandinavian design was advanced in post-war decades. Swedish Form, or Svensk Form, the name given to the Swedish Society of Crafts and Design (originally Svenska Slöjdföreningen), is a not-for-profit association mandated by the Swedish government to promote design in Sweden and was founded in 1845. Its aims were consistent with the new methods of mass production introduced in the nineteenth century, and together, Sweden's working classes were 'design-empowered with access to well-designed, beautiful and affordable goods'.[24] Now Svensk Form makes clear that designers are not only the 'natural link between manufacturers and consumers but they are highly influential in integrating sustainable development into design and enhancing the good life'.²⁵ My interest in detailing this historiography is not to provide a historically determinist perspective to explain contemporary practice (see Fallan 2012: 15). Instead, I focus on the ways in which salient narratives concretise linkages between the national imaginary and advance design practice as a structural component of Swedish domestic history and nationhood.

Design designates the self-consciously modern. It includes not only an orientation towards innovative futures but also a narration of the past. This linearity establishes the motivation for change and evokes the agents who can achieve it (Otto 2016). In Stockholm, one happens upon designed goods or environments in the most quotidian places, and respondents rarely aligned the term *design* with the remote specialised knowledge that I have found in corresponding discussions in Dublin. Integral to the most intimate domestic practice, which is appropriated in individual ways, ordinary objects are a tangible mnemonic of the multiple agencies that are marshalled in domestic composition. Industrial design was integrated into economic prosperity, and Ekström tracks its 'immense breakthrough' in the 1960s with advancements in serial manufacturing (Ekström 2010: 518; see also Robach 2010). By virtue of inexpensive mass production, and its historical longevity and the temporal framework of its establishment, Ikea is well positioned to mediate widespread narratives of product accessibility, and by implication, a kind of equality. Anthropologist Keith Murphy argues that good design and Swedish design (svensk design) carry close associations, the latter of which can be viewed as a 'powerful concrete rendering of a sort of essentialized "Swedishness" embedded in objects identifiable as emblems of nationalist pride' (2015: 3). Beyond the national, though, is a second register that subtly foreshadows moral visions tied to social democratic principles into the concreteness of designed forms. In Chapter 4, I explore the ways standardisation is pitched as benefitting vast swathes of national and global populations by making good design accessible, inflecting serial production with a moral stance. This situation is complicated, however, because normative domesticity requires that, one way or another, the particularity of each household unit is stamped on the otherwise common. Paradoxically, the demonstration of too little concern or effort in homemaking, the purchase of too many Ikea products or the replication of an Ikea showroom at home is not lauded as devoting time, energy and resources to 'more important matters' but instead harbours the potential accusation of social sterility, or 'living the brand'. Carrying both positive and negative inflection, ubiquity is posed as a problem that must be assuaged.

In Chapter 5, I follow the corporeal and affective logics entailed in an aesthetic order variously described as 'Scandinavian', 'Swedish modern' or 'modernist' styles, which Ikea design activity propagate. National iconographies picturing white-walled, light-filled, sparsely decorated rooms in broadsheet newspaper spreads and lifestyle magazines bolster the Scandinavian modern aesthetic as an object of value that originated and thrived in the twentieth century. Householders I spoke to referred to clutter, meaning objects out of place as a self-evident problem, and a contravention to an ideal domestic order. Closely associated with this order, respondents nominated a series of qualities that constitute for them the Scandinavian style:

FIGURE 1.1   The arrivals atrium in Ikea Kungens Kurva.

clean lines, blond woods, white walls, a stripped-down timber and uncluttered surfaces.[26] Against this background of the stripped-down minimalism is a globally sourced and circulated valorisation of colour and emotion as well as a shifting housing market. In recent years marketing strategies underpin experience in the home and workplace amid breathless exhortations to employ colour as a tool in activating ameliorated moods or feelings. Against these uncertainties, Swedish style, or Scandinavian modern, perpetuates a sense of stability that is belied by intense fluctuations in interior trends and the housing market.

Beyond commercial workings, however, another emotional register is evident that derives from the animation and liveliness of the Ikea tableau and here we come full circle and return to the Ikea showrooms. If domesticity is a physical and political territory entrenched in models of citizenship and state, then it also hosts the deeply subjective and affective states, realised through the embedded microroutines of quotidian life. Chapter 6 interrogates research respondents' experience of mobility and transience: many of my research respondents are on the move, strategically using Ikea products as part of their relocation. In each case, Ikea furniture and its place in the construction of home are central. Heightened transience is marked by the increasing alliance of furniture retail with fashion, but here I focus on the strategic use of transience to manifest a more relational sense of temporality and permanence. This perspective entails moving beyond Ikea-branded goods as cogs within a market economy and concerns extraneous presences in domestic composition and the finely tuned dynamic between the home as both public object and private possession. The logics of loneliness encourage some respondents to find fora where they can comfortably escape the piercing solitude of home. What results is a mix of commercial trends and emerging marketing strategies but also the structures of feeling that arise through mobility, from oscillating from home to Ikea showrooms animated with the activities that constitute household provisioning.

Setting the scene: visiting Ikea in Kungens Kurva

There are two Ikea stores in the Stockholm region, but the one under focus here is the world's largest at approximately 56,000 m2 – the size of eight football pitches – in a romantically named southern suburb called Kungens Kurva (King's Curve).[27] Located approximately 15 km south of the city centre, the area got its name following an incident on September 28, 1946, when King Gustav's chauffer-driven 1939 Cadillac skidded off the rural road into a ditch (Torekull 2000). From open countryside in the 1930s, Stockholm's Huddinge municipality sold land to the growing Ikea corporation in the early 1960s, which identified the location as a site for development. The Kungens Kurva store opened on June 18, 1965.[28]

Based on a year of participant observation in 2008 and a shorter visit in 2010 in Stockholm's flagship store – the largest Ikea in the world – this book places the retailer squarely within the realm of the homebuilding efforts of individuals. Ikea, the world's largest retailer, is the focus of intense popular fascination internationally yet is rarely subject to in-depth anthropological inquiry. Over the course of one year, I conducted ethnography in Ikea Kungens Kurva and followed the furniture to the homes and lives of individual householders in Stockholm.

Ikea's arrival in Kungens Kurva in 1965 coincided with rapid national economic prosperity and metropolitan expansion. With rural decline and increased urbanization came the development of the road network and a proliferation of cars, facilitated by enhanced disposable incomes amongst the middle classes.[29] People had more free time than before: in 1951, a law stating that all citizens had the right to three weeks' holiday was introduced, and the average working week was reduced to forty-eight hours in 1957 (cf. Ekström 2010). Furthermore, during the 1950s, fifty thousand farms were abandoned, and that number doubled again in the 1960s. Within this shifting urban context in which city populations were expanding and replacing the agricultural base, active steps were taken by government to modernise housing. In 1964, the Social Democrats announced the launch of the Million Programme, a building programme guaranteeing to place the required capital and labour at the construction sector's disposal to build a million homes between 1965 and 1974.[30] The modernist blocks built during the Million Programme proved controversial but were advantageous to Ikea firstly in creating a ready market 'hungry' for household goods (Torekull 1999: 40) and secondly in putting into practice a major expansion of Stockholm suburbs where it was envisioned residents would be able to live, work and shop in their local district. The current popular perception of the Million Programme is of less appealing high-rise blocks on the outskirts of Stockholm. Visiting the Swedish Building Service (Byggtjänst), a company that provides information on all aspects of construction, I was told that typical housing before the 1960s was built 'in the nature', surrounded by green areas and parks. Million Programme constructions by contrast were built with an emphasis on function and standardisation, lacking attention to the natural undulations and potential of the surrounding areas. Drawing attention to the heavily standardised architecture of the time, one architect in the agency Byggtjänst described his early career:

> That was during late sixties and the seventies. In ten years, people in Sweden would build one thousand apartments per year for ten years. And that was the same time as IKEA grew. Then, the installation for each apartment was enormous because it was connected to the state loans for apartment houses, and so everything was very standardized. I remember I started working in the late seventies, and then as an architect, you couldn't do anything, it was so tailor-made for these restrictions. That meant of course that IKEA had an enormous possibility to standardize the furniture to sell because they knew exactly how big is a normal living room suite, how big is a master bedroom, etcetera, etcetera.

The largest residential area in the vicinity of Kungens Kurva, called Skärholmen, was built as part of the same construction programme and represents a significant housing and commercial district in Greater Stockholm's southwest region.[31]

Inside the Ikea store

In 2002, the Ikea store in Kungens Kurva was expanded in size from 45,000 to 56,301 m2, twice the size of most Ikea stores worldwide. Already, however, the store was notable for its landmark corkscrew construction that houses the showrooms and adjoins a rectangular warehouse. The architectural inspiration for the corkscrew was museulogical in inspiration, springing from Frank Lloyd Wright's Guggenheim Museum in New York. Following a visit to the city, Kamprad is credited with the idea of creating a parallel visitor experience and enlisting his architect, Claes Knutsson, to create a Swedish response to the New York museum. Instead of the world-class art in the New York gallery, a contemporary design with prices for a wide and popular consumer base was envisioned. The building captured attention instantaneously, and indeed, respondents report that Ikea Kungens Kurva ranks amongst the most visited sites in Stockholm, ranking favourably with key city attractions such as the Vasa ship museum (Vasamuseet) and the metropole's outdoor ethnological museum (Skansen). Project leader for the reconstruction, Hans von Hijne identified that the vast glazed construction should combined a central inner platform for standard furniture display, while the semicircular glass walls would house the showrooms and restaurant.

Stepping off the escalator on the third floor and following a series of arrows projected on the floor by light fixtures overhead, one can see that the round building is an effective architectural platform for the showrooms and compact 'homes' that follow. The corkscrew shape allows shoppers to pass showrooms on the left, while a

FIGURE 1.2 Interior of Ikea Kungens Kurva, illustrating the corkscrew plan partly inspired by the Guggenheim Museum in New York.

Source: Photo by author.

vast circular glazed wall wraps around an inner glass tube that houses conventional displays, such as sofas placed in rows or office furniture. Natural light from the inner glass funnel floods the shop floor, and one can take in the full extent of the three levels of showrooms, usually animated with wandering and probing shoppers to a background of easy-listening music. Intended to make better use of the round building for furniture exhibitions, the effect is singular in allowing one to gaze between levels and across the extensive floor space.

Every aspect of the Ikea showrooms is the result of detailed planning. The standard size for the majority of Ikea stores is about 30,000 m2, which can comfortably contain fifty to fifty-five room sets and three 'homes'. The Ikea store in Kungens Kurva is considerably larger than average, and due to its vast size, walking past all the exhibits and stopping, albeit briefly, at each can take up to several hours. Unsurprisingly, international spatial analyses have focussed on Ikea stores for their circuitous route, maze-like layout and disorientation to shoppers. Often quoted in the media is the labyrinthine 'no-exit strategy' as forwarded by Alan Penn, director of the Virtual Reality Centre for the Built Environment at University College London, Ikea stores, he tells us, are 'built like a maze' so that it is difficult to deviate from the time-consuming route. Shortcuts are present purely to fulfil fire regulations, but when one opts for them, one finds oneself 'adrift in a sea of lampshades' (Tucker 2011). Most of my research respondents, while occasionally referring to the Ikea concourse in terms approaching that of an obstacle course, tended to congratulate themselves on their expert knowledge of shortcuts, hidden doors and exits. Very few I spoke to travelled to the out-of-town store with an expectation of a quick exit but instead dedicated several hours to the shopping trip.

Nothing can be purchased in the showrooms, and apart from the occasional bins with small decorative goods, actual acquisition is largely deferred to the basement department. Instead, shoppers encounter a route that tracks the furniture displays, running along the interior of the vast glass corkscrew. At regular intervals, signs hang from the ceiling advocating the benefits of thrifty design. Pictures of designers are common in showrooms, small smiling faces peering up from every angle, perched on CD holders and flowerpots. On large pieces of furniture, one finds more emphasised designer presence. For example, one of the rooms has a large Vaxholm sofa with an accompanying tag explaining the designer's plan that it could split into various sections and fit a variety of room sizes. Small labels called 'tips and ideas' similarly inform the shopper that a series of hooks can conveniently hold dishcloths or children's artwork in kitchens. Residents are continuously implied in large floor-to-ceiling posters, such as, for instance, two men cooking together under a sign 'We live in 25m squared' Children are evoked by crude sketches hanging in showroom kitchens, while parents are implied by the preservation of these artworks on a would-be family notice board. As one moves from the third floor to the second and first, one passes from the sofas to media and storage, work IKEA (Vi jobbar på 40 m2), bedrooms and children's IKEA, which is a mandatory layout, and all adhere to the same cluster of themes.

If the upper floors retain an exhibitionary ambience lent to them by the architectural plan and showrooms, the lower ground floors progressively project a fast-food atmosphere. As one moves downwards, one goes from the showroom tableaux to a decidedly self-service area in which the fruits of standardised mass production are found in kitchen utensils (saucepans and scrubbing brushes) piled high in metal wire baskets and stacked haphazardly. Goods are not only inexpensive but also arranged in abundance, a stark reminder of Ikea's formula that high-volume products lead to lessened costs. The expectation by informants as they walk around is that 'it is for nothing – until you get to the cash registers and think "that can't be right"' was a commonly made observation. Many respondents described dumping goods at the till, realising that they couldn't afford them, or purchasing in anticipation of a possible return within the three-month window.[32]

Research for this anthropological study of Ikea consumption was carried out in 2008 with shorter visits principally in 2010. Research was funded by the Irish Research Council for Humanities and Social Sciences, now called the Irish Research Council, and by the Swedish Institute. My young family and I settled in Stockholm for a year, and during that time, I conducted forty-eight interviews with householders. I decided to 'follow the furniture' (cf. Marcus 1995) from the world's largest flagship store located in Kungens Kurva (King's Curve) in the southern suburbs of the Swedish capital and followed research respondents as they rippled out from this centre to various locations in the metropole and met them in their homes for interviews. Based in the store (with kind permission from Ikea), I found a mix of households made up of diverse ages, genders and backgrounds who were willing to allow me to follow them home. Several kept in touch by email, and I had the opportunity to meet several respondents again during a follow-up trip in 2010. These are principally the people I refer to in this book. I argue that from the perspective of my informants, defining immutable boundaries of 'Ikea' is untenable. Therefore, the book removes design from the relatively abstract 'Scandinavian design' idiom and places it squarely within a range of human practice, historical trajectories and political strategies that frame its apprehension on a popular level.

Notes

1 See Garvey (2011).
2 The IKEA museum replaces a smaller 800 m2 exhibition that showed twenty different room settings furnished with IKEA products.
3 In 2010, I visited the earlier exhibition that was previously situated in an unremarkable white concrete building called Tillsammans (trans: Together) and was dedicated to Ikea corporate 'culture'. At that time, the display progressed visitors through a series of tableaux typifying each decade from the 1950s and eventually arriving at current styles. The exhibits carried descriptive labels and were cordoned off with heavy ropes.
4 Inspiration for this approach arose in the early planning of a special edition of the *Journal of Design History*, entitled 'Design Dispersed' (2016).
5 I am grateful to Henrik Wennerhag and members of the Ikea management for setting up a small desk for me in the reception area of Ikea from which I approached shoppers. The Swedish Ikea store is the engine behind the Nordic countries' largest marketplace. Soon

after returning from fieldwork in Sweden, an Ikea opened in Dublin in 2009, which I explored in order to complement my research in Stockholm. Before long, I realised that one small book would not cover two locations and decided that the Irish element of my study could be used to aid my thinking but that detailed analysis would have to wait for another time or project.

6 'The Most Important Place in the World' is an Ikea slogan I found on the exterior of Ikea stores in Dublin and Stockholm during fieldwork ('Hem, den viktigaste platsen i världen').

7 For example, Jonsson and Foss (2011) and Tarnovskaya and de Chernatony (2011). See Rugman and Hodgetts (2001) for an alternative perspective.

8 In diverse global cities since the 1990s, Ikea encapsulates modern design and benign capitalism for the emerging middle classes (see Fehérváry 2009: 28).

9 'IKEA Retailing Facts and Figures', Inter IKEA Systems BV, accessed 13/03/17, http://franchisor.ikea.com/ikea-retailing-facts-and-figures-new/.

10 Later, Tottenham MP David Lammy said, 'Ikea must have known that in opening the store next to the second most deprived constituency in London and by leafleting the area about knock-down bargains for those who arrived first, people would flock to their store in large numbers'. (Gareth Furby, 'Crush Chaos at Ikea Store Opening', *BBC News*, February 10, 2005, accessed 20/03/17, http://news.bbc.co.uk/2/hi/uk_news/england/london/4252421.stm.)

11 'IKEA Disobedients', Museum of Modern Art, accessed 19/01/17, www.moma.org/explore/multimedia/videos/235/1158.

12 DEMOCRATIC DESIGN - IKEA, exhibition running in PINAKOTHEK DER MODERNE, Munich. from 03.04.2009 - 12.07.200, See Artmap, accessed 19/01/17, https://artmap.com/pinakothek/exhibition/democratic-design-ikea-2009.

13 'The IKEA Phenomenon', Hofmobiliendopt, accessed 19/01/17, www.hofmobiliendepot.at/en/exhibition/exhibition-archive/the-ikea-phenomenon.html.

14 Medieakademins förtroendebarometer 2008. The barometer was designed by Lennart Weibull and Sören Holmberg, professors at the University of Gothenburg, in conjunction with the market research company TNS Gallup in 2008 It is published each year on MedieAkademien's web page http://medieakademien.se/#page

15 Ikea-in-the abstract is the only place where I feel it is appropriate to use all caps (IKEA) because it refers specifically to the corporation as a legal and financial entity and not to Ikea as a cultural package. For reasons of consistency however I retain the same style (Ikea) throughout.

16 As a result of investigative journalism, a television programme aired in 2011 in which the previously unknown aspects of the Ikea group were uncovered. Profits from stores were traced to a foundation – the Interlogo Foundation in Liechtenstein – and interpreted as a tax-avoidance measure. (*Uppdrag granskning*. Made in Sweden – IKEA. Producer, Nils Hansson and SVT, 2011; see also Kristoffersson 2014: 100.)

17 Ingka Holding, in turn, belongs to Stichting Ingka Foundation, also Dutch registered, which was given Mr Kamprad's shares in 1982 (Kollewe 2011).

18 *Uppdrag granskning*. Made in Sweden – IKEA. Producer Nils Hansson and SVT, 2011.

19 Most of Ikea's sales take place in Germany (21 per cent), the United States (13 per cent), the United Kingdom (12 per cent), France (9 per cent) and Sweden (7 per cent). (Tarnovskaya, Ghauri and Elg 2007).

20 In order to gain purchase on the ambiguity of global movements, anthropologist Anna Tsing advocates the adoption of two analytical frameworks. Firstly, the scrutiny of 'ideologies of scale', meaning cultural claims about the local, the regional and the global. Secondly, claims about circulation and stability and 'networks and strategies of proliferation' (2000: 347). Against this, she questions how our research respondents make sense of events and social processes, how specific projects maintain a commitment to the local. These local projects may focus on any coherent bundle of ideas and practices; even in the face of the 'biggest world-making dreams and schemes', they open up the messiness,

the incoherence and the fissures apparent in the juxtaposition of ideologies of scale and projects of scale-making (2000: 347).
21 As a case in point, take Keane's example of money. Money is instructive because from an economic perspective it should 'in essence be weightless and invisible, any concrete forms it takes remaining purely arbitrary' (Keane 2003, 2008: 38). Nevertheless something so seemingly abstract as is clearly mediated by the concepts that people have about it, by the actions that deploy it, as well by as the perspectives and moralities that direct these practices. As a social relation, money is subject to earmarking, saving, devising and gifting in diverse ways, as people engage with it to fulfil private projects (Gilbert 2005; Zelizer 1994). It may operate as a sign, but it is not an arbitrary signifier; and instead, its semiotic and material potential plays a role in the moral world of social agents. Not only is money never as abstract as it is often represented but also the very ideas of abstraction entailed in this perspective are part of a wider constellation of concepts that include moral, political and socio-historical trajectories (Keane 2008: 39).
22 White walls emphasise the lightness of the colour over the solidity of the plaster, for example (see Garvey 2013).
23 Following Slater, this means that what we consider durable, stable and meaningful does not rest on either physicality or immateriality but on 'social thingness', the conditions and contingencies 'through which things are stabilised as social materialities, or destabilised, reconfigured, problematised' (Slater 2003: 96).
24 'About Svensk Form', Svensk Form, accessed 25/01/17, http://svenskform.se/en/about-svensk-form/.
25 'About Svensk Form', Svensk Form, accessed 25/01/17, http://svenskform.se/en/about-svensk-form/.
26 This was particularly emphasised in the homes of young and middle-aged, middle-class professionals, where muted colours, unpatterned furniture, relatively few tablecloths and random personal possessions were evident in living areas. In homes such as these, traces of children – outside of bedrooms – were restricted to boxes of toys stacked neatly in living room corners.
27 The second store is Ikea Barkarby.
28 Not all Ikea stores follow the colours of the Swedish flag: this particular branding exercise replaced the earlier red-and-white exteriors that can still be found in some Swedish towns. As is now a common pattern, Ikea's establishment was quickly followed by other large retailers and major international chains, and the area is now home to an agglomeration of square store warehouses that boast the title of Scandinavia's largest marketplace, with thirty million visitors annually. At the time of fieldwork, plans were afoot to develop it further with the addition of a vast shopping mall owned by Ikea-linked company Ikano that promised to 'ensure its status as Scandinavia's biggest and most successful retail area. And it will lay the foundations for it to be unchallenged for many years to come.' ('Our Businesses', Ikano, accessed 03/03/15, www.ikanofastigheter.se/ImageVaultFiles/id_1724/cf_28/Kungens_Kurva_broschyr.PDF). The area is currently home to approximately one hundred high-volume retail stores such as housed in the large mall in Heron City, other prominent retailers and fast-food outlets and is credited with an annual turnover of SEK 8 billion and thirty million visitors.
29 Car ownership rose to two million in the 1960s, allowing retailers such as Ingvar Kamprad to develop inexpensive out-of-town locations for some (but not all) of his stores (Torekull 2000).
30 The Million Programme entailed the demolition of approximately 350,000 homes (Klinenberg 2013).
31 It is perhaps not surprising then that some of these areas, as emblems of twentieth-century massive building programmes, have since come to represent the alienating forces of the welfare state (cf. Hilson 2008). In recent decades, prosperous middle-class Swedes have increasingly relocated into more established districts or returned to the city centre, leaving some suburban districts occupied by socially disadvantaged residents, including

a high proportion of Stockholm's immigrant population. One such area called Husby, which was developed as part of the Million Programme and completed in 1972, was catapulted into international fame as the location of immigrant riots in 2013.

32 In Dublin, the arrival of Ikea was preceded by a local youth theatre staging a play entitled 'Waiting for Ikea' set in Ballymun, equally a renowned and economically deprived part of the city. The advert pictured the not uncommon scene of young women sitting in a public square in their pyjamas, a visual idiom that captures the paucity of employment in the area. The arrival of Ikea in Dublin, facilitated by a change in national planning legislation, was greeted with crowds that, according to then-manager Garry Deakin, exceeded their 'wildest dreams' and was touched with a frisson of excitement and trepidation as would-be shoppers were turned away on the first days when numbers exceeded safe levels.

References

Anderson, Benedict R. 1983. *Imagined Communities: Reflections on the Origin and Spread of Nationalism*. London: Verso.

Appadurai, Arjun. 1990. "Disjuncture and Difference in the Global Cultural Economy." *Theory, Culture & Society* 7 (2): 295–310.

Arrhenius, Thordis. 2010. "The Vernacular on Display: Skansen Open-Air Museum in 1930s Stockholm." In *Swedish Modernism: Architecture, Consumption, and the Welfare State*, edited by Helena Mattsson and Sven-Olov Wallenstein. London: Black Dog Publishing.

Arvidsson, Adam. 2006. *Brands: Meaning and Value in Media Culture*. Abingdon and New York: Routledge.

Bengtsson, Staffan. 2010. *IKEA the Book: Designers, Producers and Other Stuff*. Stockholm: Arvinius Förlag.

Benson, Peter and Stuart Kirsch. 2010. "Corporate Oxymorons." *Dialectical Anthropology* 34 (1): 45–48.

Bertilsson, Jon. 2014. "The Slippery Relationship Between Brand Ethic and Profit." *Ephemera: Theory & Politics in Organization* 14 (1): 125–136.

Bevan, Andrew and David Wengrow. 2010. *Cultures of Commodity Branding*. Walnut Creek, CA: Left Coast.

Bourdieu, Pierre and Randal Johnson. 1993. *The Field of Cultural Production: Essays on Art and Literature*. Cambridge: Polity Press.

Buchli, Victor. 2013. *An Anthropology of Architecture*. London: Bloomsbury.

Burkeman, Oliver. 2004. "The Miracle of Älmhult: Part One and Two." *The Guardian*. Available online: www.theguardian.com/lifeandstyle/2004/jun/17/shopping.retail, accessed 13/03/17.

Carrier, James G. and Daniel Miller. 1998. *Virtualism: A New Political Economy*. Oxford: Berg.

Cassell, Philip. 1993. "Introduction." In *The Giddens Reader*, edited by Cassell Philip, 1–37. Stanford, CA: Stanford University Press.

Cieraad, Irene. 2014. 'IKEA and the Dutch Domestic Landscape: Trendsetter or Trend Follower?' 'IKEA en het Nederlandse woonlandschap. Trendsetter of trendvolger?' *DASH*: Stijlkamers/ Interiors on Display, Fall issue, 62–75.

Collins, Lauren. 2011. "HOUSE PERFECT: Is the IKEA Ethos Comfy or Creepy?" *The New Yorker*, October 3, available online at http://www.newyorker.com/magazine/2011/10/03/house-perfect.

Coombe, Rosemary. 1996. "Embodied Trademarks: Mimesis and Alterity on American Commercial Frontiers." *Cultural Anthropology* 11 (2): 202–224.

Cronin, Anne, M. 2004. *Advertising Myths: The Strange Half-Lives of Images and Commodities.* London and New York: Routledge.
Ekström, Karin M. 2010. "Design and Consumption." In *Consumer Behaviour: A Nordic Perspective*, edited by Karen M. Ekström. Lund: Studentlitteratur.
Fallan, Kjetil. ed. 2012. *Scandinavian Design: Alternative Histories.* London: Berg.
Fehérváry, Krisztina. 2009. "Goods and States: The Political Logic of State-Socialist Material Culture." *Comparative Studies in Society and History* 51 (2): 426–459.
Foster, Robert J. 2007. "The Work of the New Economy: Consumers, Brands, and Value Creation." *Cultural Anthropology* 22 (4): 707–731.
Foster, Robert J. 2008a. "Commodities, Brands, Love and Kula: Comparative Notes on Value Creation in Honor of Nancy Munn." *Anthropological Theory* 8 (1): 9–25.
Foster, Robert J. 2008b. *Coca-Globalization: Following Soft Drinks From New York to New Guinea.* New York: Palgrave Macmillan.
Foster, Robert J. 2010. "Corporate Oxymorons and the Anthropology of Corporations." *Dialectical Anthropology* 34 (1): 95–102.
Garsten, Christina and Anette Nyqvist. 2013. *Organisational Anthropology: Doing Ethnography in and Among Complex Organisations, Anthropology, Culture and Society.* London: Pluto Press.
Garsten, Christina, Jessica Lindvert, and Renita Thedvall, eds. 2015. *Makeshift Work in a Changing Labour Market: The Swedish Model in the Post-Financial Crisis Era.* Cheltenham: Edward Elgar. Giddens, Anthony. 1990. *The Consequences of Modernity.* Stanford, CA: Stanford University Press.
Garvey, Pauline. 2011. "Ikea as Folk Museum." In *Ikea Butter Churn for Gneeveguilla*, edited by Gareth Kennedy. Invited contributor to the catalogue that forms part of this art installation, funded by Kerry County Council and on tour throughout Ireland during 2011/2012.
Garvey, Pauline. 2013. "'Ikea sofas are like H&M trousers': The Potential of Sensuous Signs." *Journal of Business Anthropology* 2 (1): 75–92.
Garvey, Pauline and Adam Drazin, eds. 2016. *Design Dispersed: Design History, Design Practice and Anthropology. Journal of Design History* 29 (1): 1–7.
Gilbert, Emily. 2005. "Common Cents: Situating Money in Time and Place." *Economy and Society* 34 (3): 357–388.
Habel, Ylva. 2010. "The Exhibition Modern Leisure as a Site of Governmentality." In *Swedish Modernism: Architecture, Consumption and the Welfare State*, edited by Helena Mattsson and Sven-Olov Wallenstein, 122–133. London: Black Dog Publishing.
Hannerz, Ulf. 1996. *Transnational Connections: Culture, People, Places.* London and New York: Routledge.
Hartman, Tod. 2007. "The Ikeaization of France." *Public Culture* 19 (3): 483–498.
Hilson, Mary. 2008. *The Nordic Model: Scandinavia Since 1945.* London: Reaktion Books.
Holt, Douglas B. 2004. *How Brands Become Icons: The Principles of Cultural Branding.* Boston, MA: Harvard Business School Press.
Hoskins, Janet. 1998. *Biographical Objects: How Things Tell the Stories of People's Lives.* New York and London: Routledge.
Hoskins, Janet. 2006. "Agency, Biography and Objects." In *Handbook of Material Culture*, edited by Christopher Tilley, Webb Keane, Patricia Spyer, 74–84. Los Angeles, London, New Delhi, Singapore, Washington DC, and Melbourne: Sage.
Jonsson, Anna and Nicolai J. Foss. 2011. "International Expansion Through Flexible Replication: Learning From the Internationalization Experience of IKEA." *Journal of International Business Studies* 42 (9): 1079–1102.
Julier, Guy. 2014. *The Culture of Design.* 3rd ed. Los Angeles: Sage.
Keane, Webb. 2003. "Semiotics and the Social Analysis of Material Things." *Language & Communication* 23 (3): 409–425.

Keane, Webb. 2005. "The Hazards of New Clothes: What Signs Make Possible." In *The Art of Clothing: A Pacific Experience*, edited by Susanne Küchler and Graeme Were, 1-16. London: University College London Press.

Keane, Webb. 2008. "Market, Materiality and Moral Metalanguage." *Anthropological Theory* 8 (1): 27–42.

Klein, Naomi. 2000. *No Logo: Taking Aim at the Brand Bullies*. 1st ed. Toronto: Knopf Canada.

Kollewe, Julia. 2011. "The Secret of IKEA's Success: Lean Operations, Shrewd Tax Planning and Tight Control." *The Economist*. Available online: www.economist.com/node/18229400, accessed 17/02/17.

Kopytoff, Igor. 1986. "The Cultural Biography of Things: Commoditization as Process." In *The Social Life of Things: Commodities in Cultural Perspective*, edited by Arjun Appadurai, 64–91. Cambridge: Cambridge University Press.

Krause-Jensen, Jakob. 2010. *Flexible Firm*. New York: Berghahn Books.

Kravets, Olga and Örsan Örge. 2010. "Iconic Brands: A Socio-Material Story." *Journal of Material Culture* 15 (2): 205–232.

Kristoffersson, Sara. 2014. *Design by IKEA: A Cultural History*. London: Bloomsbury.

Lee, Benjamin and Edward Li Puma. 2002. "Cultures of Circulation: The Imaginations of Modernity." *Public Culture* 14 (1): 191–213.

Lien, Marianne E. 1997. *Marketing and Modernity, Explorations in Anthropology*. Oxford and New York: Berg.

Lindqvist, Ursula. 2009. "The Cultural Archive of the IKEA Store." *Space and Culture* 12 (1): 43–62.

Lury, Celia. 2004. "Marking Time With Nike: The Illusion of the Durable." In *The Blackwell Cultural Economy Reader*, edited by Ash Amin and Nigel Thrift, 384–403. Oxford: Blackwell.

Manning, Paul. 2010. "The Semiotics of Brand." *Annual Review of Anthropology* 39: 33–49.

Manning, Paul and Ann Uplisashvili. 2007. "'Our beer': Ethnographic Brands in Postsocialist Georgia." *American Anthropologist* 109 (4): 626–641.

Marcus, George. 1995. "Ethnography in/of the World System: The Emergence of Multi-Sited Ethnography." *Annual Review of Anthropology* 24: 95–117.

Maurer, Bill. 2006. "The Anthropology of Money." *Annual Review of Anthropology* 35: 15–36.

Mauss, Marcel. 1970. *The Gift: Forms and Functions of Exchange in Archaic Societies*. [S.l.]: Cohen & West.

MedieAkademiens förtroendebarometer, 2008 http://medieakademien.se/#page, accessed 2/02/2012.

Meneley, Anne. 2004. "Extra Virgin Olive Oil and Slow Food." *Anthropologica* 46:165–176.

Miller, Daniel. 1987. *Material Culture and Mass Consumption*. Oxford: Blackwell.

Miller, Daniel. 1998. "Coca-Cola: A Black Sweet Drink From Trinidad." In *Material Cultures: Why Some Things Matter*, edited by Daniel Miller, 169-188. Chicago: University of Chicago Press.

Miller, Daniel. 2005. *Materiality*. Durham, NC: Duke University Press.

Moeran, Brian and Christina Garsten. 2012. "What's in a Name? Editors' Introduction." *Journal of Business Anthropology* 1 (1): 1–19.

Moore, Robert. 2003. "From Genericide to Viral Marketing: On Brand." *Language and Communication* 23 (3–4): 331–357.

Murphy, Keith M. 2015. *Swedish Design: An Ethnography*. Ithaca: Cornell University Press.

Otto, Ton. 2016. "History in and for Design." *Journal of Design History* 29 (1): 58–70.

Rajak, Dinah. 2011. *In Good Company: An Anatomy of Corporate Social Responsibility*. Palo Alto: Stanford University Press.

Ritzer, George. 2011. *The McDonaldization of Society*. 6th [rev. and updated] ed. Thousand Oaks, CA and London: Pine Forge.

Robach, Cilla. 2010. *Formens frigörelse: konsthantverk och design under debatt i 1960-talets Sverige*. Stockholm: Arvinius.

Roberts, Tom. 2012. "From 'new materialism' to 'machinic assemblage': Agency and Affect in IKEA." *Environment and Planning A* 44 (10): 2512–2529.

Rugman, Alan and Richard Hodgetts. 2001. "The End of Global Strategy." *European Management Journal* 19 (4): 333–343.

Slater, Don. 2003. "Markets, Materiality and the 'new economy'." In *Market Relations and the Competitive Process*, edited by Stan Metcalfe and Alan Warde, 95–113. Manchester: Manchester University Press.

Smart, Barry. 1999. *Resisting McDonaldization*. London and Thousand Oaks: Sage.

Stenebo, John. 2012. *The Truth About IKEA: The Secret Behind the World's Fifth Richest Man and the Success of the Flatpack Giant*. London: Gibson Square Books.

Stolle, Dietlind and Micheletti Michele. 2013. *Political Consumerism: Global Responsibility in Action*. Cambridge: Cambridge University Press.

Suchman, Lucy. 2011. "Anthropological Relocations and the Limits of Design." *Annual Review of Anthropology* 40: 1–18.

Tarnovskaya, Veronica, Pervez N. Ghauri and Ulf Elg. 2007. "Market Driving Supplier Strategy: IKEA's Global Sourcing Network in Two Developing Markets". Paper presented at the International Conference "Novye napravleniya razvitiya marketinga: Vzaimodeystviya i partneskie otnosheniya" [New Directions of Marketing Development: Interactions and Partner Relations], Moscow, Russia, November 15–16. Available online at www.snee.org/filer/papers/482.pdf, accessed 03/03/14.

Tarnovskaya, Veronika and Leslie de Chernatony. 2011. "Internalising a Brand Across Cultures: The Case of IKEA." *International Journal of Retail & Distribution Management* 39 (8): 598–618.

Tilley, Christopher, Webb Keane, Susanne Kuüchler, Mike Rowlands, and Patricia Spyer, eds. 2006. *Handbook of Material Culture*. London and Thousand Oaks, CA: Sage.

Tomlinson, John. 1999. *Globalization and Culture*. Chichester: Polity Press.

Torekull, Bertil. 1999. *Leading by Design: The Ikea Story*. London, New York: Harper Collins.

Tsing, Anna. 2000. "The Global Situation." *Cultural Anthropology* 15 (3): 327–360.

Tucker, Ian. 2011. "Adrift in a Shopping Maze: It's a Successful No-Exit Strategy." *The Guardian*. Available online: www.theguardian.com/business/2011/jan/30/ikea-like-a-maze-ian-tucker, accessed 16/09/15.

Urban, Greg, and Kyung-Nan Koh. 2013. "Ethnographic Research on Modern Business Corporations." *Annual Review of Anthropology* 42: 139–158.

Weiner, Annette B. 1985. "Inalienable Wealth." *American Ethnologist* 12 (2): 210–227.

Weiner, Annette B. 1992. *Inalienable Possessions: The Paradox of Keeping-While-Giving*. Berkeley: University of California Press.

Zelizer, Viviana A. Rotman. 1994. *The Social Meaning of Money*. New York: Basic Books.

2
BENIGN INTERVENTION
Ikea showrooms as tableaux vivant

'No one does branding quite like the giant blue and yellow furniture company' announces *Form*, the foremost Nordic architecture and design publication running since 1905 and the vehicle for the organisation Svensk Form. Resolutely hitched to what it calls 'Nordic display', the magazine features Ikea and several well-known department stores in Stockholm. In this issue, Ikea is emblematic of specific Scandinavian display practices that have 'moved beyond the mannequin' in cultivating a life filled with 'surface, scenes and disguises' (Cirelli 2012: 59; see also Garvey *forthcoming*; Hultén 2012). In marked contrast to conventional display strategies that 'rely on eye-catching window displays that ratchet up the drama in an endless cycle of oneupmanship, Ikea does the opposite. Their sales strategy requires that customers recognise themselves and their homes in IKEA's displays' (Cirelli 2012: 68). In other words, Ikea showrooms 'strive for the familiar' (Cirelli 2012: 68; see also Garvey *forthcoming*). For example, deliberately placed items of personalia indicate family members in showrooms such as knitting needles and wool on a shelf or a cup and saucer on a coffee table. In one showroom in Ikea Kungens Kurva, a breakfast tray on a bed suggests a recently departed resident while a baby's cot sits in the corner.

Ikea stores are frequently presented as stages for experimentation in domestic practice. It is relatively common, for example, to find images in social media that picture Ikea showrooms as the fitting backdrop for romantic expression, family outings and household provision. In a critical appraisal of such media depictions, historian Mark Sandberg draws attention to a series of quirky Wes Anderson-directed Ikea advertisements aired in the United States in 2003, which were supposedly based on typical shopping practices adopted by Ikea consumers (Sandberg 2011). In these adverts, fictional family members try out Ikea furniture through sampling how well arguments can be conducted in the showrooms. The kitchen showroom, for example, provides the scene for marital discord, the wife accusing her husband of 'prowling the streets' while she is 'stuck in here like some prisoner' (Sandberg 2011: 63).¹ In the second advert, the Ikea living room is used as a prop for a teenager breaking the news of her unexpected pregnancy to her parents (Sandberg 2011). In each scene, the showroom is deemed sufficiently lifelike to imagine a familial row by these make-believe consumers. In relatively high-profile advertisements such as these, we encounter not only the extension of Ikea into the emotional territory of the conventional nuclear family but also its place at the level of everyday domestic praxis.

Internationally circulating sketches intensify the betwixt-and-between sensation that is actively encouraged in Ikea showrooms and frame it as globally comprehensible. Showrooms (or room sets as Ikea managers call them) have been described as an 'enormous prop room', potentially leading 'into the realm of pure theatre and high camp – as when a subject-consumer is truly "playing the part"' (Hartman 2007: 484), but more than this, they demonstrate the fragile boundary that separates spectatorship from participation that one routinely encounters in shopping trips, particularly in Ikea (Sandberg 2011). There is a performative basis to routine shopping, Sandberg suggests, which is part and parcel of the shopper's repertoire. When purchasing a bed, most people hover between sitting on it awkwardly or lying down on it for a few moments, demonstrating that the internalised boundary distinguishing public and private space is as tentative as its physical counterpart (Sandberg 2011).

Satellite-based sketches commonly lampoon both this boundary and its transgression such as in the cliché of the romantic couple who set up home in Ikea showrooms. In one Hollywood movie, *500 Days of Summer*,² this caricature is particularly evident in one scene where a young couple is pictured cavorting around the Ikea store. Literally skipping and holding hands, they linger over the kitchen fittings, stir non-existent food in saucepans and predictably finish up in the bedroom. Clearly, the showrooms are being used as a kind of prop, but beyond being a backdrop for romantic expression, they are employed by the protagonists to light-heartedly conjure and imitate routine household activities. Although the banality of domestic regimens seems far removed from blossoming romance, mimicking them does acknowledge their salience in forging relationships for the long term. Indeed, the twinning of coupledom and Ikea in one way or another is so amenable to soap opera that a small serial soap opera, *Ikea Heights*, represents one melodrama filmed entirely in the Burbank, California, Ikea store.³

It is not surprising, then, to find prominent stories in global media translated into the Ikea idiom. Concurrent with the movie *Gravity*'s high profile in the run-up to the Oscar awards in 2014, for instance, I was sent a humorous clip that was based on the theme of outer space but set in an Ikea store.⁴ The clip showed a young couple who lose sight of each other while shopping in Ikea. Pretty soon, they are lost, cut adrift and meandering amid the vertiginous cornucopia of products and unfamiliar Swedish labels, disorientated in a vast space. These light-hearted clips rely on a fairly standard theme, stressing the umbilical link between romantic relationships and Ikea while also satirising it as a cliché. One episode of the American situational comedy *30 Rock* provides a neat demonstration of this in which the female lead is mistakenly perceived as a lesbian and set up with a woman.⁵ When the confusion is cleared, a platonic friendship develops only to be muddled and ultimately discontinued when the lead suggests they visit Ikea.

In these – always humorous – sketches, we find romance coupled with the enactment of domestic practice in a way that is framed, intensified and parodied. The force of this parody derives from the juxtaposition of the Ikea backdrop within an intimate relationship, transposing the public and commercial into a personal idiom with which the spectator can identify. Humour is elicited through the juxtaposition of unlikely scenarios in unlikely places, again found in the movie *500 Days of Summer*, in which the two lovers lie languidly in an Ikea showroom bed and observe in passing that 'Darling, I don't know how to tell you this, but there is a Chinese family in our bathroom'. In order for the comic absurdity to be effective, the individual must appreciate the contrast and identify with it. This template provides one characteristic that research respondents describe as the Ikea experience. By this, they mean experiencing showrooms as staging posts to try out a domestic scene that operates as a kind of tableaux vivant, entailing store staff, shoppers and material culture. Significantly for this book, this type of tableau necessarily entails enacting and intensifying the intimate and ordinary within a common, public and corporate medium.

Exhibitionary techniques found in Ikea include the showroom tableaux and the actions of visitors located in them, both of which respondents describe as evoking 'inspiration'. The crafted arrangement of furniture in showrooms is salient to their work as stimuli for ideas and plans on the part of customers, but my point here is aimed to counter a prevailing belief that inspiration devolves from the virtuoso acts of exceptional individuals. Instead I contend inspiration is embedded squarely within a nexus of social practices and distributed agency rather than being evoked purely through the choreographed actions of management. Consumers attribute particular human intentions to objects deemed *designed*, and for my respondents designers are described in terms of a benign but largely anonymous collective whose creativity is foreshadowed in specific objects and arrangements of furniture – 'the Ikea designers are very clever' was a frequent refrain during fieldwork.

Designed environments and objects intensify and materialise benign intervention, and render a distant set of professional practices actual and concrete. The showrooms, moreover, extend a legacy of housing theatre found and widely encountered in museological, home expo and commercial exhibitions (see the next chapter). However, in this instance, the evocation of agency is not only designer focussed but also heightened and intensified through the tableaux vivant, the animated showrooms and the activities of consumers. What this implies is that Ikea showrooms integrate people – actual, distant and imagined – with their goods, thus animating the scenes, rebounding on ideas of design. Set up as living spaces, which are lifelike but not quite real, showrooms do not merely signify or reflect domesticity but operate as different kinds of spaces against which respondents understand and mimic mainstream practice. Through such means, Ikea showrooms provide an immediate visual shorthand for the practice of domesticity as a globally intelligible concern.

'Now Ikea is into design!'

Let me introduce one research respondent who I'll call Johanna. Johanna and her husband, Marius, are young professionals who had recently returned to Sweden when I met them. Johanna is a mother of three in her late thirties who worked in a state agency, while Marius worked in the foreign service. They had returned from a stint abroad, and my request for an interview coincided with their efforts to furnish their newly acquired home.

In order to purchase bathroom and kitchen furniture in Ikea, Johanna needed to 'think about it for half a day beforehand, it being such a big effort'. She continued, 'We certainly needed a strategy, you see, you need to plan it. It isn't nice shopping. It isn't like going to a posh shop'. On their first visit, after returning to Sweden, they didn't have a plan:

> We just left the kids in the play area, and we brought the baby with us, and we didn't quite think, and we just looked everywhere, and we didn't buy a thing and then we needed lunch . . . Okay, next time, we'll make a plan and just focus on two or three things.

For the following visit, they first consulted the catalogue, made a list and realized that fitting a kitchen and bathroom would have to be achieved sequentially. They decided to take just one room per visit. Johanna left the children with her husband's parents, and they arrived at Ikea very early in the morning. Despite all her plans, the result was chaos:

> It was an awful day, the twenty-seventh of December, and everyone had the day off work, and everyone was there. All ten cashiers, everything was open. It was a nightmare realizing that this was the 'wrong day' to be here and you had all the kids screaming, people were desperate – you could see it in their eyes. It was crowded, even though it is huge. It wasn't a nice experience.

Undaunted, and with some time and effort, however, Johanna devised her own system: 'Yes, the more times you go there, you get a habit, and you know how to plan and you get a bit more. . . *tactics* is the word'.

Despite Johanna's obvious dislike of shopping in the store, she describes a visit there as inevitable: 'It is inevitable to go to Ikea'. I find this comment surprising because when we go through her furnishings, we find that she has purchased nothing substantial there. At most, she could point to one leather armchair and blinds for her boys' bedroom: 'I put Ikea blinds in the boys' bedroom because they are going to get thrashed anyhow'. The result of four trips and a lot of effort was 'small things for the household like hooks, where you put the curtains, really just practical things'. For everything else, she chose 'solid furniture that will last' and has a particular preference for a second-hand site called Blocket:

> I am very into second hand, for many reasons. It is good for the environment, and it is cheaper, and so yes, I would probably rather go for solid wood … That bookshelf we bought for three hundred SEK, and it really is not anything that would impress people, but it appealed to me because it is solid wood rather than Ikea that is just veneer.

In the same vein, she looked carefully at Ikea sofas but later decided to purchase two mid-century Folke Ohlsson Dux sofas that cost 35,000 SEK. Her husband's grandmother had them for four decades, and in that time they required no maintenance beyond changing the covers. Nevertheless, they traipsed out to Kungens Kurva located in Stockholm's southern suburbs in order to view its offerings, quickly arriving at the conclusion that Ikea sofas wouldn't last forty years. Besides, she admits, 'I wouldn't be proud to have a sofa from Ikea', the first hint on her part that as a professional middle-class household, it is preferable not to have too many Ikea purchases, at least amongst statement furnishings.

Of all my respondents, Johanna seemed the least likely to describe herself as an Ikea customer. She has clear ideas about the environment and purchasing furniture that is 'solid' and that will 'last forty years'. She has followed these ideals with her major purchases, such as her kitchen and living room. The expense of these items is placed alongside the saving they made with their second-hand occasional purchases. She claims she would be embarrassed to own certain items of Ikea furniture, such as a sofa, and she clearly dislikes her previous experiences of shopping there. Despite all this, she describes the Ikea trip as 'inevitable' when sourcing items for their newly acquired home. 'Why inevitable?' I ask. 'Price-wise, I would say, it is efficient shopping as well, but it is certainly the price', she responds but notes 'there are lots of things I would never buy in Ikea, and since we can afford to buy sofas elsewhere, we went to Ikea, and we realized they weren't good enough or they weren't nice enough. I never liked the beds'. Referring to her Ikea bed as a child, she recalled, 'My Ikea bed was really cheap and hard – it didn't even have a proper mattress – but we couldn't afford better. But I think it has changed now. It is different now than the 1970s. Now they are more into design'.

Johanna is interesting as a research participant, not because she sees herself as an Ikea consumer but because she doesn't. It is clear that her memories of growing up with 'quite a lot' of Ikea furniture in a household with minimal financial resources has a bearing on her attitudes to it today, coupled with her preference for furniture that will stand the test of time. Why, then, should a visit to Ikea be inevitable? What attraction makes it so inexorable? Johanna's own explanation premised solely on thrift is swiftly undercut by her recognition of very inexpensive second-hand shelving purchased on a popular website. Also relevant is the suggestion that Ikea showcases contemporary design, providing a worthwhile template for broad comparison, if not for purchase. For Johanna, reference to 'design' seems a sufficient explanation to communicate to me some standard of quality or fashionability that marks the brand as altogether better than in the 1970s. Amongst other things, the designation of design implies a tangible connection between individuals' own priorities that have been identified by designers and mass-produced, homogeneous products. Johanna compares the experience of shopping in Ikea as ultimately falling short of her hopes and deterring her from finding just the right stuff to furnish her new home. Nevertheless, as indexes of Swedish design, Ikea goods objectify professional practice that has a long tradition in domestic intervention.

Setting up the showrooms: international modernism, traditional, Scandinavian modernism and young

In building the showrooms, managers start with a consideration of the furniture to be showcased, called the range. IKEA of Sweden AB develops the IKEA range and advises individual stores on which items to display. Located in the southern Swedish town of Älmhult, the range strategist, and his or her team, decide on product development several years in advance, including which domestic spaces should be prioritized or how to promote themes such as small-space living. All products are designed in Älmhult, chiefly by in-house designers. Although external designers may be employed for occasional pieces, they too must travel to Älmhult to be briefed. These designs are inspired, range strategist Lea Kumpulainen told me in 2010, by a mix of international modernist design blended with twentieth-century Swedish influences. It is in Älmhult that products are initially handmade and presented to members of the 'Product Council', who decide if it should be progressed onto production, meaning outsourcing to one of Ikea's many producers worldwide.[6] Pieces of furniture are envisioned as sites of potential. It is not only about the wardrobe, Kumpulainen tells me, but also what you can do with it, what you need to fit in it, how many pairs of shoes global consumers have these days and how many items contemporary householders have to fit in this one wardrobe. The range should look typically 'Ikea' for Scandinavian shoppers, but further afield, the same look should appear as typically 'Swedish', she said.[7] When I met Kumpulainen, she was considering how to recycle Ikea goods, such as encouraging consumers to return goods for gift cards and so on. In addition to the items of furniture that must be included are the sales priorities that might encourage a manager to place a specific sofa and storage item within the modern-themed room. To do this, managers must consult with the Ikea range and retail offices in Ikea located in Älmhult and Helsingborg as well as with common store planning offices in Malmö that offer advice on the construction and planning of showrooms. The Common Store Planning group in Malmö works with the management of new stores, providing recommendations that cover 90 per cent of the first five room sets, presenting the basic framework for new stores (such as in Dublin) with the 'right combination', protecting the 'Swedishness' of the brand but allowing for a minimal amount of tweaking to suit the local market.

The range covers approximately nine thousand items, only three thousand of which can be viewed in the catalogue, so the primary mechanism to sell Ikea goods is by putting them on show and 'in function', meaning within the mise-en-scène of the showrooms. In Ikea Kungens Kurva, furniture ranges could be read as signifying specific styles broadly homologous with discrete constituencies of global consumers (see Garvey 2013). During fieldwork, these furniture themes were described to me as modern, country, Scandinavian and young Swede but have been categorised more recently as international modernism, traditional, Scandinavian modernism and young (Kristoffersson 2014: 64). Each showroom in global Ikea stores is organized in accordance with these themes, or roughly comparable ones, and all Ikea furniture should conform to one theme or another.

Modern is the most important theme. It is closest to the brand and is showcased prominently in Ikea showrooms on entry. Modern, or international modern, will be encountered first in Kungens Kurva as one steps off the escalator onto the third floor. It is signified by bright primary colours – green, blue, red, white, black – by contrasting graphics or occasionally single dominant colours and lastly by a prevalence of angular shapes (such as Klippan sofas). Modern is similarly identified by a high-gloss paint, bold contrasting colours on soft furnishings or specific wood hues. Variations on modern (modern-white) is also signified by a play of light on surfaces, by a dominating white complemented by textures provided by plastic, metal, glass and natural fibres. Young, by contrast, is also amongst the first rooms to be showcased in Ikea stores worldwide but aims to attract a different purchaser, such as young householders with limited economic resources. Bunk beds and white Billy bookshelves might fit this group as signs of youthfulness or the young at heart. Indicating this theme are bright-yellow banners announcing one can buy the whole room 'for a steal' at 8,000 SEK, complete with extremely low-cost 'breathtaking items', bright fabrics and colourful furniture. If young is identifiable by its bright primary colours and knock-down prices, then the theme Scandinavian is closer in style to modern and less identifiable to the untrained eye. Visiting the staff offices in Ikea Kungens Kurva while meeting Per Lundgren, who is responsible for furnishing showrooms and interior decoration, we pass items produced in Asia on display for Ikea staff and trade partners. Despite the provenance of the wicker lampshade, he describes it to me as 'very, very typical Scandinavian, which would go with the red Karlstad – because of the fabric and the shape of the lamp'. Karlstad sofas fit very well into the Scandinavian theme, then, but this designation is not wholly dependent on the item of furniture but also relates to the other items in the room. Karlstad sofas could equally be found in modern rooms, whereas traditional (country) tends to give name to furniture styles that have rounded edges and unpainted or lightly varnished wood shelving (Garvey 2013).

Theme names change slightly over time and may be signified by – and can alter depending on – the colour of wood, the glossiness of fabrics, the coarseness of textiles and the colours or contrasts employed so that few pieces of furniture are exclusively aligned with one theme. Some colours bring furniture to life. An Ektorp sofa with its rounded arms would never be placed in a modern-themed showroom, Garry Deakin, manager of Dublin's Ikea in 2009, tells me: of its twelve possible covers, one might be 'pure country', another might prompt the question 'Is it country?' while a third cover might 'give it a different expression'. Country, in recent years, he continues, might be characterised by reds, blues and washed white, whereas previously, the style was characterised by stained woods. Now, shoppers are purchasing 'solitaire' pieces of bright red or yellow in different fabrics, which when placed against a white wall, 'has an amazing impact on a room'. By these means, furniture is increasingly judged with an eye to the relationship amongst colour, texture, shape, sheen, fabric and contrast that dictates how certain stylistic themes complement one another and how colours create expression (see Chapter 6).

Individual shoppers are not expected to recognise the international modernism theme for example, but be 'inspired' by it, while showrooms are deemed to work well if they comport with the preferences of different lifestyle clusters. To delineate and understand these clusters, extensive annual market research is conducted in Stockholm to elicit and understand 'brand capital', which focuses on the customers within the store's catchment area. Market research professionals then sort and delineate the surrounding area into shopping groups, and furniture ranges should appeal to projected consumer lifestyles. Shoppers' lifestyles may be distinguished on the basis of their status as parents, singles or cohabiting, their economic resources, average apartment size and ethnic composition. As Lundgren commented:

> We have to have the four style groups. If we look into the first five living rooms, then we have all the four styles in the first five rooms. We have to have them so we can show our different customers – for country or modern – so they feel like IKEA has a lot to offer.

In deciding on the design of a showroom, managers place themselves in the shoes of fictional householders, taking a hypothetical moment such as an evening and then discussing the activities these individuals are engaged in:

> On this side of the city, it's smaller apartments, so we try to adjust to the local market . . . But when we have the families, we also have things called activity, needs and solutions. If we look into a family – Svensson. . . [with] three children . . . then we have to look into the living room with children. So we have to focus upon what are the main things they are doing at one time in the room – like maybe it's a Wednesday looking at [television]. Two children are painting or something – so we have more for a specific time. And then we look into the functions and the family's needs. They need bookshelves for storage, and then we have maybe the mother working from home, so she studies and needs a workplace; the children are very small, so that is part of the living room – playing – so what solution do they need to work in that area? Then we go more and more and more into detail when looking at the function, so it works with the family that lives in that room. There's a lot of thought put into every room.

FIGURE 2.1 Children's drawings hanging in one of the 'houses' in Ikea Kungens Kurva.

Source: Photo by author.

FIGURE 2.2 Photographs of fictional family members in showrooms in Ikea Kungens Kurva.

Source: Photo by author. Also in Clarke, A. J. 2011. *Design Anthropology: Object Culture in the 21st Century.* Wien: Springer Verlag.

FIGURE 2.3 Knitting needles and wool on a shelf in a showroom in Ikea Kungens Kurva.

Source: Photo by author. Also in Clarke, A. J. 2011. *Design Anthropology: Object Culture in the 21st Century.* Wien: Springer Verlag.

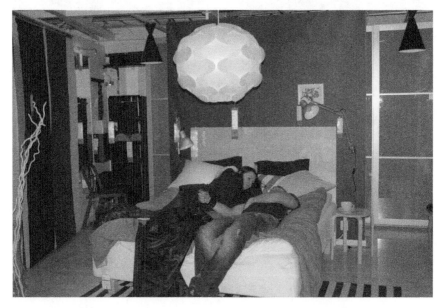

FIGURE 2.4 Shoppers trying out furniture in Ikea Kungens Kurva.

Source: Photo by author.

Inspiration

Within design consultancies and cultural industries, qualities of creativity and innovation often entail assumptions regarding the innate creativity of individuals (Garvey *forthcoming*; Reimer and Leslie 2008). Questions of creativity, innovation and the 'new' are particularly prized in get-ahead corporate environments where constant pressure is applied to outperform competitors (Suchman and Bishop 2000) and increasingly, questions of innovation and inspiration have come under focus amid arguments that there is little understanding of how innovation actually operates (Hallam and Ingold 2007; Sunley et al 2008). Although anthropologists contend that ideas of innovation in corporate environments operate within a 'cultural imaginary', evoking both vision and fantasy, individual experience and socio-historical conditions (Suchman and Bishop 2000: 1, following Marcus 1995), nevertheless, conventional perspectives frequently exaggerate the gifted individual over collaborative environments, to the degree that inspiration is described in terms of an asocial process moving from external prompts to internal states, such as in renditions of the 'eureka moment'.

One prompt for inspirational epiphanies is seemingly couched in the skilled manipulation of the material environment. Known as brandscaping this approach describes corporate strategy surrounding 'lights, design, music and the demeanour of personnel to encourage consumers to co-perform a particular ambience' (Arvidsson 2006: 80, in Manning 2010: 43–44). Already by 1974, Kotler coined the term *atmospherics* to describe the physical environment of commercial outlets in order to emphasise the importance of the senses in retail, and more recently, this emphasis has escalated. Current branding dictates that contemporary store atmosphere should engage the olfactory, tactile, aural and visual senses (see Howes 2003, 2005; Hultén 2012; Malefyt 2012; Malefyt and Moeran 2003), which is clearly evident in Ikea store planning.[8] Through the mechanics of putting goods on show, shoppers should see products 'in function' allowing them according to in-house manuals, to 'come alive'.[9] Considering inspiration from this perspective, the staging of Ikea stores complies with late twentieth century marketing trends that valorise experience as the route to selling goods. The 'Ikea experience' could thus be explained as simply part and parcel of a store choreography that attempts to control the customer's passage, triggering positive emotions and opening wallets. Abstracted from other people and from the vagaries of everyday life, inspiration is thus pitched as an outcome of positive experiences acquired through browsing on the shop floor and engaging with pieces of furniture in Ikea showrooms. We see this perspective again on the Ikea website, where it is written, 'Inspiration is free: Visit an IKEA store and sit, lie down, test, touch and try things out. Look inside our closets and under our beds. (Who knows what good ideas you'll find there.) Even if you walk away empty-handed, you'll be taking home a whole lot of fresh ideas', implying that inspiring customers depends solely on a skilful arrangement of the tableaux.[10]

Brandscaping models of inspiration are inadequate, however, because they are presented as separate from the vagaries of social life. As if hermetically sealed from experience and encounters external to the store, what is neglected in this scenario is the performative and physically engaged quality of these practices. In contrast, several respondents report that inspiration emerges from cross-referencing Ikea showrooms with private domestic arrangements, such as perusing showrooms to gauge what is 'out there'. Regularly, people impute innovative inspiration to Ikea through the layout and organisation of showrooms, the arrangement of furniture and eye-catching posters proclaiming good deals. But these same people derive inspiration from diverse locales, including their own home environments or that of friends and neighbours, public exhibitions, commercial expos and shop floors, none of which are isolated from one another. Moreover, browsing in this way, the elicitation of inspiration emerges as a tactile, corporeal experience in which householders 'try out' different domestic appliances and arrangements.

Brandscaping approaches, furthermore, reify the polarisation of subject and object, which is, I argue, contradicted by the idea of designed objects in the peopled showroom setting. Challenging these dualities, designed things are distinctive because they manifest an implied but absent intentionality, separate and apart from the jetsam of nondescript stuff. Ikea-designed products were often described to me as capillaries of some distant creative potency, as a canny skill captured in ordinary things, underlining the abiding material bond bridging designer, object and householder.

Design and agency

Alfred Gell's posthumously published book, *Art and Agency*, is significant here because it advances an argument that, in certain situations, art objects are agents, not because they have minds but because they have effects on their immediate environment (1998: 5).[11] Intentionality may be sourced in designed objects to the degree that they act upon others (as an agent) or are acted upon (occupying a 'patient' position). Artworks, therefore, may be regarded as a physical trace of the artist's creativity, effecting those in its orbit or alternatively subject to the actions of others, if, for example, someone was to alter or break it. Therefore, the source of agency is not fixed, nor is it restricted to humans, but it is context dependent and relational. In this respect, the idea of a 'causal nexus' attempts to undermine subject/object distinctions while underscoring the place of the artwork in a network of relations. Depending on the series of actions, relationships and effects of which it is a part, anything, including persons, can operate like an art object. In some instances, objects act on people in a way that seems comparable with human work on things. Consequently for Gell, both persons and objects may possess agency, although he discriminates between primary or secondary agents, confirming a kind of anthropomorphism whereby primary agency is found in people and their actions within the object world (Miller 2005: 13; see also Leach 2007). In an analogous way, the showroom carries the distributed efficacy of its creators. It successfully recreates ideal living environments (the prototype) that should act upon shoppers (who encounter it as recipients of its agency). Agency is realised through the designed object and through its placement in the particular configuration of furniture. As a totality, then, the personal features in showrooms, the storage solutions, the notes on tips and ideas carry the trace of Ikea design.[12]

Several scholars have criticised Gell's theory as narrowly confining agency within the 'originating intention' of an individual's mind (Hallam and Ingold 2007; Ingold 2013; Layton 2003; Leach 2007; Sabeti 2015). Hallam and Ingold argue, for example, that the abduction of agency is back-to-front and advocate a departure from the language of causality in which agency derives from improvisation instead of intention. Agency possesses people, they insist, and emerges through movement and action rather than deriving from the removed but inferred intentions of the maker. Despite these criticisms, the inferred causality inherent in designed works as material extensions of their authors is salient in this example, particularly when considered in the light of Gell's analysis of art objects as traps.

As a foundational theory preceding *Art and Agency*, Gell postulates that a trap not only materialises the skill and creativity of its designer but also significantly acts as a stand-in for the person, captivating the mind and will of others, extending the capacity of their creative brokers over time and space. An effective trap must not only embody the intention of its creator but also disperse it in a network of relations that extend his or her efficacy through a clever manipulation of the target's own behaviour. Agency is twofold, not only as a model that manifests the inventor's intentions but also in mirroring its user's habits, behaviour and characteristics. Here one sees the adduction of agency as deriving from the work of a creative inventor but situated within a series of relationships.[13]

Showrooms as traps

Only through detailed knowledge of its object can a trap allure and captivate. To do this, one must have a level of intimate knowledge of one's target to skilfully mimic its behaviour. The showroom is a model of its creator, manifesting his or her skill and allowing the designer to 'act from a distance'. Indeed, the work of design is lauded as an exercise in intentional action, but here the inferred agency is carried by the objects and their arrangement in which agency is visible in its calculable effects. Skill and knowledge are objectified in the showroom, magnifying and enhancing the work of design as a collective capacity. To be successful, the designer must be intimately familiar with habitual behaviour and conspire to subvert it. Analogous to a trap, a showroom is not deceitful or clever but objectifies the ability of designers to closely understand and thereby mimic habitual consumer behaviour. The trap manifests a triadic relationship, modelling the hunter and the victim and embodying the scenario. A 'dramatic nexus' binds the protagonists together in both time and space (Gell 1998: 201). Effectively mimicking household practices, the Ikea showroom carries the 'imprint' and 'parody' of natural behaviour (Gell 1998: 200). One technique that is pivotal in this regard is the 'spatial effigies' or missing persons evident in showrooms that encourage the imaginative emplacement of the shopper, which we turn to in the next chapter.

Garry Deakin, manager of the Dublin Ikea in 2009, described how showrooms gain purchase with shoppers, how they should successfully mediate the relationship between designer and Ikea interior manager and the browser. Pitched within the global corporate strategy and edicts from head offices elsewhere, Dublin's store managers were occupied with navigating a middle path between conforming to the Ikea range strategy as dictated by the relevant offices in Sweden and the United Kingdom while catering to the trends of the local market in the first ever store in the Irish republic. Based on the local demographic, which covers an area within a three-hour drive from the store, the personnel tasked with creating the showrooms must balance a sensitivity to the local market while simultaneously incorporating the 'Swedishness' of the brand entailed in the 'strong recommendations' from the Common Store Planning office in Malmö. One manager Gill Reilly responsible for the showrooms in Dublin explained that 'basically, we are given ninety per cent, and we just finish the rooms off. Sometimes we can refuse them – for example, history has shown that an all-white room set is a disaster here'. She continued:

> When I retuned back from training, we then pretty much launched into the design of the store. We were given a layout of the store, the actual shape of how the store moves around, and from that you can then get in as many rooms as possible . . . and they'll probably fall into a specific dimension because once a room goes below a specific dimension then people won't go into it – it's too cold, too small, you can't get as many people in – and so we settled on fifty-five room sets, including three homes. From there, the marketing team has a part to play to try to decide what is our market. Is it more of a country-feel market or is it a modern market, or will we have some hope to have a Scandinavian-feel market? And modern is the number one for us. Then, within our percentage, we weighted that modern would be our highest scene room set. Then followed by country, and then you'll start to see the Scandinavian where we're kind of introducing this to the Irish market . . . Once we have decided, yes we are going to have a modern room or a Scandinavian room, we then decide who is going to live in those rooms. And the reason we do this is, OK, if there is going to be a young married couple or an older established couple, then that gives us the basis of who we are designing for. There is no point in designing a room if you don't know who is living in it because you don't know what their needs are. If there are children in the room, then we're not going to have pointy furniture, or we wouldn't have it all white and non-washable – it would be a disaster. People wouldn't be interested in that. They want to picture themselves in it, they need to have the toy storage, and they need rounded corners and they need removable covers but still trendy and stylish. When we decide who would be in the room, we can start the design process because then we get under the skin of what they need. And it's easier to design because then you get into the shoes of the young married couple or older person.

Parents speak of their children lying on beds in Ikea showrooms in amused tones, as if they are being somehow transgressive. In fact, sitting on beds and sofas or at tables is not only permitted by Ikea management but is positively encouraged. In Ikea stores, customer interaction with furniture is measured in colour codes: the more people physically locate themselves in, on and around exhibits, the more successful they are deemed to be. This human infusion is so important that it is actively monitored by store management, as outlined by then-manager of the Dublin store:

Garry: We do customer traces. So we'll go to the front of bedrooms ... and we follow one hundred customers with a piece of paper and pencil, and we check how many go into each room set and check how many sit on the bed, lie on the bed, bounce on the bed, and we do customer traces ... And then if we decide the fourth room set we built, with a bed in it called Vikram, was wrong, and the next week we shut that room down, and within forty-eight hours, we'll open it in a totally new bed expression, still in the same style group.

Pauline: So it is a good sign if people are in there and they are sitting on the –

Garry: Oh very good. If it's a hot room set, we leave it alone – and without giving secrets away – depending on the number of people who go in, we give it a colour.

In tracking customers' movements, their actions, what they pick up and leave down, the store management can identify hotspots and cold spots. If children are not trying out the beds or shoppers are not sitting at tables, then the rooms are regarded as unsuccessful. Moreover, contrary to web-based sketches that provide playfully burlesque domestic enactments outside of its conventional home, actual Ikea showrooms retain richer sensorial dimensions than the visual pastiches found on the Internet. Whilst standing in showrooms such as an Ikea kitchen, one immediately registers a panoply of decorative devices, such as the children's paintings that hang on fridges or teacups on tables. These devices remind us of the showroom's capacity to imitate: they are curiously similar but not the same as actual households, but the mimicry is sufficiently lifelike to invite participation by browsers.

Missing from the analogy of the trap is the vital ingredient of people vitalising showrooms as part of the overall design. This ingredient is an integral component of the showrooms in Dublin and Stockholm and reminds us that inspiration emerges from highly socialised contexts, neither 'traditional or innovatory in any absolute sense' (Gell 1998: 256). Certainly, instead of focusing on objects of design as finished products that are appropriated by users, it makes more sense to consider showroom exhibits as activated by multiple participants, both present and distant. The Ikea showroom provides an interactive space for the consultation, browsing and occasional keen awareness of other domestic arrangements, other people, other couples and other families. Partnered with designed things is the mimetic capacity of the showrooms that carry consequences in their potential to copy and persuade. Mimetic capacity implies not only reflecting but also carrying the power to transform. Taussig, for example, describes imitation in terms of the 'faculty to copy, imitate, make models, explore difference, yield into and become Other' (1993: xiii). The copy is compelling in its power to affect the original to such as degree that the representation shares in or acquires power over the represented (1993: 47).[14]

The faculty of both close imitation and its consequent effect on original households is commonly ascribed to the store. Unlike other corporations that strive to fit into new markets, Ikea is credited with transforming markets and altering domestic trends, extending homogenous interiors throughout the globe (see Boşcor and Brătucu 2009; Lewis 2008). At a local level we see this in the example of Andreas, a thirty-seven-year-old sheet-metal worker, who described his enthusiasm for Ikea in terms of the guidance he receives in furnishing his home. Ikea provides Andreas with standard, reliable products without demanding specific flair in mixing and matching, decorating or upholstering he told me and even with the catalogue in hand, he prefers to visit Ikea and browse. Lacking expertise in interior planning, which he expresses by saying, 'I'm not a designer', he praises the advantage of having room arrangements on display, plus in-house interior designers on hand to advise and guide householders. Andreas has moved home 'four or five times' in thirteen years, and in each case, his move necessitated complete refurbishment 'and a fresh break'. On those occasions, he purchased 'bookcases, bed, kitchen, couch, even if it comes from Ikea, so I bought it from someone who bought it at Ikea. We can say that my home is made up of seventy-five per cent Ikea. It's rugs, lamps, everything'. Probing a little further, I asked him to describe his typical visit:

Pauline: You always find something at Ikea?

Andreas: Yes (giggle), sorry, it's that it's so nice at the King's Curve. You can walk around, you can grab a snack, you can move on, you eat a piece of food, you can plan, you can write, you can spend a whole day there! It is not just to go in and look and then you go out, whether to make a major change. I've done that many times when I'll plan my kitchen, so that is how I have done it. I have spent hours at Ikea, between six and eight hours at Ikea. Or gone just for a particular purpose as well. If I were to go there today, then I would probably go through quickly and get what I'm after.

Discussing flea markets and other furniture stores, Andreas continued that he might think of an alternative to Ikea, but he has difficulty knowing what might go together:

Andreas: I'm not a designer. I have difficultly seeing what might go together. I can see that this might go, and so I buy it and it is OK, but to go to a flea market and buy an old chair, that demands in any case that I have some decorating ideas, that yes, this would go with that, and I don't have much of that. It is easier at Ikea. Besides, eight million people cannot be wrong.

In its capacity to captivate and entrap, the showroom extends the efficacy of Ikea design outwards in time and space, made and re-made in various configurations across the city and spanning across the globe. Actual and implied householders are ubiquitous in Ikea showrooms. And although the rooms are uninhabited of course, the implied occupants of these living spaces are not entirely absent. They are peopled in the aggregate of householders milling about, touching, testing and comparing, which provides the transposition of 'family' that showrooms might otherwise lack.

'It is like a designer is in my home'

Derek: For the first couple of months, the staff seem to take you by the hand to show you it is a warm environment, not a cold Swedish warehouse. And it has a great communal feel. We met a nice Polish couple in the restaurant last time, and we talked about baby furniture, which was great, and then OK, coffee over. You have the mentality that you are there for the day unless you are there in the evening with a shopping list. We talk to people definitely. Can't go for a few minutes without talking to people.

Pauline: Can you tell me a bit about when you first went to Ikea?

Lisa: We went to Belfast first. We just wanted to have a look because we had heard so much about it, and we just wanted to have the experience. We knew the brand from being in Australia.

Pauline: What was your first contact with it then?

Derek: From work, I think. Katrin started by giving us the catalogue.

Lisa: He brought it home, and we had a look and started getting excited. We heard some horror stories, people saying that we wouldn't have a clue what to do when they went in there, but we actually found it good.

Derek: Once you get your head around it, the experience is very good.

Pauline: What do you mean when you say the 'experience'?

Lisa: Seeing the different kind of showrooms, the displays. We were expecting to walk into a warehouse, so to see all the different rooms and styles was great.

Soon after Ikea's opening in Dublin's Ballymun, I met with Derek and Lisa, and we had the conversation just shown. Derek and Lisa are a couple living in a purchased apartment block in the south-western outskirts of Dublin city. Derek had just celebrated his thirtieth birthday, and they had an infant daughter – Emma – who was just a few months old. The family lived in a modern apartment block erected during the 1990s and early 2000s construction boom in Ireland. As with most apartment blocks constructed in this period, these apartments were built with scant provision for storage. In Dublin, and in Ireland more generally, there is a widespread expectation that one must own one's own house, especially if one has children. As we sat in Derek and Lisa's living room, baby toys and paraphernalia surrounded us. The pram jutted out into the central living space, making the living room feel small and cluttered. As we chatted, Lisa and Derek expressed their happy anticipation of

Ikea's recent arrival to Dublin that was articulated in terms of the 'Ikea experience' and their hopes for efficient storage solutions to their growing household. 'It is so colourful', they told me. 'And everything is explained'.

For Derek and Lisa, Ikea furniture represents affordable mid-range goods in a market where either insubstantial bargain-basement or high-cost options from expensive department stores were the primary options of the past. Most of their large items of furniture, such as sofa and kitchen table and chairs, were purchased as gifts by in-laws in one such bargain store, but the table was problematic because it could not be extended for dinner parties. It foreclosed the opportunity of having friends over for a meal, Lisa noted, and their out-of-town location made socialising problematic. Derek, meanwhile, hoped he could find some wall storage for his bicycle – he was an avid cycler – which, in the meantime, was temporarily housed in the spare room.

Dublin householders, such as Derek and Lisa, and especially those in small city apartments, emphasised less the hopelessly inadequate storage provision made available to them by the construction industry and instead marvelled at the canny knick-knacks found in Ikea Ballymun to help them contain their expanding collection of personal and childcare-related possessions. This they attributed to astute design creativity:

> The small things are really clever. And you wonder why you can't get that down the road in any shop. It's those little extras – you just know that someone looked at what was generically available [and] they sat down to design it to make it more functional. Function and design.

FIGURE 2.5 Shoppers trying out furniture in Ikea Dublin.

Source: Photo by author.

FIGURE 2.6 Beds in the Ikea showroom in Dublin with a sign encouraging shoppers to try them out.

Source: Photo by author.

Picking up a plastic fork that he was using to feed his infant daughter, Derek waved it at me, showing me that its wide base sticks to her tabletop. 'It's like a designer is in my home and can see all the problems', he said. Design here represents a positive interventionist presence, linked by Derek to the experience they found in Ikea showrooms. Similarly to Derek's feeling of having a designer in his home, he talks of the displays in terms of his reaction to them. These presentational devices are termed as 'inspiring', not only because they represent a kind of stage filled with Ikea merchandise but also because these props are inhabited with shoppers who often use them to try out an item before purchase. As a result, a series of tableaux vivant is conjured based on a mimetic enactment, a kind of imitation that enlivens an otherwise inert scene and exerts power over it. Based on a performative rather than a purely display modality, we see an emphasis on engagement and human participation. As with an exhibition, it is both model and implement; it houses and manifests a series of intentions, and design is framed as capturing the creativity of its maker, meditating between the household and the Ikea creative. The dynamic is relational, as both spheres are changed through it. In waving the spoon at me, Derek elects to use it as a stand-in for the designer who stands behind it; it assumes the role of a particular kind of technology that entangles designers, objects and consumers.

Tableaux vivant

Ikea stores and their display strategies undoubtedly conform to a global commercial strategy emphasising inspiration and experience. However, in imitating 'real' domesticity and hosting domestic performance, the showroom traverses actual life and staged settings. This feature strikes an exhibitionary note, but one infused with people and bodily engagement. Ikea showrooms are experienced as sites that are intrinsically vitalized by unknown, unseen persons who are imagined through a mix of designed objects and absent presences encountered there (Chapter 3). Seeing and being seen, mass experimentation with domestic arrangements in Ikea is comparably enlivened and is mistakenly branded as solitary. This sensorial injection serves to populate the showroom so that a visit to Ikea is commonly associated with collective action and significant others. There is a distinct kind of housing theatre at play in global showrooms, animated with actual householders as both the subjects and the objects of the shopping experience. Through imagined others created in display tableaux and actual others milling through these same showrooms, a quality of inspiration binds Ikea products (as material indices of Swedish design) to aggregate experience.

Ikea-in-the-abstract is conventionally described as changing markets rather than as adapting to them. Inter IKEA Systems B.V., the owner of the Ikea concept and global Ikea franchisor monitors individual Ikea stores in order to ensure that they comply with the standard Ikea look and store layout. Despite this intervention, one finds negotiations back and forth in the face of constant shifts in corporate policy and local circumstances. In this respect, the showrooms in Dublin and Stockholm are the same in mediating the benign transformative potential of design goods on singular households, but also being subject to influences from households in their composition and form.[15]

Influences are bidirectional rather than purely sourced in a corporate centre and in the next chapter we see that juxtaposed against homogenous corporate planning is historical contingency. This is evident when Ikea in Stockholm is situated within a history of housing theatre through which the domestic has been long been purveyed, displayed, scrutinised and consumed and in which the minutiae of domestic material culture has had far-reaching effects. Marking Ikea Kungens Kurva out as distinct from seemingly homogenous global stores, the consequence of this for my respondents is not only a familiarity with the staging of vernacular architecture and design but also on the traversal of public and private domains through these exhibition spaces.

In corporate settings, trade shows and sites of cultural production, publics in Stockholm have encountered home and housing exhibits in which participants were enlisted as witnesses or participants in perfunctory domestic practices at various junctures during the twentieth century. Imitation is enlisted not as an exact copy but through a play on similarity and dissimilarity that lies at the crux of the showroom's efficacy. In imitating homes as inexact but compelling copies, displays cross the boundaries that separate the intimate household interior from the public exhibition space. In destabilising the otherwise polarising boundaries between public and private, they underscore the home's significance on the national stage. Next we will look at the trajectory and mechanics of housing theatre in Sweden and the implied aggregate contained in these exhibitory techniques.

Notes

1 The adverts in question: "IKEA: Living Room" can be viewed at https://www.youtube.com/watch?v=0CCL-vhEtf4 and "IKEA: Kitchen" at https://www.youtube.com/watch?v=CcpzVs_94Z0, accessed 14/07/17. Andersen directed films including *Rushmore* (1998), *The Royal Tenenbaums* (2001) and *The Darjeeling Limited* (2007).
2 Comedy released in 2009 from Twentieth Century Fox Film Corporation starring Joseph Gordon-Levitt and Zooey Deschanel. Director Marc Webb.
3 Shooting for these sketches is obviously undertaken without the permission of Ikea management (www.Ikeaheights.com).
4 Thanks are due to my colleague Thomas Strong for this.
5 Satirical situational comedy created by Tina Fey and run by NBC Television from 2006 to 2013.
6 Up to two thousand at the time of this writing.
7 'Product Development', Inter IKEA Systems BV, accessed 04/08/17, www.ikea.com/ms/en_US/jobs/business_types/product_development/.
8 Sitting in Ikea back offices in Dublin one day, I glanced through showroom in-house manuals and noticed that inspiration is valorised as an integral element of the showroom experience. Inspiration should spring from the dual mix of demonstration and enactment, it reads. Familiarity with householders in their homes is necessary, along with presentation of the range, in a way that maximises its visibility. Through the mechanics of

48 Benign intervention

putting goods on show, shoppers should see and interact – engage – with Ikea products. This allows goods, according to in-house manuals, to 'come alive'.
9 *Range Presentation in the Store. The IKEA Way*, Inter IKEA Systems BV, 2007; *Selling in the Showroom. The Ikea Way*, Inter IKEA Systems BV, 1995, 2002.
10 'Inspiration Is Free', Inter IKEA Systems BV, accessed 01/02/17, www.ikea.com/ms/en_SG/the_ikea_story/the_ikea_store/ideas_and_inspiration.html.
11 Gell distinguishes between the *primary* agency of intentioned actors and the *secondary* agency of objects. He cites the example of the landmines placed by Pol Pots soldiers as components of Pol Pots person and objects that function as secondary agents. Landmines are not simply tools but part of the material index that defines the soldiers themselves. They do not initiate actions through acts of will but nonetheless are objective extensions of the people. Artworks can be regarded as external extensions or objectifications of mind, and it is this that is the focus of his work rather than any claim for an intrinsic aesthetic quality of artworks.
12 This causal relation has been critiqued by Ingold, who argues for a departure from a perspective that looks for causes deriving from fully formed and complete entities. Ingold advocates that instead of objects and persons possessing agency, we should consider agency as possessing people and things: 'The constituents of this world are not already thrown or cast before they can act or be acted upon. They are in the throwing, in the casting' (2011: 215). My perspective lies closer to Gell in that agency is only ever indirect, as an index of human intention (Leach 2007).
13 Applied to Ikea, the creative skill of a body of designers finds concrete realisation in the object world but only when apprehended by recipients. The process is not straightforward, however, and often, the originator of designed objects may be ambiguous. Not only are designers named but also pictures of them tangle over items of furniture as if to press home their claims as originators and personifying the thing itself. Often, the aggregate of designers therefore is subsumed into one person who stands behind and makes claims to the originating idea (Leach 2007). Potentially displaced is the creative body – 'Ikea design' as an abstraction – for one mediated in material things and claimed by a named author. Although this suggests that an apparent distillation between a collective body is personified in single designers, this argument is contradicted by the fact that respondents spoke of 'Ikea designers' rather than of named personalities.
14 This is demonstrated through the ways colonial subjects mimic their colonisers for the purposes of manipulation and control (Taussig 1993).
15 It is worth noting also, that the capacity of showrooms to influence can be seen to operate in both directions, in homes and showrooms. For example, fireplaces in Ireland manifest a traditional nostalgic domesticity, which is generally valorised as an integral element of the household. Fireplaces are present in the majority of rural and urban free-standing houses in Ireland but are generally absent in urban apartments. Although apartment blocks don't have chimneys comparable with free-standing houses, one can occasionally find fireplaces without a grate, built in wood, stone or a marble substitute, in apartment living rooms constructed during the 1990s/2000s construction boom. Replacing the warmth of the living flame is an electric socket for a heater. Fireplaces were equally missing in Irish Ikea showrooms at first, although some respondents commented that the large floor-to-ceiling storage units could not fit around the central fire. For one Dublin manager, the removal of the fireplace was read as a progressive sign towards having a modern interior: 'My parents don't have a country lifestyle, but they're not modern. They have a more traditional lifestyle, sort of in the middle. But they got an Ektorp sofa, which would never be included in the modern range, but they put an adventurous cover on it, and they put the TV in the corner, and they let the three-two-one suite go and had the fireplace taken out. And for Mum and Dad, they've become modern'. By 2012, Ikea had worked fireplace spaces into their Irish showrooms, relenting on a local preference

that is out of step with international apartment-living trends. This example reminds us that the vicissitudes of actual circumstances confound the hyper homogeneity with which Ikea is credited.

References

Arvidsson, Adam. 2006. *Brands: Meaning and Value in Media Culture*. Abingdon and New York: Routledge.
Boşcor, Dana and Gabriel Brătucu. 2009. "Transnational Strategies Adopted by Furniture Manufacturers. Case Study: IKEA." *Pro Ligno* 5 (3): 55–61.
Cirelli, Julie. 2012. "Facing the Street." *Form: Nordic Architecture and Design Since 1905,* 5: 60–9.
Clarke, Alison, J. ed 2011. *Design Anthropology: Object Culture in the 21st Century*. Wien: Springer Verlag.
Garvey, Pauline. 2013. "'Ikea sofas are like H&M trousers': The Potential of Sensuous Signs." *Journal of Business Anthropology* 2 (1): 75–92.
Garvey, Pauline. Forthcoming. "Consuming IKEA: Inspiration as Material Form." In *Design Anthropology: Object Cultures in Transition*, edited by Alison J. Clarke. London: Bloomsbury.
Gell, Alfred. 1998. *Art and Agency: An Anthropological Theory*. Oxford: Clarendon.
Hallam, Elizabeth and Tim Ingold. 2007. *Creativity and Cultural Improvisation*. Oxford: Berg.
Hartman, Tod. 2007. "The Ikeaization of France." *Public Culture* 19 (3): 483–498.
Howes, David. 2003. *Sensual Relations: Engaging the Senses in Culture and Social Theory*. Ann Arbor: University of Michigan Press.
Howes, David. 2005. *Empire of the Senses: The Sensual Culture Reader, Sensory Formations*. Oxford: Berg.
Hultén, Bertil. 2012. "Sensory Cues and Shoppers' Touching Behaviour: The Case of IKEA." *International Journal of Retail and Distribution Management* 40 (4): 273–289.
Ingold, Tim. 2011. *Being Alive: Essays on Movement, Knowledge and Description*. Abingdon and New York: Routledge, Taylor & Francis.
Ingold, Tim. 2013. *Making: Anthropology, Archaeology, Art and Architecture*. London and New York: Routledge.
Kotler, Philip. 1973. "Atmospherics as a Marketing Tool." *Journal of Retailing* 49 (4): 48–64.
Kristoffersson, Sara. 2014. *Design by IKEA: A Cultural History*. London: Bloomsbury.
Layton, Robert. 2003. "Art and Agency: A Reassessment." *Journal of the Royal Anthropological Institute* 9 (3): 447–464.
Leach, James, ed. 2007. "Differentiation and Encompassment: A Critique of Alfred Gell's Theory of the Abduction of Creativity." In *Thinking Through Things*, edited by Amiria Henare, Martin Holbraad and Sari Wastell, 167–188. London and New York: Routledge.
Lewis, Elen. 2008. *Great Ikea! A Brand for All the People*. 2nd ed. London: Marshall Cavendish Business.
Malefyt, Timothy Dwight de Waal and Brian Moeran. 2003. *Advertising Cultures*. Oxford: Berg.
Malefyt, Timothy Dwight de Waal. 2012. "Touching Consumers, Engaging the Senses in Consumption." *The Senses and Society* 7 (3): 350–355.
Manning, Paul. 2010. "The Semiotics of Brand." *Annual Review of Anthropology* 39: 33–49.
Marcus, George, ed. 1995. *Technoscientific Imaginaries*. Chicago: University of Chicago Press.
Miller, Daniel. 2005. *Materiality*. Durham: Duke University Press.

Reimer, Suzanne and Deborah Leslie. 2008. "Design, National Imaginaries, and the Home Furnishings Commodity Chain." *Growth and Change* 39 (1): 144–171.

Sabeti, Shari. 2015. "'Inspired to Be Creative?': Persons, Objects, and the Public Pedagogy of Museums." *Anthropology & Education Quarterly* 46 (2): 113–128.

Sandberg, Mark B. 2011. "The Interactivity of the Model Home". In *History of Participatory Media: Politics and Publics, 1750–2000*, edited by Solveig Jülich Anders Ekström, Frans Lundgren, and Per Wisselgren, 63–80. New York: Routledge.

Suchman, Lucy and Libby Bishop. 2000. "Problematizing 'innovation' as a Critical Project." *Technology Analysis & Strategic Management* 12 (3): 327–333.

Sunley, Peter, Steven Pinch, Suzanne Reimer, and James Macmillen. 2008. "Innovation in a Creative Production System: The Case of Design." *Journal of Economic Geography* 8 (5): 675–698.

Taussig, Michael T. 1993. *Mimesis and Alterity: A Particular History of the Senses*. New York and London: Routledge.

3
HOME STAGING, HOUSING THEATRE

Design, domesticity and the People's Home

In September 2007, Casa Cor, the largest decoration, architecture and 'trend-setting event' in Latin America, inaugurated its first exhibition in Europe in Stockholm's famous T-house at Engelbrektsplan. The T-house is a 2,000 m2 historically listed building whose high profile enhanced the influence of Casa Cor's long-awaited arrival in Europe. As part of its twenty-first-anniversary celebrations, it was nothing if not flamboyant, covering thirty-five rooms and depicting the fictional, lavish and sometimes outlandish interior of a family of thirteen individuals. Casa Cor translates as 'House of Colour' in Portuguese, and the highly ornate exhibition, organised with the assistance of the Swedish-Brazilian Chamber of Commerce (Swedcham), enlisted over sixty Swedish and Brazilian architects and designers to create bright and ostentatiously wealthy showrooms. Media attention focussed on the exhibition's over-the-top quality, the exuberant lavishness it brought to 'design-crazed Scandinavia' (Stadler 2007). Distinguishable from mainstream design fairs, the event created a fictitious home occupied by a family composed of a Swedish father and Brazilian mother, their three children, a grandfather and the owner's ex-wife. The fictional family was represented through their unorthodox possessions. The husband, for example, was presented as somewhat eccentric, a man who loves hunting evidenced by the gallery of trophy animal heads. One room held a giant bed, black glass walls and a remote-controlled lighting system. Another, the fictional ex-wife's room, was decorated with bespoke wallpaper and a chandelier garnished with twenty thousand handmade spheres. As is now common in housing exhibitions, everything on show was available to purchase, and proceeds from auctioned items were given to Childhood, an international children's charity. Furthermore, in an electronic magazine produced by Swedcham, it was reported that Maíra Lot, marketing manager of Casa Cor, noted that Sweden is a reference point in terms of creativity and innovation and is renowned for being open to new ideas, technologies and products (Reid 2007: 22–23). 'The Nordic market is a benchmark for design', stressed Roberto

Dimbério, director of Casa Cor, whose objective is for Stockholm to be the first of many European cities to host the event (Reid 2007: 22–23).[1]

Publics in Stockholm have encountered home and housing exhibits throughout the twentieth century. In creating the mise-en-scène for domesticity, these displays figuratively – and occasionally literally – traverse the boundaries that separate the intimate household interior from the public exhibition space and underline the home's significance as a national institution of public interest and a commercial concern. Although Casa Cor spotlights the untouchability of the design piece in relatively abstract ways, Ikea showrooms and the housing exhibits I present here occupy very different modus operandi.

Exhibitionary techniques that use tableaux of furniture to simulate real-life situations are found globally in Ikea stores, but they also sit within a regional history of housing theatre. Swedish museums led the world in inaugurating lived domestic spaces as sites of public consumption (Arrhenius 2010: 136; see also Naylor 1990), and although not invented in Sweden, housing exhibitions and model homes became 'a cultural specialty in Scandinavia', rivalling popular interest in the living-history folk museums and providing a platform for envisaging and transforming societal relations (Sandberg 2011: 67).[2] In order to capture the resonances of this staged vernacular, I throw a wide interpretative net to cover diverse institutions, including public institutions, private homes and corporate settings. In drawing comparisons between a series of model homes and interior exhibitions, my intention is to illustrate and compound an argument that, through these means, the Swedish vernacular home operated as a 'public object of inspection' (Arrhenius 2010: 149). Ikea showrooms are different sorts of 'object institutions', operating either as model homes representing a normative domesticity or as different kinds of spaces through which one can contemplate the actual, and which rebound on the original in profound ways (see Habel 2009; Murphy 2015). Showrooms represent a compelling feature that distinguishes Ikea retail warehouses from their competitors, but what is interesting and somewhat unique about them is that they build on a matrix of housing theatre that became something of a feature of Scandinavian countries, equipping the model home with particular social and political stakes (Sandberg 2010: 67).

Pivotal to this argument is the idea of the effigy (Sandberg 2003).[3] The effigy refers to absent corporeality, a missing person whose presence is nevertheless signalled through object stand-ins or arrangements. Sandberg traces the expansion of mannequins in wax museums during the nineteenth century as one example of an effigy that contributed to an enhanced sense of displacement, part and parcel of a more general accelerated mobility – people on the move – that European urban publics encountered. Replacing previous taxonomic displays in favour of 'living contextualised scenes', natural history museums, wax museums, folk ethnographic museums and zoological gardens turned towards the intricate building of a scene, 'a compensatory project of mise-en-scène that gave displaced objects and bodies a new kind of scenic home' (Sandberg 2003: 8, 2011). As part of the trajectory of the model home exhibit that followed early vernacular museums, the idea of the effigy was adopted with frequency, requiring the spectator to place himself or herself within the scene.

Placing the home centre stage

Exhibitions emerge with frequency in studies of the mid-twentieth-century economic boom in Sweden and its burgeoning national modernity (Ekström 2010; Mattsson and Wallenstein 2010; Robach 2002). Integral to a confluence of state and corporate actions to bolster and enhance domestic consumption, exhibitions also promoted specific templates of the standard home on the national stage. There was a 'veritable flood of courses and exhibitions' (Kristoffersson 2014: 60) during the post-war era, and the combination of mass production, industrial design and elevated household consumption fed into a national economic buoyancy. More recently and more prosaically, many respondents refer to a raft of home decoration programmes that emerged in the 1990s that focus on home improvement as providing the impetus to a perceived home-decoration trend. During fieldwork, respondents referred to television programmes that advised viewers how to recycle and revamp tired-looking furnishings in inexpensive ways, such as how to change the fabric on bedroom headboards and apply coloured glass studs in varied patterns. Another programme aired on a commercial channel, TV4, called *Rent Hus* (Clean House) documented the task of two middle-aged women (Marlene and Marie-Louise) to find the filthiest households in the city, and with a kind of glee, report just how dirty they were while instructing the inhabitant how to maintain sufficient hygienic standards in the future.[4]

Distinguishable from formal expositions that stage ideal interiors, or television programmes that promote public participation in decorative practices, young individuals recounted how they were recruited to participate in practices of home staging in less formal ways. Kristen, the sixteen-year-old teenage daughter of a research respondent who lives in the town of Uppsala, outlined a school project that her class was given in which they were instructed to decorate an apartment on a fictional budget. As part of this exercise, the Ikea website was recommended as a helpful resource to complete the project. When quizzed by her mother, a lawyer who specialises in corporate law, whether students were specifically directed to Ikea, thus giving the company directed and endorsed publicity by the state educational system, Kristen responded that it wasn't stated that they *had* to look at Ikea web pages but that Ikea *might* provide a good resource. This exercise is more widespread than Kristen's school, as one thirty-year-old man, Khaled, living in Stockholm, recounted a similar task but remembered with amusement that, although he furnished his fictional space with Ikea merchandise within budget, the teacher showed some disapproval of his choices:

> I got an assignment to furnish a room, no – your first home. Everyone got a budget for twenty thousand kronor, and the assignment was to last for one week. I remember how I had solved it because the flat was one bedroom

> with a kitchen, and I used the Ikea catalogue. I remember the teacher admiring me for using the Ikea catalogue. I don't know if the other classmates used it too, but I remember that my teacher was very happy with how I had solved it. But I also remember that she was quite unsatisfied with my choices of things (laughs). I don't remember the details; it is too long ago. I mean, I bought – I simulated – that I would need a bed, a chair, a table, but she, like, thought that I had not chosen. She kept asking me these questions all the time: 'Are you sure that you are happy with your furnishing?' and things like that. I don't know what she didn't like about it.

Although these examples seem far removed from an established tradition of housing theatre, they are notable in perpetuating a novel approach to the visitor/exhibit dynamic that one finds in early Swedish exhibitions dedicated to vernacular housing. Despite their diverse objectives and articulations, one finds nevertheless that Ikea showrooms and the open-air housing museum of Skansen show an unlikely kinship.

Skansen and spatial effigies

Speaking to a man employed in the world's first ethnological museum, which is located in Stockholm and called Skansen, I was interested to hear him make the following statement:

> Ikea, they don't sell furniture, they sell a lifestyle. They sell something that you think you will live in, as a whole environment. Connect that to Skansen, to Artur Hazelius, who started Skansen when museums were growing in 1880s . . . All over the world, they built big institutions, they showed museum items under glass so you could look at it, but he had an idea of putting all these items in a total environment and put people, real clothes and behaviours in there. When you come in here, it is another kind of museum . . . The same thing is what Ikea did, maybe they knew, maybe they didn't . . . the first shop in Stockholm is the round house, which is the concept that you walk around. You go into the room, and the room is full of books on the shelves. So you don't just say, 'That is a beautiful chair. I'll buy that chair'. You say, 'Wow, I'll buy this and this and this'. You start to create something yourself. That is the main thing that they really sell. That was the new thing – you see a nice chair and decide to buy it – you can start to create something yourself . . . that was the new thing. They sell a lifestyle, and you choose the lifestyle at the level you want. From the beginning, they had the reputation of having bad quality, so you had to go two or three times, and that has changed. They have much better quality. Now they say OK to designers to put the names on furniture. Now there is a person behind the design.

The staging of experiences is an apposite description of Ikea, and showrooms provide a typical example of how these staging strategies are borne out in practice.

In addition, the blurring of boundaries between cultural production and the market is well documented. Within museum practice, it is now recognized that strict designation of the binary model between department store and museum is a product of the past (Cumming and Lewandowska 2004). Such encroachments are more typically illustrated as moving from the corporate world into museum practice (Duncan 2002), but what initially surprised me about this respondent's comments is not the connections between his museum and Ikea display practices but the longevity of these practices. Skansen – the world's first outdoor museum – was a pioneer in inaugurating a national design tradition that advanced the unique cultural value of peasant culture (Naylor 1990). In the creation of Skansen, regional houses from all over Sweden were dismantled, rebuilt and conserved in an area of Stockholm called Djurgården with the aim of creating a national architectural vernacular. This required that substantial wooden houses, farms and outhouses, including their furnished interiors, had to be moved wholesale in order to allow museum visitors to enter into a whole domestic environment, a lived home replete with a hive of human activities. What was starkly novel at the time is that the curator, through trial and error, succeeded in evoking this sense of immersion, facilitating visitors to put to one side their positions as intruders and to instead imagine themselves to be in actual homes. Skansen incorporated the vernacular experience into Swedish heritage at a time when farming society was irrevocably changing through emigration, modernisation, industrialisation and urbanisation (O'Giolláin 2012; Stoklund 2003). It legitimated a peasant past but also required, as Sandberg expertly elucidates, a distinctly new mode of spectator participation that increasingly came to feel natural. This naturalisation, this process of wilful forgetting, was created initially through the juxtaposition of costumed mannequins against a background of folk houses, but later, was replaced by something altogether more successful.

Skansen was founded by Artur Hazelius in 1891 and until 1965 and was linked with the Scandinavian-Ethnographic Collection (Skandinavisk Etnografiska Samlingen).[5] In the Nordic Museum (Nordiska Museet), the creation of a national imaginary was manifested in artefacts and exhibitions, but in Skansen, the emphasis was more architectural in the assemblage of whole environments (Silvén 2008: 9; see also Bergman 2000). At first, it was unclear what would be showcased: ethnographic collections could include anything from crania to a cultural history of all social groups in Sweden. Hazelius, eventually, opted to prioritise rural, peasant (allmoge) culture through the medium of the lived domestic environment. Replacing mannequins, Hazelius and his successors hit on the effective use of spatial effigies or the evocation of an absent person, which allowed the individual to 'enliven' the scene with his or her own imagination (Sandberg 2003: 223). Central to this strategy was the adoption of a rhetoric of the home in naturalising the display space. The interior was emphasised as being a real home, one that the viewer could imagine inhabiting. By encouraging spectators to think of each museum visit as a homecoming, the folk museums could override the representational basis of display and create a continuity of the depicted scene. The way this theatricality is played out in contemporary scenes is found in the finely tuned balance between being both a spectator and a participant, which is required of trade fairs, model home expos and furniture showroom visitors. This tentative liminal feeling is suggestive, Sandberg notes, in photographs taken beside reconstructed houses, where individuals stand by open doors or perch on stairs, mimicking the one-time resident (Sandberg 2003).

Under Hazelius's stewardship, Skansen was exceptional not only in its assemblage and reconstitution of an archive of vernacular domesticity but also in actively mobilising the engaged imagination of the visitor through display practices. Witnessing a vacated presence and reading into it an imagined person, the visitor is transmogrified into a participant, placing himself or herself in the scene, inhabiting it imaginatively. Furthermore, in actively constituting a tension through displacement, the visitor found himself or herself elsewhere, not firmly rooted in one place but rather at the interstice of home and not-home, tradition and modern (Sandberg 2003). Expanding and extending, rebuilding and refiguring vernacular housing, this open-air museum foreshadowed model home exhibits that followed, its prescience forming one strand in a wider weave in which the domestic was placed centre stage in the late nineteenth century, rendering the home a public object in novel ways (Arrhenius 2010: 149).

Living history museums were superseded by various model home exhibits, whose persuasive force lay not in the disassembling and reconstruction of regional artefacts and architecture but in a boiling down of this sense of a lived environment in a playful back and forth between perused object of display and lived home. Model homes were substantial crowd-pullers in the Stockholm exhibitions of 1909 and 1930, as they were in the Baltic exhibition in Malmö in 1914 and in the 1917 Home exhibition held in the Lijevalchs art gallery in Stockholm. Model home exhibits were launched by the Swedish Society of Applied Arts (1917, 1955), and housing exhibitions sponsored by the Stockholm Association of Building Engineers were held annually during the 1920s. The commercial aspirations of the exhibitors is evident by the sale of the model homes after the exhibition (Sandberg 2011) and the fact that model houses were inhabited for the duration of the 1909 Stockholm exhibition. The emphasis here is not on the quantity of housing exhibits that were launched in Sweden so much as on the co-option of the spectator to place himself or herself within the scene, to envision the material environment as one's own.

The home and social reform

The Swedish home as cipher for the state-citizen contract was a fitting advancement of a long-standing social commentary. The home had been eulogised in nineteenth-century nationalist literature – such as in the works of the national poet Gustaf Geijer – but was consolidated and politicised in unifying the nation within the new political landscape of the twentieth century (Witoszek 2002: 58). The publication of a book in 1899 featuring work by the artist Carl Larsson and the subsequent commentary that surrounded it placed it firmly within a burgeoning social reform movement.[6] In contrast to the excesses of nineteenth-century

Where Swedish 19th century art meets modern Nordic design.

NATIONALMUSEUM
THE NATIONAL MUSEUM OF FINE ARTS www.nationalmuseum.se
OPENING HOURS: TUESDAY 11 AM–8 PM, WEDNESDAY–SUNDAY 11 AM–5 PM. CLOSED MONDAY.

FIGURE 3.1 A Carl Larsson painting used by the National Museum of Stockholm in an advertising campaign in 2008. The pairing of the painting with an icon of modern design (Jonas Bohlin's concrete chair) signifies a bridge from past to present.

Oscarian ostentation, Larsson's watercolour and oil paintings depicted a domestic craftsmanship that combined handwoven textiles, simple wooden furnishings and rustic ideals. Carl and his wife, Karin, who was responsible for much of the handicraft, advocated a simplicity that was avant-garde and international; it characterised a minimalist style but combined Swedish folk design with international Arts and Crafts influences. The Larssons' efforts were not intended as political statements, but under the stewardship of social reformer Ellen Key, they became highly charged with a resonant symbolic capital that is still instantly recognisable today. Larsson prints not only adorn calendars and souvenirs for tourists but also can be found in advertising images that showcase perceived national strengths in art and design. An image advertising the National Museum during fieldwork shows two popularly recognisable examples of symbolic capital: the Larsson paintings and the cutting-edge designs of the Jonas Bohlin's concrete chair.

It was when Key, one of the most well-known social reformers within Sweden but little recognised internationally, saw Larsson's images that they were immediately catapulted onto the national stage as an example of ideal homes for the people. Not until the sublime is as inexpensive as the ugly, she thundered, can beauty for all become a reality. In her pamphlet entitled *Beauty for All* or *Skönhet för Alla* in Swedish (1913), Key proposed that by refining people's tastes and enhancing their appreciation of aesthetic issues, design standards could be raised to such a level that they would bring about a programme of wide-ranging social reform.

Key was part of a wider nineteenth-century phenomenon of utopianism, in which ideas of the public good and social contract were actively questioned. She advocated an alliance between the benefits of mass production and the beauty of artisan craftsmanship, and her promotion of design reform was wide ranging. Key's call for inexpensive yet beautiful domestic objects formed a platform for a concomitant argument that tabled equality amongst social classes and independence for women. Her arguments proved prescient without entailing indiscriminate rejection of the past. She referred to traditional farming houses as providing a limited form of inspiration, a point that would re-emerge in the twentieth-century design movement. It was not necessarily a radical break from the past, she espoused, so much as a realisation of incipient potential centred on the home that would, in time, refract onto the national stage. Key once noted, 'Beautiful home surroundings would be sure to make people happier'; the home was 'fatherland in miniature' and a primary site for social reform and women's emancipation (Witoszek 2002: 58).

The fin de siècle utopianism of a unified taste founded on simplicity and accessibility mediated by everyday things was, however, already in circulation amongst a small group of craft and design professionals. Svenska Slöjdföreningen (Swedish Society of Craft and Industrial Design and later named Svensk Form), the world's first design organisation founded in 1845, sprang from a concern regarding the negative influence of mass industrialisation on handicrafts, in line with the British Arts and Crafts movement. The organisation was originally established in reaction to the perceived threats posed by modern industrial methods but soon came to focus more exclusively on the benefits of mass production. Led by Gregor Paulsson,

Svenska Slöjdföreningen published its propaganda piece under the title *More Beautiful Everyday Things* (*Vackare Vardagsvara*) in 1919, arguing that the purpose of the Swedish design industry should be focused on the creation of functional, beautiful and affordable objects. Formative to Paulsson's perspective was an international movement, and particularly the German organisation Deutscher Werkbund, that advanced a similar reformist goal. Paulsson's ideas developed while living in Germany, where he was exposed to the Werkbund, but he made international ideas regarding the modern movement his own in his landmark publication. Although *Vackare Vardagsvara* was a one-off piece, its legacy remained current in different fora throughout the twentieth century.

Individuals such as Key and Paulsson were part of an international movement that focussed on the rudiment domestic materiality as a route to social reform, and they were part of a professional elite who, in the early twentieth century, showed little success in alleviating the poverty or overcrowding of housing in Stockholm. The vision of social reform through housing percolated to the mainstream through several routes, however. One highly resonant form can be seen in the series of housing exhibits and fairs through which the dynamics of household living were planned and probed. Housing exhibitions were part of a broader trend in which housing was seen, perused, inspected, visited and refracted through the medium of housing exhibits, and as a consequence, the home acquired the expediency of political strategy and mobilisation through the burgeoning social democratic party. Although the welfare state became visible in large-scale modernisation projects, such as in sewage projects and road construction in twentieth-century Europe more generally, what is striking in Sweden is that concomitant with the monumental state interventions, designed environments emerged through a valorisation of the ordinary, showcased through popular and public scrutiny of domestic organisation.

The material culture of social democracy

It is not surprising that there is a saying in Sweden, 'Per Albin Hansson [party leader of the Social Democrats, 1926–1945] built Sweden, and Ingvar Kamprad [founder of Ikea] furnished it'. The legacy of the political avant-garde cannot easily be disentangled from the modernist domestic aesthetic it progressed. Modernist design from its earliest European expression was mobilised by its proponents as an active tool in utopian social change, and aspirations for a social revolution through intimate domestic infrastructure was emphasised early.

Sweden remained neutral during World War II and was well placed to develop rapid industry in the post-war period. But even much earlier – from 1932 and the ascension to government of the Social Democratic party – one finds fundamental changes in economic and social policies, ideologically linking 'the small world of the everyday with the big world of the state and its economy' (Hirdman 1994: 76). The Swedish Social Democrats dominated Swedish politics from 1932 to the 1970s and launched the first Keynesian economic policy in their foundation of the first phase of the welfare state. This collaboration causes some to refer to the social democratic *movement* rather than a party (Hirdman 1994), based on collaboration between state bodies and those representing the interests of businesses and workers. Premised on a promised efficient management of the economy (Hilson 2008: 105; Lujanen 2004: 20), 'needs' and a universal standard of living available to all was pledged, and in the main, provided.

Early twentieth-century housing provision was urgent. Migration into cities, accelerated urbanisation and high-profile radio broadcasts in 1938 describing 'filthy Sweden' (Lort Sverige) highlighted the shortage of adequate housing. A high standard of living in the form of domestic provision and consumption therefore was central in early political posturing. In 1928, Prime Minister Per Albin Hansson famously argued in the parliament (Riksdag) that the welfare state should be conceptualised as the 'People's Home', in which democratic principles would ensure equality for all, thus transmogrifying a social policy statement into an ideological milestone:

> The foundation of the home is community and solidarity. The good home knows no privilege or neglect, no favourites and no stepchildren. There, no one looks down on another, no one strives to gain advantage at the expense of others, the strong do not repress and rob the weak. In the good home equality, thoughtfulness, co-operation and helpfulness prevail. Applied to the great peoples' and citizens' home this would mean the breakdown of all social and economic barriers that now divide citizens into privilege and deprived, into the rulers and the ruled, into rich and poor, the propertied and the destitute, the robbers and the robbed. Swedish society is not yet the good citizen's home ... if [it] is to become [so] class differences must be an economic levelling out, the workers must be accorded a share on economic administration, democracy must be introduced and applied to the social and economic life.
> *(quoted in Hilson 2008: 106)*

'The People's Home' has remained highly resonant throughout the twentieth century and is a popular byword for the Swedish welfare state. It now transcends mere social democratic policy to refer to national sentiment (Hilson 2008: 105) and has been filled with a certain nostalgia since the 1990s (Mattsson and Wallenstein 2010). Similarly, the Key and Paulsson legacy to the future progression of Swedish design and its panoply of values continues to carry resonance on a popular and professional level.[7]

Building on an already established tradition of model home exhibits (see Zetterlund 2012), one salient milestone is the Stockholm exhibition of May 16 to October 9, 1930. The exhibition, called Acceptera! (Accept!), represents the first official launch of functionalist architecture and design to the general public. Funkis – the Nordic version of functionalism – was presented as 'less an aesthetic than a principle' (Linde-Laursen 2010: 158; see also Woollen 2012), the advancement of a new era that, according to one of its foremost architects, will inspire through its 'light sides, its outstanding technical inventions, its freer humans' (Linde-Laursen 2010: 158). Not only that, with light interiors, the relinquishment of former social pretence would follow, according to the exhibition organisers. The benefits of

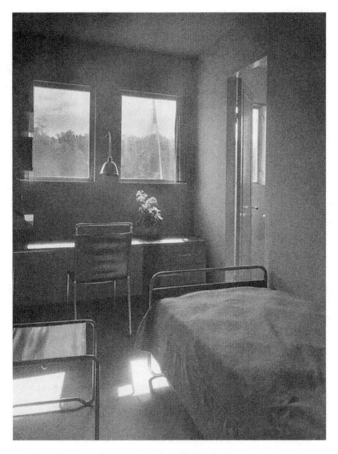

FIGURE 3.2 A bedroom from the Accept exhibition.
Source: Nordiska Museet. Reproduced with kind permission.

standardisation as the 'deliberate development of types' (Creagh et al 2008: 223) would also follow. Affordable, quality homes and furniture were primarily showcased here but also incorporated were presentations on gardens, streets, transport and burial grounds (Linde-Laursen 2010: 157). The main thoroughfare of the Stockholm exhibition was called the Course (*Corson*), off which exhibitions halls were located and that terminated in a building called Paradise (*Paradiset*). Here was housed the fair's restaurant and exhibition halls, which displayed everything from traditional handcrafts to lamps, electric goods, books and printing presses. There were halls dedicated to high-end goods, but these were dwarfed by those that promoted mass-produced furniture, showcasing cutting-edge, inexpensive domestic furnishings for the masses, ready to go into production. Beyond Paradise could be found a presentation of these goods, placed in model apartments of various but standardised sizes, advocating the beauty of simple, functional solutions to domestic organisation.

Sandberg points to northern Europe as a place where one finds an acute juxtaposition between old and new, modern and tradition, as played out in Nordic museums, espousing old techniques of preservation and collection while pursuing pioneering agendas of living scenes and active spectatorship. Due to relatively late modernisation in Scandinavian countries, one finds a striking co-existence of modern and traditional experience, where large swathes of the population moved in worlds that were both forward-looking metropolitan centres and rural farmsteads offering very traditional ways of being. Out of this seeming disjunction of living in two worlds precipitates modernism and ideas of the modern Sandberg argues (2003: 11), recognising that this marks no unequivocal march to the future. Instead, one finds a constant dynamic back and forward in which traditional and modern ways of living co-exist. Regional farming and peasant homes therefore became an unlikely point of reference for the onward creation of modern homes, most perspicaciously in the 1930s Accept exhibition, located just across the water from Skansen. In launching architectural modernism with a heavy political investment in design, the Accept exhibition favoured mass production and standardisation by referring to the simple modesty of traditional vernacular homes. The lack of originality of the folk home, furnished without personal expression, was held as a forerunner to the repetition of the mass-produced object. In fact, one traditional peasant home was redrawn in the Accept manifesto as a functionalist villa. And although Accept was looking to Skansen vernacular traditions, the museum was being thoroughly modernised. In the same years as the Accept exhibition, the site was made sanitary, restaurants were provided, the exhibits were reshuffled to better represent 'Sweden in miniature' and ease of passage was facilitated by the provision of Europe's longest escalator. Although not focused upon in this work, one cannot but ponder the high number of second homes, called *stuga*, in Sweden. These rural homes reiterate a sense of traditional rural basic living that flourished in number at the same time as the modern social democratic state was under construction, reminding us that the family home is not necessary unary and that the binary of modern and traditional is an illusion: the cabin is as much an outcome of daily life and modern domesticity as it is a product of its escape (see Garvey 2008).

A year after the Accept exhibition, a manifesto was published that presented the key aspirations of the event and its organisers, which propounded the values of the beauty inherent in functional things, in democracy as social equality and in the mass production of homes (Linde-Laursen 2010: 157). Standardisation promised to fulfil the needs of quality and quantity simultaneously. The political associations with the architectural and design style were apparent from the start. Magazines that promoted the new aesthetic included the social democratic women's magazine *Morning Breeze (Morgonbris)* and the Cooperative Consumer publication *Konsumentbladet*. Moreover, the manifesto for the Accept exhibition was published in the social democratic publication *Tiden* (Nilsson 1991: 73). In 1936, Prime Minister Per Albin Hansson – who coined the word *folkhemmet* – moved into a functionalist house twinning a specifically Scandinavian version of functionalist design with a specifically Scandinavian version of the welfare state.[8] Not to be forgotten, however, and dovetailing with these more spectacular initiatives, were the panoply of policies that materialised the architectural visions established in the exhibitions. These standardised domestic architectures and interiors actively choreographed domestic practices in closely scripted ways. Women were central in driving forward an intensive domestic modernisation programme in which profound focus intensified on the minutiae of domestic material culture, on everything from correct mattress maintenance to children's toys, earning social democratic women the title 'mattress socialists' as a term of ridicule by communist women's groups who saw instead middle-class aspirations out of step with life (Hirdman 1994: 88, see also Hirdman 1992). These reforms were not only aimed at adjusting the political landscape and housing market but also more profoundly catapulted the private sphere into the limelight of political strategy, causing the home to become the harbinger of a new society. 'Revolution came from below' (Mattsson 2010: 79).

Revolution from below

Within the political climate of the post-war period, the mobilisation of a highly positivistic form of design developed in line with a symbiotic relationship with state-sponsored housing development and research projects. Post-war housing policy explicitly drew on the vision of the People's Home as deliverable through the equitable distribution of modern standardized housing. Allmännytta, meaning 'for the benefit for everyone', is the name given to national housing policy originating in the interwar years when municipalities first created their own housing companies (Christophers 2013: 891). Municipal housing companies were instrumental in ensuing that public rental was public, rather than 'social': 'It should not be directed at certain groups with special needs but should be for everyone (Hedman 2008: 12, in Christophers 2013: 891). As a non-profit sector, state municipalities oversaw the bulk of Stockholm's housing and granted housing loans to construct extensive and standardised building projects during a post-war period of economic expansion (Caldenby et al 1998: 143).[9] The advantage to residents of the non-profit housing sector was that it was almost entirely owned by municipalities, open to everyone and not means tested, and the rents it set served as the norm for the entire sector, including private housing companies, as enshrined in law in 1974. Epitomising the 'Swedish model', the golden age of public rental extended from 1945 to 1970, culminating in the Million Programme (see Chapter 1). But the state's interest in housing did not stop at the front door: concomitant with the provision of housing was its transformation into a researched-based terminal.

With an unprecedented collaboration between the state and science-based industry a raft of agencies were established to research and regulate the construction and interior decoration of homes. Research progressed by the Home Research Institute therefore combined the dual purpose of defining a domestic pedagogy while concomitantly solving more prosaic problems, such as storage solutions, kitchen planning and sleeping requirements. One of the most important goals of this research was to develop housing norms (*bostadsnormerna*) in order to rationalise

FIGURE 3.3 Research into efficient kitchen practices.

Source: Nordiska Museet. Reproduced with kind permission.

The Home Research Institute (Hemmens forskningsinstitut) was founded in 1944 and funded by the state with the dual goal of rationalizing housework through research and consumer education. The housewife-as-expert was at the centre of this research, but her work was scrutinised by domestic teachers, chemists, nutritionists, sociologists, architects and engineers. In 1957, the Home Research Institute became the National Institute for Consumer Affairs, now the Consumer Agency (Konsumentverket). Photographer: Ateljé Hernried.

housework and elevate the housewife into an expert of domestic skills.[10] Meanwhile, in 1944, the Swedish Society for Crafts and Design (*Svensk Form*, formerly known as *Svenska Slöjdföreningen*) started a Committee for the Home in association with Swedish Co-Operative Union (KF), the Home Research Institute (*Hemmens Forskningsinstitut*), and the National Association of Tenants Savings and Building (HSB), funded by industry and the trade union movement (LO). The committee aimed to 'raise awareness of the importance of interior decoration and sought to accomplish this task through educational courses and exhibitions' (Robach 2002: 198). The courses were designed as 'study circles' aimed to advise young couples, often in receipt of state loans, on how to equip a new home (Robach 2002).

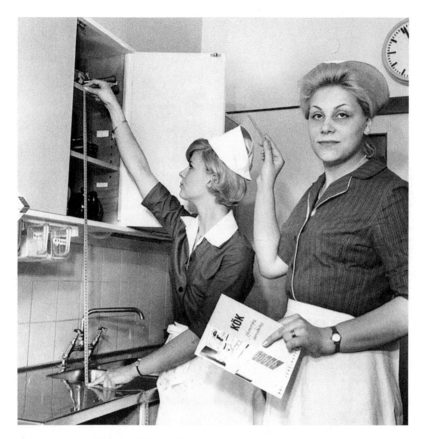

FIGURE 3.4 Research into efficient kitchen practices.

Source: Nordiska Museet. Reproduced with kind permission. Photographer Okänd.

In 1954, the National Housing Board (*Bostadsstyrelsen*) published a book, *Good Housing* (*God Bostad*), thus establishing the norms that dominated home design until the 1990s. *Good Housing* set the regulations for minimum living space and thoroughly outlined the requirements for every part of a dwelling: utility room, kitchen, hall and so on. Designs entailed close measurement of domestic activities to facilitate the most efficient use of space, but other significant considerations included access to direct sunlight, room climate, sound isolation, electric installations, elevators and building and room dimensions. Precise measurements resulted from observations of household activities, such as washing-up or preparing food, leading to official recommendations as to height or width of kitchen worktops and the distance between stove and kitchen sink. The result was a series of enforced architectural norms that were not only endorsed by the state but also proscriptive for the building industry to procure municipal funding. Such efforts were directed to managing domestic spaces, standardising sizes and shapes of rooms and facilitating the storage of burdensome objects in small spaces (Eriksson 2000: 53). Within

66 Home staging, housing theatre

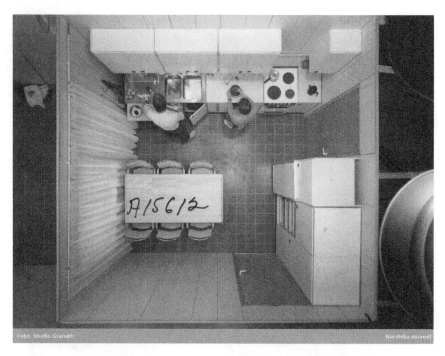

FIGURE 3.5   Konsumentverket (the Consumer Agency). Two people in the test kitchen, seen from above. 1971, Studio Granath.

Source: Nordiska Museet. Reproduced with kind permission.

a decade, several guidelines included in the booklet 'Good Housing' were added to state housing norms, marking something of an apex in housing norms: kitchens should have a stove, sink, workbenches, and cupboards. Workbenches should be 85–90 cm high based on the assumption that the individual working there was 164 cm tall, implying a woman. At least 110 cm of free space is required in front of the stove, sink, and workbenches (*God Bostad* 1964: 20, in Hård 2010: 121), and provision should be made for the later installation of a dishwasher if desired. Many apartments have storage space in hallways for linen storage, and these should adhere to a 60 cm by 60 cm standard, or alternatively, an 80 cm width, if the cupboard includes an ironing board (Hård 2010: 122). This third edition of *God Bostad* presciently preceded a government announcement that one million homes would be constructed in the coming decade. Ikea opened a store in Stockholm in 1965, just in time to furnish them.

Ikea in Kungens Kurva opened its doors, then, when domestic construction and consumption practices were entering a new moment. Domestic consumption was formative in the consolidation of the social democratic welfare state, giving form to the promise of ameliorated welfare, explicitly entwining individual life chances with the wider social economic policies (Mattsson and Wallenstein 2010: 8). From the 1950s, political mandates were designed and then implemented to make

FIGURE 3.6 Kitchen in the 1957 Without Borders exhibition. Lennart Holm (no. 7 on Plate 2.1.4).

Source: Kooperativa Förbundet bibliotek och arkiv.

it financially easier for people to marry, have children and move into better homes, while an aesthetic template of 'modern living' was popularised in the 1950s and 1960s as 'a shared aspiration' as well as a design export (Kälvemark 1980; Löfgren 2010). Both liberal capitalism and universal welfare were marketed through democratic access to goods. Encouraged by both the state and the market, then, specifically, domestic consumption lay at the heart of the progression of national modernity. Individuals were encouraged to purchase appliances, services and goods, which were either said to facilitate the development of the individual or to help rationalise the home, household chores and immediate environment (O'Dell 1997: 132–133).[11]

With growing prosperity, the commercial potential of exhibitions kept pace. In the summer of 1955, the international exhibition H55, organized by the Swedish Society of Industrial Design, opened in Helsingborg. As much trade fair as cultural show, it set out to demonstrate how modern design could be integrated into everyday commercial products that used new technologies and materials (Ekström 2010: 519). Soon after, the 1957 Without Borders exhibition was launched by the Swedish Cooperative Movement and aimed to highlight the global world of commodities available to the post-war world. In it, the visitor moved from an architectural globe with mirrors to an exhibition of a multitude of standardised commodities hanging or arranged in repetitive groups to de-emphasise the singular object and to create a new environment or mass ornament. Toilets or wash basics, for example, were stacked to create walls (Mattsson 2010: 90), making the most unlikely things into eventful stages for a dramatic environment. The exhibition progressed from an architecture constructed with mirrors to an exhibition space for commodities, finishing in a standard family apartment. Such exhibits underscore the promise of domestic consumption as a participatory practice, which extends beyond the exhibitionary moment. The commodities on show are not enclaved or cordoned off but create an environment that blurs the boundaries between spectator and participant. The use of the domestic scene, described at the time as 'shocking in its complete absence of shock' (Paulsson 1957: 238, in Mattsson 2010: 95; see also Figure 3.7), is telling in its showcase of a frozen moment of ordinary life portrayed by the stocked fridge in the kitchen, the laid table, and the pullover hanging on a plastic clothes line in the bathroom. (Mattsson 2010: 95).

Home staging

Visiting a research respondent – who I'll call Khalad – in his new home one chilly November evening, he told me about the advice he had been given by his estate agent regarding how best to sell his house. Instead of the spatial effigies of Ikea showrooms, Khalad emphasised the presentational strategies he enlisted to transform the intensely personal space of the home into an altogether more public place. He was advised on 'home staging', and he rhymed off, 'It should be as empty as possibly, and you shouldn't have any personal possessions lying around. Try and clear it out and not make people uncomfortable with too much personal stuff'. As a tactic in successful sales, then, home staging hinges on the transversal of public and private boundaries but in a way that differs from public exhibitions. Home staging of private space is markedly different from the housing theatre of public displays, but both are based on a similar series of themes.

The frozen moments of lived experience that are particularly perspicacious in model home exhibits are avidly avoided in buying and selling transactions. In a book published in 2012 entitled *High on Housing* (*Hög på Hus*) one man, Alexander Norén, describes in detail how he navigated Stockholm's housing market, chronicling his efforts to purchase a home amid intense popular interest and rising house prices. This he attributes to the sale of public housing, low interest rates, the added ingredient of the Internet and twenty years of economic affluence. Plus, he adds, seventy-five different interior magazines are available at the local store, ramping up interest and dictating that suddenly 'everything should be bright and fresh'.[12] The book itemises ten myths regarding the housing market, one of which underscores that emotions always trump rationality when purchasing a home. Although home staging is often subject to humour or derision, he reports that creating a successful stage – the halo effect – can add 10 per cent to the sales price and create a sale for reasons that are not necessarily clear to the buyer.[13] Following the launch of the book, Alexander Norén appeared on radio stations and added his recommendations on home staging on a dedicated blog, under the heading '14 Truths about Home Staging'.[14] These pointers emphasise the importance of clear surfaces, empty spaces and the clever use of light and colour in establishing scenarios and moods. Most important is to lend the prospective buyer an aspiration of home life, and as such, it should never be messy. Realism does not sell houses, he dictates. In the late 2000s, light and fresh is now hopelessly passé, he remarks (possibly replaced with 'dark and drab', he quips in Norén, 2012: 158), but the emotive undercurrent that determines the sale of a home remains constant.

Home staging starts by eliminating elements that risk ruining the mood, such as overly unique, individualistic items like untidy books on bookshelves, brash colours on walls or children's toys. On the other hand, a complete absence of furniture looks sterile. The trick, according to Norén, is to clear clutter, remove the noise of actual everyday life and make surfaces look as big as possible. The hotel room is a good guide, Norén claims, because it is sufficiently neutral to allow residents to place themselves within a home-like environment, and for however long, feel comfortable there. Intimate possessions such as photographs create a barrier to viewers placing themselves within the scene, preventing their imagination to territorialise the home on view. Home staging facilitates an imaginative emplacement and enlists the viewer to place himself or herself in the domestic environment but does so through a carefully choreographed environment. Instead of the personal items or children's drawings that we have seen in commercial home stages, domestic spaces need to dampen personal style, actively create a public environment and secure the right balance between private and impersonal when courting the social audience.

Design legacies

Arriving in Helsingborg in 2008 to meet Ikea's then-marketing manager Nils Larsson, I was swiftly gifted a small booklet outlining the company style progenitors in which historical figures Ellen Key and Gregor Paulsson and milestone events such as the Accept exhibition are detailed. The booklet, produced by Ikea, places the company at the culmination of these historical trajectories in which Key and Paulsson represent the founding members of an era that twinned design with national aspiration and modernity.

Milestone events in which design legacies were established, such as the Stockholm exhibition during the summer of 1930, have been described in terms of a national monument, a monument to the New Star of Swedish modernity, and the manifestation of a utopian agenda (Linde-Laursen 2010). As with any monument, it is the narratives that are constructed around it by a relatively small number of individuals as much as the thing itself that is active in identifying the temporal benchmarks that define a before and after. The homogenisation of the Scandinavian design narrative is increasingly acknowledged (Fallan 2012; Zetterlund 2012), and Linde-Laursen points out that it did not take long before the Accept exhibition's significance seemed to be credited with marking a line in the sand. Accept is often represented as a revelatory ritual, a practice in which the future was manifested. Soon after the exhibition, it was already credited as a fait accompli, less an image of the future as a baseline for revolution that had already happened (Linde-Laursen 2010: 163). In conversation, I noticed that the 1930s was used as a kind of temporal shorthand for policies pertaining to social engineering and urban planning that were put in place from this time. But during those months from May to September in 1930 when 4.1 million people visited the Accept exhibition, only 5,767 catalogues were sold (Linde-Laursen 2010: 163; Pred 1992, 1995: 151). For most visitors, the exhibition was a pleasurable day out more than a didactic instrument, and the lessons learned were not necessarily what the organizers hoped.

The significance of the Accept exhibition, I suggest, should not be considered as an isolated phenomenon but instead as a part of the wave of exhibitions that staged national modernity within the intimate environments of people's lives. Events such as these worked to crystallise the ideas of various actors advocating political intervention, scientific and technical excellence and mass production in the creation of a specific domestic environment. In so doing, it disturbed immutable distinctions between public and private, individual and collective, and rallied the political rhetoric of the People's Home. Designed environments showcased as a category continue to consolidate multiple actors and visionary programmes, and the emphasis on domestic immersion emerges in the most unlikely of places. Larsson images as progenitors of an essentially Swedish domestic style still evoke social commentary within an aesthetic display, and these images are frequently associated with domestic exhibitions. In 1997, the Victoria and Albert Museum in London staged a Carl and Karin Larsson exhibit, pitched as 'quintessentially Swedish' and a 'beloved' part of national heritage in the launch of a Larsson retrospective exhibition. The commemoration named the artistic couple as 'creators of the Swedish style'. The exhibition was partially funded by the Swedish government and Ikea, which is pitched as an informal continuation of that style in Ikea marketing literature.[15] Interestingly, the inheritors of the Larsson house insisted on a live, lived-in exhibition that the museum professionals reported as 'somewhat surreal': 'We sat on the chairs, slept in the beds and used the table, which we will next see carefully installed as museum objects in our exhibition'.[16]

This potential as part of the Larssons' 'symbolic production' (Bourdieu and Johnson 1993) can again be found internationally. In Dublin in 2012, a small exhibition featuring work by artist Veronica Forsgren and funded by Swedish Women's Educational Association (SWEA) opened which displayed examples of the rich Swedish tradition of handicraft, or hemslöjd. Furthermore, in the opening statement, the artist suggests that the Larsson ideal, comprising small, light, unpretentious rooms, family-oriented and economically furnished, has come to epitomise Swedish style.[17] Continuing to draw links with today, she suggests the following:

> These ideals fit in with modern attitudes and lifestyles and also had an impact on the creation of folkhemmet, of the People's Home, the social housing reform movements of the 1930s through the 1970s, as well as influencing IKEA, which cites the couple as having a strong historical impact on its design. Parallels can be drawn with society today. It is interesting that in this time of a volatile economic situation, there has been an upsurge of interest in sustainable living, do-it-yourself crafts, going back to basics and TV programmes promoting innovative architecture and the merits of relocating to the countryside from the city. With many young families stuck in negative equity, the home is again a contentious subject.

Housing theatre continues to rally, even when adopted in unexpected contexts. Here, against the backdrop of the global economic crash, acutely felt and applied to an Irish context, mingled with nostalgia for a geographically, temporally and socially distant folkhemmet, I find myself one wintry afternoon in a small backstreet city-centre exhibition centre, reading about the alliances between negative equity in the Irish housing market and twentieth-century Swedish housing reform movements. Ikea is pitched as a benign manifestation of distant housing reform and carrier of future ambition. In Dublin, one wonders how such statements are received, to what degree the visiting public is aware of the significance being hinted at and the politically laden aesthetic of the Swedish style that seems to collapse complex historical actions into an aesthetic shorthand. But again, housing theatre has been applied in diverse ways before now. Exhibitions showcasing home interiors and dwellings were a feature of contemporary consumer culture as much as a harbinger of national modernity. Expos and fairs were again mobilised in reaction to the housing slump of the 1990s: visiting the Swedish Building Service (Byggtjänst), a company that provides information on all aspects of construction, I was told that the organisation of expos was funded by state bodies such as Byggforskningråd to reinvigorate the industry 'to show what we can do'.[18] In other words, to give form and material manifestation to an aspiration for an invigorated economy and to remind visitors of past successes. In these measures, design mediates not only past successes but also indexically connects design expertise with public aspiration.

To recap, Ikea showrooms participate in this long history of housing theatre through the invocation of experiences that 'establish cross-contextual links and resonances' and that 'powerfully persuade' (see Kratz 2011). Ikea showrooms employ both the trope of design and the instrument of spatial effigies in their organisation. The trace of missing persons was already a dominant trope in home exhibits when Ikea was established, and corporate marketing publications and the store's web pages allude to the Accept and Skansen exhibitions. It is worth remembering that although the history of Swedish design tends to pivot on these individuals and the social democratic party that followed it as the centre of gravity that shackled design and social policy, the stripped-down minimalism of funkis did not gain purchase with broad popular appeal until the mid-twentieth century. Nevertheless, Ikea showrooms perpetuate this trajectory, both architecturally, in that the store at Kungens Kurva was based on the plan of the Guggenheim Museum in New York, conceptually and materially, in the manifestation of the home as a public object, and strategically, in its adoption of the decorative logic of the effigy. My point, however, is concerned less with tracing a direct lineage than with underscoring the traversal of public and private domains in which domesticity may be experienced as a matrix of experiences and locations. Fundamentally, the design of interior spaces and its attendant material furnishing provided one forum for the entanglement of intimate routines with the workings and priorities of broader collectivities and the imaginings of national modernity. Boundaries between public spectacle and private property continue to be actively transgressed in order to refract on ideas of the social. The microroutines of daily life, then, became not only pedagogical instruments of national and political expression but also the mechanism through which modern subjectives were crafted.

Notes

1 Maíra Lot, marketing manager of Casa Cor and responsible for the European project, noted that Sweden was picked for being the number one test market in Europe, since Swedes absorb new products three times more quickly than the rest of Europe. Furthermore, we are told, Sweden is a reference point in terms of creativity and innovation and is renowned for being open to new ideas, technologies and products (Reid 2007: 22–23).
2 This was in large part due to the specific role that architectural policy and design research played in the early formation of the welfare state (Sandberg 2011: 67).
3 Sandberg's observation was that bodily effigies proliferated from the late nineteenth century in various museological, international fair and cinematic settings.
4 'Rent Hus,' TV4, accessed 03/08/17, www.tv4.se/rent-hus#.
5 This was founded by Artur Hazelius in 1873. In 1880, it was renamed the Nordic Museum (Nordiska Museet).
6 The national poet was influential in his argument that the home is the 'only environment to promote the ideal of the Christian-liberal personality, which later came to imbue the dominant educational and ethical foundation of Sweden' (Witoszek 2002: 57–58).
7 As in Svensk Form's mission statement, which includes the following: 'A better life through good design. Increasing knowledge about the benefits of good design to the development of society has been the key theme throughout the history of Svensk Form. Today, the goal of achieving a long-term sustainable society and improved quality of life is more urgent than ever. Designers are a natural link between manufacturers and

consumers and can influence how social, environmental and economic aspects are integrated into a product's design, manufacture, marketing and market communications. Good design solutions can contribute to sustainable development. Svensk Form participates in a number of projects on the theme of good design.' ('About Svensk Form', Svensk Form, accessed 01/03/15, http://svenskform.se/en/about-svensk-form/.)
8   Uno Åhrén, one of the Accept exhibition's architects, designed his house.
9   In addition to these were cooperative housing companies (the HSB) and the Cooperative Housing Union (Svenska Riksbyggen) that were founded in the 1930s and entitled to give housing loans. Less favourable terms were offered to private-sector housing companies that had earlier represented the main builder of homes.
10 Kristoffersson notes the very many 'courses and exhibitions, as well as columns of advice in magazines aimed at "irrational" habits' (2014: 60).
11 Löfgren notes the centrality of the state campaigns 'for better living and modern interior decorations; an educational tradition that companies like Ikea would carry further' (2010: 70). For example, in the immediate post-war era, young couples were given housing but were encouraged to attend home decoration classes first, while a rise in the standard of living for the working classes pitched the Swedish style of modern living as a popularly homogenous movement within a 'highly international rhetoric' (Löfgren 2010: 69). Less evident in historical treaties is the emphasis on the unassuming quality of domestic design that was advanced at this time. Scandinavian design tended to be associated with an unassuming ordinariness characteristic of the Scandinavian home.
12 Alexander Norén, 'Hög På Hus: Vägen Till det Perfekta Boendet', Adlibris, www.adlibris.com/se/bok/hog-pa-hus-vagen-till-det-perfekta-boendet-9789100127961, accessed 03/08/17
13 'Vi har lärt oss att skratta åt home-staging-klyschorna i bostadsannonserna. "Ljust oh fräscht" är hopplöst pass, nu ska det tydligen vara "mörkt och murrigt"'.
14 See Alexander Norén's home-staging tips at http://sverigesradio.se/sida/artikel.aspx?programid=103&artikel=5755694 as well as his blog on home staging at https://hogpahus.wordpress.com/2014/01/12/darfor-funkar-home-staging/, accessed 03/08/17.
15 The Larsson house receives sixty thousand visitors annually and deliberately defies a strict definition of either home or museum because the Larssons' descendants decided it should be both.
16 Tina Manoli and Nicola Costaras, 'Preparations for "Carl and Karin Larsson: Creators of the Swedish Style"', Conservation Journal 25, www.vam.ac.uk/content/journals/conservation-journal/issue-25/preparations-for-carl-and-karin-larsson-creators-of-the-swedish-style, accessed 03/08/17.
17 The exhibition was put together by the artist Veronica Forsgren.
18 These fairs took place every two years in cities such as Stockholm, Malmö and Göteborg.

References

Arrhenius, Thordis. 2010. "The Vernacular on Display: Skansen Open-Air Museum in 1930s Stockholm'." In *Swedish Modernism: Architecture, Consumption, and the Welfare State*, edited by Helena Mattsson and Sven-Olov Wallenstein. London: Black Dog Publishing.

Bergman, Ingrid. 2000. *Artur Hazelius: Nordiska museets och Skansens skapare*. Stockholm: Nordiska Museet.

Bourdieu, Pierre and Randal Johnson. 1993. *The Field of Cultural Production: Essays on Art and Literature*. Cambridge: Polity Press.

Caldenby, Claes, Jöran Lindvall, and Wilfried Wang, eds. 1998. *20th Century Architecture: Sweden*. Munich and New York: Prestel.

Christophers, Brett. 2013. "A Monstrous Hybrid: The Political Economy of Housing in Early Twenty-First Century Sweden." *New Political Economy* 18 (6): 885–911.

Creagh, Lucy, Helena Kåberg, and Barbara Miller Lane, eds. 2008. *Modern Swedish Design: Three Founding Texts*. New York: Museum of Modern Art.

Cummings, Neil and Marysia Lewandowska. 2004. "Collision." In *Grasping the World: The Idea of the Museum*, edited by Donald Preziosi and Claire Farago. Aldershot: Ashgate.

Duncan, Carol. 2002. "Museums and Department Stores: Close Encounters." In *High-Pop: Making Culture Into Popular Entertainment*, edited by Jim Collins, 129–133. Malden, MA: Blackwell Publishers.

Ekström, Karin M. 2010. "Design and Consumption." In *Consumer Behaviour: A Nordic Perspective*, edited by Karen M. Ekström. Lund: Studentlitteratur.

Eriksson, Jan. 2000. "Bostaden som kunskapsobjekt." In *Hem i förvandling: Arkitekturmuseet, årsbok 2000*, edited by Bitte Nygren, Christina Enfors, and Eva Rudberg, 44–73. Stockholm: The Swedish Museum of Architecture.

Fallan, Kjetil. 2012. *Scandinavian Design: Alternative Histories*. London: Berg.

Garvey, Pauline. 2008. "The Norwegian Country Cabin and Functionalism: A Tale of Two Modernities." *Social Anthropology* 16 (2): 203–220.

Habel, Ylva. 2009. "Beside Myself With Looking: The Provincial, Female Spectator as Out of Place at the Stockholm Exhibition 1897." In *Strange Spaces: Explorations Into Mediated Obscurity*, edited by André Jansson and Amanda Lagerkvist, 123–148. Farnham: Ashgate Publishing.

Hård, Mikael. 2010. "The Good Apartment: The Social (Democratic) Construction of Swedish Homes." *Home Cultures* 7 (2): 117–133.

Hedman, Eva. 2008. *A History of the Swedish System of Non-Profit Municipal Housing*. Stockholm: Boverket.

Hilson, Mary. 2008. *The Nordic Model: Scandinavia Since 1945*. London: Reaktion Books.

Hirdman, Yvonne. 1992. "Utopia in Everyday Life – Problems and Background." *International Journal of Political Economy* 22 (2): 5–19.

Hirdman, Yvonne. 1994. "Social Engineering and the Woman Question: Sweden in the 1930s." *Studies in Political Economy* 44 (1): 73–94.

Kälvemark, Ann-Sofie. 1980. *More Children of Better Quality? Aspects on Swedish Population Policy in the 1930's*. Uppsala: Acta Universitatis Upsaliensis.

Key, Ellen. 1913. *Skönhet för alla*. Stockholm: Albert Bonniers Förlag.

Kratz, Corinne, A. 2011. "Rhetorics of Value: Constituting Worth and Meaning Through Cultural Display." *Visual Anthropology Review* 27 (1): 21–48.

Kristoffersson, Sara. 2014. *Design by IKEA: A Cultural History*. London: Bloomsbury.

Linde-Laursen, Anders. 2010. *Bordering: Identity Processes Between the National and Personal*. London and New York: Routledge.

Löfgren, Orvar. 2010. "Historical Perspectives on Consumption." In *Consumer Behaviour: A Nordic Perspective*, edited by Karin M. Ekström, 57–73. Lund: Studentlitteratur.

Lujanen, Martti. 2004. *Housing and Housing Policy in the Nordic Countries*. Copenhagen: Nordic Council of Ministers.

Mattsson, Helena. 2010. "Designing the Reasonable Consumer: Standardisation and Personalisation in Swedish Functionalism." In *Swedish Modernism: Architecture, Consumption and the Welfare State*, edited by Helena Mattsson and Sven-Olov Wallenstein. London: Black Dog Publishing.

Mattsson, Helena and Sven-Olov Wallenstein, eds. 2010. *Swedish Modernism: Architecture, Consumption and the Welfare State*. London: Black Dog Publishing.

Murphy, Keith M. 2015. *Swedish Design: An Ethnography*. Ithaca: Cornell University Press.

Naylor, Gillian. 1990. *The Arts and Crafts Movement: A Study of Its Sources, Ideals and Influence on Design Theory*. London: Trefoil.

Nilsson, Jan Olof, and Anders Linde-Laursen. 1991. *Nationella identiteter i Norden: ett fullbordat projekt? sjutton nordiska undersökningar, Nord (København).* Stockholm: Nordiska rådet: Allmänna förl.

Norén, Alexander. 2012. *Hög på hus vägen till det perfekta boendet.* Stockholm: Albert Förlag.

O'Dell, Tom. 1997. *Culture Unbound: Americanization and Everyday Life in Sweden.* Lund: Nordic Academic Press.

Ó'Giolláin, Diarmuid. 2012. "Archives and Artefacts: Collecting, Collections and Ethnography in an Irish and Comparative European Context." In *Exhibit Ireland: Ethnographic Collections in Irish Museums*, edited by Séamas Ó'Síocháin, Pauline Garvey, and Adam Drazin. Dublin: Wordwell Press.

Paulsson, Gregor. 1957. "Utan gränser." *Byggmästaren* 11: 234.

Pred, Allan and Michael J. Watts. 1992. *Reworking Modernity: Capitalisms and Symbolic Discontent, Hegemony and Experience.* New Brunswick, NJ: Rutgers University Press.

Pred, Allan. 1995. *Recognizing European Modernities: A Montage of the Present.* London: Routledge.

Reid, Laura. 2007. "Casa Cor Holds Its Very First European Edition in Stockholm." *Swedcham* 4: 22–23.

Robach, Eva. 2002. "Design for Modern People." In *Utopia & Reality: Modernity in Sweden 1900–1960*, edited by Cecilia Widenheim and Eva Rudberg. New Haven: Yale University Press.

Sandberg, Mark B. 2003. *Living Pictures, Missing Persons: Mannequins, Museums and Modernity.* Princeton, NJ: Princeton University Press.

Sandberg, Mark B. 2011 "The Interactivity of the Model Home". In *History of Participatory Media: Politics and Publics, 1750–2000*, edited by Solveig Jülich Anders Ekström, Frans Lundgren, and Per Wisselgren. New York: Routledge.

Silvén, Eva. 2008. "Cultural Diversity at the Nordiska Museet in Stockholm: Outline of a Story." In *Scandinavian Museums and Cultural Diversity*, edited by Katherine Goodnow and Haci Akman, 8–22. New York and Oxford: Berghahn Books.

Stadler, Erika. 2007. 'Casa Cor Design Exhibition Hits Europe', *Wired*, October 12, available online at www.wired.com/2007/10/casa-cor-design/, accessed 03/11/16.

Stoklund, Bjarne. 2003. "Between Scenography and Science: Early Folk Museums and Their Pioneers." *Ethnologia Europaea* 33 (1): 21–35.

Witoszek, Nina. 2002. "Moral Community and the Crisis of the Enlightenment: Sweden and Germany in the 1920s and 1930s." In *Culture and Crisis: The Case of Germany and Sweden*, edited by Lars Trägårdh and Nina Witoszek, 48–74. New York and Oxford: Berghahn Books.

Woollen, Malcolm. 2012. "The Stockholm Exhibit 1930: Reinventing the Everyday." *Environment, Space, Place* 4 (2): 130–162.

Zetterlund, Christina. 2012. "Just Decoration? Ideology and Design in Early Twentieth Century Sweden." In *Scandinavian Design: Alternative Histories*, edited by Kjetil Fallan. London: Bloomsbury.

4
STANDARDISATION, DEMOCRACY AND EQUALITY

Design for the many people

On the Ikea.se web page in 2009, the question was posed, 'What does IKEA mean by democratic design?' to which it replied, 'This is the design philosophy at IKEA. Having a limited budget should not prevent people from creating a beautiful home, with practical and sensible furniture. Therefore, IKEA offers good-quality design that the many people can afford' (Inter IKEA Systems BV 1999–2009).[1]

There is a story I have heard on three occasions during fieldwork, which emerged in such diverse settings that I am beginning to wonder if it ranks as an urban – or Ikea – myth. In 2008, while visiting then-marketing manager Nils Larsson in one of Ikea's head or 'service' offices in Helsingborg, a scenario was recounted to me whereby a woman's children were jumping on the display beds in one of their unspecified stores. When a staff member eventually intervened, the annoyed parent responded, 'Look, I pay my taxes like everyone else'. The second time I heard this story was in an apartment in Stockholm, where the girlfriend of a former employee described the same. The situation evoked on both occasions was identical, although the point differed for each of my interlocutors. The manager's intention was to illustrate the dominance of Ikea on the Swedish market, describing Ikea's presence in furniture retail as 'saturated'. So saturated, it seems, that for a tiny sector of its consumer base, Ikea was considered a 'right', or public service. For Sophie, on the other hand, while we sat on her sofa in her white-walled cosy apartment devoid of clutter or kitsch, she complained of the ubiquity of Ikea and Ikea-linked (Ikano) services and products and gave voice to her exasperation that there are people 'out there' who think Ikea is part of the state system. 'There can't be many', she qualified, 'because that would be stupid'.

> I just get the feeling that they want to be the head of Sweden who decides what to put in your homes ... It feels like a sect, it feels like that. Ikea has their own bank, their own daycare centre. In Älmhult, they have their own daycare

and their own houses for the workers so they can only be in Ikea. And their bank is called Ikano, and I have seen houses being built by Ikano. I think it is really, really big. That is kind of scary, I think. It is too much.

Sophie and I had been talking about democratic design, an idiom I had originally noticed in Ikea catalogues, later seeing it acknowledged as Ikea's 'design philosophy' on its web pages and finally registering this term in several publications dedicated to Swedish design. As we chatted, Sophie volunteered the previous anecdote and claimed it was, to her knowledge, based on fact. Finally, the story arose again on a third occasion in 2010 when I met Lea Kumpulainen, range strategist in the Älmhult head office dedicated to the design of Ikea products and catalogue production. It is in Älmhult where decisions regarding the trajectory of the Ikea range take place, and this trajectory is set several years in advance. Speaking to Kumpulainen, I was mildly surprised to hear the situation recounted because it sounded far-fetched and was told with a slight smile, and it struck me that everyone who mentioned it was in some way employed by the store, or in the case of Sophie, the partner of a previous employee. What was unclear, however, was whether this anecdote emerged from individuals situated within the retailer itself – and had become a corporate myth – or alternatively was giving name to a broader, popular vision of design in which Ikea merchandise and the Ikea store are implicated.

Ikea has been described as an example of a corporate 'hegemonic consumptionscape' (Kjeldgaard and Ostberg 2007: 185), meaning that a small number of businesses in the corporate or state sector in Sweden are 'acceptable to a point' because they are local or establish legitimacy through a 'close connection to "the people"' (Kjeldgaard and Ostberg 2007: 185–186). An example of such popular connections may be found, for example, in cooperative movements that are major players in the dairy and meat sectors, or as in the case of Ikea, 'having the good of the people as a basis for business philosophy' (Kjeldgaard and Ostberg 2007: 186). The allegory of 'the people' is persuasive but also elusive. How are such alignments and connections forged? On the one hand, there is a clear national basis to the idea of 'the people', still fundamental to contemporary expressions of identity. Calhoun places particular emphasis on imagination and creativity in the constitution of the nation in the everyday lives of individuals. The nation is integrated into collective systems, such as public transport and health care (2007: 159), and design in the abstract provides a suitable medium for a nationalizing rhetoric, although most respondents did not routinely consider their Ikea purchases within a national framework unless they themselves were living abroad.

In this chapter, I aim to illustrate how circulating versions of the democratic are unshackled from formal political institutions and extended to designed goods. Whereas the state was heavily invested in the past in providing standardised and equitable housing, now commerce is playing a key role in various aspects of domestic provision. Significantly, the reference to design blurs distinct boundaries between commerce and state, and by virtue of their very ubiquity, ordinary things become the manifestations of lofty qualities. According to this logic, standardization creates a kind of social equality through the appropriation of accessible and common goods, shedding light on the fact that while the majority of my respondents claimed that Ikea is 'for everyone', a caveat was often made for 'high earners'. This narrative is salient in the face of increased income disparity in Sweden, against which consumption choices may be read as expressions of differential resources and class distinction (Isenhour 2010: 520). The democratic in this sense need not refer to strict political terrain but may be expanded to encompass specific values, national imaginaries and practical applications as a 'key symbolic operator' more suited to 'ideological fields, rather than organisational realities' (Verdery 1996: 105; see also Paley 2002).[2] As part of this symbolic currency, I argue that democratic design implies the benefits of an affluent modernity that comes with serial production. Carrying a peculiarly Scandinavian cadence when married to notions of equality, mass production is thus not only accessible materially but also ideologically. Running through this chapter is the idea of consensus as harnessed to democratic design: in the face of perceived consensus, ambivalences emerge regarding how much is too much.

Democracy and consensus

It sometimes appears universally agreed that Sweden occupies the apex of a well-functioning democracy. This association has a long history, from early twentieth century politicians linking the social democratic model of cradle-to-grave welfare to a Swedish capacity for having 'democracy in their blood' (Trägårdh 2007), to more recent and global eulogies of Nordic democratic culture on the international stage. As a case in point, *Economist* magazine ran an article in 2007 naming Sweden 'the most democratic country in the world'.[3]

At a time when democracy is most lauded, is also when it is under fire.[4] Neoliberal market reforms and international free-trade agreements work to the advantage of corporations by reducing regulation and advancing flexible forms of production so that transnational corporations constitute a potential challenge to the nation state and governmental forms of regulation (Garsten and Jacobsson 2007, 2012). Paradoxically, it is not unusual for these same corporations to be framed as not opposed to, but rather complementary to the roles and responsibilities of the government so that activities traditionally reserved for the state, such as health provision or the pursuance of sustainable policies, are adopted by commerce. In addition, corporations increasingly embrace international aid interventions targeting the global south. Sitting in Älmhult with range strategist Lea Kumpulainen and an Ikea designer in 2010, I am told of the feeling of pride that surges when witnessing the benefits that result from Ikea-sponsored projects, including Ikea Foundation's partnership with UNICEF and the World Health Organisation promoting child welfare in India.[5] I ask about social projects in Sweden, to which I am given an incredulous look.

Transnational corporations often occupy the self-styled role of guardians of sustainable development and transglobal social initiatives (Rajak 2011). And although laudable in itself, Garsten and Jacobsson point to the underbelly of this consensus,

Standardisation, democracy and equality **79**

FIGURE 4.1 'We call it democratic design' from the *Ikea Family* magazine.

whereby previous distinctions between 'us and them', so crucial to political thinking are steadily unravelling. What we are left with, they argue following Mouffe, is an illusion of consensus and agreement that constrains the voicing of alternatives, a situation they term 'post-political' (Garsten and Jacobsson 2012, following Mouffe 2000, 2005). Post-political implies a position whereby such antagonisms can be transcended, particularly in regulatory practices (2012: 422). In the case of democratic design ideas of the political are working to form collective subjectivities outside of formal politics and beyond corporate claims, acquiring new expression through their circulation.

Democratic design

I first came across democratic design while leafing through an *Ikea Family* magazine from the 1990s from a vast stack of backdated catalogues and family magazines that one of the Ikea managers – Henrik Wennerhag – in Kungens Kurva lent me. We had spent some time talking when he disappeared from the office, only to return with his own personal and weighty collection. When faced with the huge stack and aware that catalogues are supposed to be the same or virtually the same internationally, I opted first to peruse the family magazines from the 1990s. It was in one of these that I came across a double-page spread dedicated to some familiar Ikea products such as Klippan sofas and Billy bookcases arranged in a large, spacious area, obviously intended as an exhibition area or showroom. The room holds only Ikea furniture in an otherwise undecorated, minimal and white-walled setting.

Underneath the sales pitch runs the headline 'We call it democratic design' ('Vi kallar det demokratisk design'; see Figure 4.1). What exactly is democratic is left unsaid, but some time later, Lea Kumpulainen, range strategist in Älmhult, describes this image to me with reference to the Milan show design fair in 1995. As international designers were vying for attention, Ikea creatives differentiated themselves through flagging their show as democratic, low cost and in direct defiance of the others. It provided the banner for Ikea's celebration of its fiftieth year since foundation. It was a big hit, she added.

Although Democratic Design Day, a day dedicated to Ikea design and the promotion of corporate transparency, was launched in the Swedish town of Älmhult and epicentre of Ikea service offices in 2014, the coupling of the democratic with Ikea design has older roots.[6] In a biographical work published in 1999 dedicated to Ikea's founder, one finds a telling quote from Kamprad: 'Our business philosophy contributes to the democratising process. It makes good, handsome and cheap everyday articles available to the great many people at a price they can afford. That seems to me to have something to do with down-to-earth democracy' (Torekull 1999: 153). And he goes further: 'We have big ambitions... We know in the future we can make a worthwhile contribution to the democratic process, not just here at home'.[7] 'It is our duty to democratize', Kamprad suggests, conflating an unlikely turn of phrase with furniture retail (Torekull 1999). Ikea marketing trades under an equality as sameness banner (Gullestad 1992), extolling the power of the many and provision to the person of low income and difficult means. We find this in Ingvar Kamprad's slogan to provide 'a better everyday life for the many people', meaning to provide accessible design for the purchasing masses. This phrase is emblazoned in large letters on the stairs leading to the staff offices in Dublin and was continually reiterated by Stockholm managers and general staff I spoke to in Sweden.

The stress on this idiom waxes and wanes from the 1990s to the present time, although it remains humming in the background of corporate strategy, occasionally interchanged with the aim to benefit 'the many people'. This latter priority semantically links democratic design with the shop-floor strategy of providing shoppers with a variety of options. 'The many people' includes the cash-strapped students, the elderly and the apartment-dwelling families, who should see in the room sets, in the catalogues and in the advertisements something that appeals specifically to them.[8] The phrase democratic design therefore implies not only inexpensive, quality design but also a non-hierarchical, non-elitist message to the degree that Ikea creatives and their products foreshadow benign intent.[9]

Once one looks, one can find design framed as democratic in corporate, academic, popular and governmental publications, including Ikea magazines, web-based media, books dedicated to Scandinavian design and publications by state bodies within Sweden. International publications make bald claims: Scandinavia or the Nordic countries are often constructed as a single, unified place – an imagined nation in its own right. Aynsley (1993: 42), for example, has argued that Scandinavian modern design has been regarded as representing the ultimate in social democracy, 'pioneer[ing] successful forms of national intervention in town planning, building and design for manufacture' while at the same time achieving a fusion of 'foreign traditions ... with national strengths' (quoted in Reimer and Leslie 2008: 155). A normative discourse runs as an undercurrent in literature such as this that romanticises and legitimises Scandinavian design history as ultimately dedicated to 'the people' (Gregory 2003).[10] And although it might not be too surprising to find emancipatory claims in international picture books that eulogise perceived national strengths, Zetterlund uncovers it closer to home to a statement in a Government Official Report published in 2000 claiming that 'more than anything, Swedish interiors, architecture and design have been distinguished by a democratic intention (2010: 103).[11] Low-cost accessibility sounds familiar to those describing Ikea merchandise, but the conflation with democratic is not automatic. Indeed, the twinning of democracy with furniture, or democracy *as* furniture (DeFazio 2004; see also Lindqvist 2009), has been a dominant theme in the company's brand for many years. This overt political resonance has not escaped critique by Nordic design historians intent on unmasking the assumptions that lie behind such rhetoric nor by social scientists who point to the harnessing of design in corporate ideology for financial gain (Fallan 2012; Zetterlund 2012, see also Halén and Wickman 2007).[12]

Possibly surprising then, and despite the extant discourse that circulates in design publications or Ikea-produced marketing literature, the phrase democratic design was unfamiliar to my research respondents who do not habitually read design publications and whose familiarity or interest in the Ikea web page does not stretch to oblique references to its design philosophy. Nevertheless, when I probed, many respondents attributed to it the more common phrase 'everybody should be able to have a nice home'. This refrain arose with frequency during fieldwork and was recounted in interviews as a self-evident claim, particularly arising with reference to mid-twentieth-century social democratic aspirations to provide universal housing. In providing standardised furniture that fitted neatly into the major construction works from the 1960s, Ikea played a prominent role in fashioning the look of modern domesticity in Sweden. At the same time, Ikea stores are efficacious in carrying the fame and capacity of Swedish design across global borders. In boomerang style, the corporation thus occupies the role of cultural brokers in mediating international influences and organising diversity into familiar styles and themes.

Everyday design

Unlike my impressions of design in Dublin, Swedish design is not relegated to impenetrable cultural capital and specialised knowledge but is attributed to common material culture and practice. This was brought home to me one summer's day when I was dropping off my twin toddlers to their day care in Stockholm. A middle-aged staff member welcomed them and approached me: 'Where did you get those sun hats?' she asked me, nodding in their direction. 'They are not Swedish kids' hats'. She was correct. As it happened, I had purchased them while overseas but noted that she was the second person in a matter of weeks who had remarked on them. A neighbour who I used to meet at the local sandpit and whose children

82 Standardisation, democracy and equality

were about the same age as mine had admired the sun hats and again observed that they didn't look like they had been purchased locally. Now, on this second occasion in an environment with so many children and varieties of outdoor wear, I was curious. When I inquired what didn't look Swedish about them, she responded, 'Oh ... umm ... the colour ... the pattern and the form – or design', she qualified. Of course, the popularity of certain types of toddler hats has more to do with the availability of inexpensive, mid-range children's ware in large department stores than with anything essentially Scandinavian. When I arrived in Stockholm, other mothers had given me a choice of three such stores for kitting out my toddler twins: one for expensive brands, two for middle range in the centre of the city (Åhléns) and H&M for cheaper but equally good ware, and finally, the thriving second-hand market for items that can be thrashed with a clear conscience. Nevertheless the twinning of children's clothing with ideas of design was less surprising to me as fieldwork continued.

Designed environments in one form or another are pretty ubiquitous as one moves through Stockholm. One encounters the word *design* as part of the nomenclature of high-end furniture retailers, clothing brands and canny knick-knacks for the home (Design House Stockholm).[13] Equally, design features are far more pervasive, more ostentatiously present in everyday situations in Stockholm. In addition to the high-end design goods, Bruno Mathsson chairs or upmarket furniture stores such as Nordiska Galleriet and Svensk Tenn, there is also the utterly

FIGURE 4.2 Advertisements for Ikea's 'Long Live Diversity' campaign posted in Stockholm train stations during 2008.

Source: Photo by author.

ordinary, everyday material culture through which daily life is facilitated. Attention to detail comes in discrete packages: ramps can be found on staircases in public areas to facilitate prams and buggies. A takeaway coffee might have a drinking spout that can be opened and closed to avoid spillages while walking. Fluorescent light switches are ubiquitous in public hallways, allowing them to be easily found on dark evenings. Student accommodation near the university possessed triple-glazed glass windows with internal blinds that can be turned to either white or black on the inside to allow more or less light in. There are gadgets in kindergartens to assist young children in removing shoes and boots or to prevent them injuring fingers in doors. More mundanely and more pervasively, design is encountered in less profiled contexts as found in the publication espousing folk design practices such as an array of body tattoos or interesting hairstyles, for example (Londos 2005). Sitting with marketing manager Nils Larsson in the Helsingborg office in 2008, he points to the coffee cup I'm drinking from. Most people think of design in terms of the form or shape of the cup, he tells me, but we see design in the small groove at the base of it. The groove prevents water gathering on the cup's base in the dishwasher and spilling while it is being unstacked. At this everyday level, design features imply other presences, other individuals and agents who intervene for the good.

The launch of diversity

Because of its myriad and widely dispersed products and corporate longevity, Ikea operates as a lightning rod for social commentary, especially on issues such as ethnic diversity or gender equality. With the launch of the catalogue each year comes media fanfare and interviews with key members of the Ikea marketing team. The catalogue represents the primary marketing arm of Ikea within individual households. It is strategically employed to heighten consumer familiarity with the store. Arriving in new markets such as Dublin, the catalogue drop provided one means of familiarising the population with the company. Brand recognition jumped from 18 per cent when the Ikea corporation first considered entering the Irish market to 63 per cent in the three months running up to the opening of the Ballymun store, purely because the UK catalogue had been dropped into Dublin homes.[14] During research, the launch of the catalogue was avidly anticipated and surrounded with a hive of media fanfare. When the day approached for the catalogue drop, householders were reminded to remove their 'no junk mail' sticker or to use a common replacement that states 'no advertisements, thanks, but would gladly have the Ikea catalogue'. Such moves reinforce the awareness of universal domesticity, while the images of purposeful householders presented in the catalogue carry a universalising imperative. Commenting on the catalogue, Erik, an architect, says:

> Because in the beginning, maybe it's not that long, but it still had an enormous impact in Sweden in the beginning because everybody has or owns their own catalogue because they've distributed to everybody. And this is not a big country, so they can reach everybody. And that means that more or

less everybody has it. I don't know how it is there far north. So everybody's referring to the catalogue, and people are keeping this catalogue lying in their room, their apartment, the whole year more or less. And now the catalogue is coming next week, and everybody's [making a] big deal, newspapers writing about the new IKEA catalogue because that is like saying, 'What are the trends in furniture in the world at the moment?' When it was during the sixties and seventies, it was the trends in Sweden, and now it's the trends worldwide. It's not the real top level, of course, because that's [competitor]and those furnishing players. But Ikea, when it comes to normal people, is directly underneath the top level so to speak, nowadays.

In autumn 2008, a new Ikea advertising campaign was twinned with the launch of the new catalogue and based on the 'long live diversity' banner. Adding flamboyance to the launch, marketing manager Nils Larsson was positioned in Stockholm's central train station with a group of assistants, distributing Ikea catalogues to rail travellers. It was followed up by a full-page ad in Sweden's largest daily, *Dagens Nyheter*, in August 2008, running the headline 'There is not a single normal person in this country' ('Det finns inte en enda normal människa i det här landet'). The text ran as follows:

> We are all different. Our skin tones come in thousands of shades. We believe in different things (or in nothing at all). Some guys are attracted to guys, some gals to gals. And there are nearly as many kinds of families as there are families. Isn't it glorious?

It continues:

> That is why you find 9,537 totally different products at this year's Ikea, a bunch of new ideas and a number of lower prices (to lower the threshold to your dream home even more). Welcome to IKEA. Whoever you are.
>
> *(quoted in Lindqvist 2009: 58)*

With the launch of diversity, we find the connection between social and material distinction made manifest. In 2008, the diversity campaign was accompanied with an 'Ikea throws out minimalism' slogan, arguing that the sterility of a minimal aesthetic should be replaced with a vibrant reawakening to colour. But there is an interesting sleight of hand here, in which Ikea is presented less as an agent of corporate capitalism and more as a delegated commentator – and validator – of an altering social context. It starts by renouncing the label of the 'normal person' while postulating the commonness of sexual, religious and ethnic divergences, which are naturalised within a matter-of-fact tone. The campaign posters reflect an ethnic, gender and generational mix in subway stations and built-up areas, where portraits of ordinary smiling faces launched the diversity theme. On closer inspection, the faces were cleverly composed of tiny images of Ikea products, the montage made local through the Swedish language caption. In these images, and as defined in internal Ikea circulations promoting the new diversity theme, difference is codified along a distinct series of categories, specifically focusing on age, gender and ethnic background but neglecting income and class differentials. This is not lost on my informants who pass the heavily posted images in underground train stations. Sitting, waiting for the T-Bana train one day, a friend named Mona commented, 'Diversity within limits though. I think it would be good if they had real diversity like punk Ikea or ironic Ikea or something'. Diversity espoused here consolidates rather than disturbs mainstream domesticity. No matter the differences, the ad seems to say, we are all set in dedicated activity towards the same goal.

Through a focus on diversity, the slogan includes all groups within the encompassing function of the 'we'. Congruent with the long live diversity slogan came the sales pitch 'Ikea throws out minimalism' as outlined by Nils Larsson at the launch of the new catalogue. Minimal decorative themes, popular in middle-class professional homes in the 1990s, should be replaced with a more eclectic, colourful fashion, the public was informed.[15] In launching the upcoming season, the slogan thereby established Ikea as the vanguard of home-based trends. The degree to which the Ikea catalogue is deemed, in some measure, representatively mainstream can be found in Swedish media's commentary on the catalogue's portrayal of a healthy mix of multi-racial, mixed gender, colour blind or sexual minorities. Under the title 'All different, all equal, Ikea celebrates diversity in the new catalogue' ('Alla olika, alla lika, Ikea hyllar mångfalden i nya katalogen', Madestrand 2008), we find reports in the national broadsheets covering the call to diversity beyond the multiracial models used in the catalogue. Here the article notes the introduction of the 'digital folkhemmet' and an upgrade of the Ikea website to allow householders to upload images and films of their own homes, providing a direct link to allow visitors to the site to 'snoop' around other people's living rooms and to find inspiration for their own projects.[16]

But ambivalence is signalled too when clear disjunctures arise between corporate claims and global practices. Diversity as a corporate theme and management strategy is not unique to Ikea or Sweden, and it spread from international business literature into a Swedish corporate vernacular by the 1990s (Wigerfelt 2012). Diversity here implies an acknowledgement of the increasingly diverse ethnic mix that comprises Western market economies. In addition to recognition of the diasporas that settle in metropolitan centres, pluralism is pitched as a resource. Within business literature, influential authors emphasise the benefits that come with an ethnically mixed management team. (Wigerfelt 2012). Meanwhile, diversity is espoused in internal Ikea documents that incorporate primary differences, such as ethnicity, age or gender, as well as 'secondary dimensions', such as sexual orientation, parental status or personal skills (Wigerfelt 2012). A seminar dedicated to the new corporate theme in Ikea in the year 2000 brought together six hundred managers and then-chief Anders Dahlvig in order to push home the need to adopt diversity and as a core value. Not lost on the management was the discrepancy in actively espousing the purported unique, local Swedishness of the Ikea brand as sourced in the small town of Älmhult and the actual corporation that is international in every respect: 'There is a certain paradox between Swedishness and diversity, but the whole IKEA organisation is full of paradoxes' then-manager of Ikea Kungens Kurva concedes, but he continued that there need be no conflict between both (Wigerfelt 2012: 22).[17] As if to underline that diversity sits within an overarching theme of cohesion, the cover of the 2010 Swedish catalogue – differing from the UK issue – states, 'We all live alike differently' ('Vi lever alla lika olika').

Within the context of heightened consumer mobility and companies whose head offices and managers are distributed across the globe, the emphasis on corporate culture is increasingly deemed outdated. The distinctiveness of culture is predicated on 'seemingly unproblematic divisions of space' (Gupta and Ferguson 1997: 65), leading to corporate organisations adopting less substantive metaphors, less grounded in a particular place, less defined on identifiable membership. Anthropologist Jakob Krause-Jensen suggests that, during the 1990s, corporations started to espouse 'values' over corporate 'culture'. Whereas norms suggest collective pressure, values are more individually based (2010: 157). These changes, he notes, conform to Anthony Giddens's (1991) argument that modernity enhances a feeling of disembedding of time and space. Individuals are ever-more mobile, and social interaction is enabled by media to cross temporal and geographical boundaries (Krause-Jensen 2010: 157). In the context of a vast and dispersed organisation, values seem to offer a unifying web of cohesion without the strictures implied by the word *culture*. Previous valorisation of a corporate community, or a 'culture', seemed to signal a distinct place, a rootedness that no longer captures the fluid boundaries that characterise contemporary corporations. Additionally with an ever-mobile customer base and an expanding organisational structure, the replacement of culture with values captures the fluidity that seems to characterise everyday life, both within and outside large corporations.

'Long Live Diversity' provides a suitable sound bite for a global retailer, but one can see the disjuncture between democratic design as a global and local value when placed in the context of a series of controversies in which the corporation was embroiled in recent years. For example, one idiomatic expression of Sweden's democratic credentials concerns gender equality, which was thrown into sharp relief when images of women were removed from Ikea catalogues in Saudi Arabia, leading to lively critical debate and media commentary on satellite-based and broadsheet media. Journalistic commentary argued that the Ikea corporation cannot simultaneously use the word democracy in its advertising while turning a blind eye to the activities of one of its franchises (Madestrand 2012; see also Malik 2012).[18]

Amid these controversies, the specific meaning of the democratic remains uncharted, as does its semantic currency. Returning to the images that featured heavily in primary train and underground stations, Lindqvist argues that the advertisement suggests that 'Ikea's product line actually constructs the social diversity that has come to mark 21st-century Sweden' (Lindqvist 2009: 57). Conversely, I contend, the image implies that Ikea creates a unifying cohesion from myriad individual elements. Ikea here is advertised not through singular merchandise but through

FIGURE 4.3 Advertisements for Ikea's 'Long Live Diversity' campaign posted in public places in Stockholm.

Source: Photo by author.

a convergence of people and things, undermining any clear separation between either. In this poster, Ikea both composes, and is distributed through, thousands of individual households up and down the length of Sweden. With the catchphrase 'long live diversity' and its accompanying imagery is the transposition from domestic interiors to their residents.

Post-standardisation

Waiting for the bus to Ikea in the Skärholmen bus station one day, I got talking to Liv. Liv was in her late forties and on a shopping trip to Ikea in preparation for a visit to relatives in Portugal. As we talked about her purchases, she commented, 'If you want to know about design, then you should do some interviews in the area where I live'. Describing herself as an actress, and with limited financial resources, Liv rents an apartment in a salubrious part of the city and has been lucky thus far to have found rent-controlled municipal accommodation in such an upmarket location. She worries because public housing is increasingly liberalized, and apartment blocks are sold off to those residents who can afford to buy. To counter what she perceives as a sinister trend, she volunteers her time on a left-wing website dedicated to protesting against the changes in housing policy put in place by successive governments since the 1990s.

As someone who self-identifies as a left-wing activist, Liv is aware that Ikea merchandise is part of a vast commercial enterprise and professes to hold an ambivalent regard for the store. On this particular day, she was in Ikea to buy pizza slicers and knick-knacks that her Portuguese in-laws cannot, she says, find in Portugal: 'I think it is nice to bring something from Ikea to my family there because it is something special, exotic like typical Swedish, and they like rust-free steel utensils'. She had chosen pizza slicers that her husband particularly liked and decided to buy one for all her relatives. Ikea has changed in the last decade, Liv claims, attributing this change in the company to the arrival of a Canadian manager and the liberalisation of the housing market. The North American influence contributed to Ikea's lack of flexibility and increased drive for profits, which alienated customers like herself, she informed me, and after that, she tried to avoid the store. So much so that she decided to boycott it after she was dissatisfied with customer service after the purchase of a sofa.[19]

In recent decades the ideals and the benefits of universal provision are in demise. In her criticism of housing liberalisation, Liv endorsed the idiom 'everyone should be able to have a nice home', the 'should' implying a recognition of accelerated social change. Not only is housing pivotal in social and cultural terms in Sweden but also politically it has been a platform for the state-citizen contract throughout the twentieth century. For many years virtually coextensive with the state, housing remains an identifiable example of the 'quasi-utopian vision' of the social democratic tradition (Christophers 2013: 886). The social democratic aspiration of the People's Home entailed a state guarantee of good living conditions for all (see Lujanen 2004: 20), perpetuated by a system in which all housing production – including owner-occupied and rented apartments – were given state financial assistance.[20]

Post war housing policy tended to regard private renting as a speculative activity that should be regulated and until the early 1990s, the vast majority of Swedish housing production was receiving state subsidy and characterised by a high degree of standardisation (Lujanen 2004: 20). However, since the financial crisis of that decade and shifts in political and economic policy, property law and housing policy have been liberalised, leading to what Turner and Whitehead term a 'grand restructuring' of housing (2002: 209).[21] With these economic shifts, which were felt most keenly since the 1990s, there is a general awareness that universalist aspirations are in demise in line with the increasing privatisation of housing. In the same period, spending power has dramatically increased but is both unevenly distributed and focused on more ephemeral types of expenditure, notably on home decoration, leisure and clothing (Isenhour 2010: 459). In the late 2000s, the disparity between past and present was acute, and the production of housing in Stockholm was amongst the lowest in Europe. People talked of the difficulties in securing an apartment: some respondents managed through inheriting rental leases from grandparents, by being on housing waiting lists since they were children or resorting to apartment swapping between different buildings and housing agencies. Moreover, Turner and Whitehead report that in the years following the restructuring of housing,

> Very few middle or lower-income earners have access to owner-occupied houses sold on the regular market while new construction is also targeting higher-income households. The situation is exacerbated by a very tight private rental market, where increased demand has removed almost all vacancies and has also created a black market for rental contracts.
> *(Turner and Whitehead 2002: 209)*[22]

From 2000 to 2010, the price of housing jumped from a national average of 390,000 Swedish crowns to 1.3 million on average – an increase approaching 200 per cent (Christophers 2013). Individuals like Liv could afford to rent in salubrious areas of Stockholm, however, because municipal rents were still based on a cost-price principal, which means that private landlords must adhere to the same price-setting as found in municipal housing (Christophers 2013). The problem now is not the cost of these sought-after apartments but queuing for many years to have access to them. As Liv explained to me:

> The situation in Stockholm is really so difficult, you know, they haven't built houses, they are building very little. The government ... they don't give subsidies, they aren't subsidising anything for the building companies, making them not build anything, of course. We have a very, very difficult situation. It is this market economy [that] they want to have few possibilities for people to find houses, why they pay so much ... This is a catastrophe, a real catastrophe, so therefore, I am so tired of this whole situation. Me and a lot of other people. I would like to move out to the country, but then, I have a child. If I was alone, then that would be very easy, but then, I have a child, and we have to have a job.

Liv's neighbours who own property have definite ideas of design and style, and one that she implies does not converge with Ikea consumption. Tellingly, she says, 'If you go to NK, then you'll find these people'. NK, or Nordiska Kompaniet, is a high-end department store in central Stockholm and more than once nominated as oppositional to Ikea.[23]

It is interesting that Liv and several others variously pose NK and high-end design stores such as Svensk Tenn as oppositional to Ikea, implying a structural homology between the professional well off and the popularising mass production of Ikea goods. Undermining this opposition, of course, is that fact that NK's flat-pack Trivia range designed by Erik Wørts (with Elias Svedberg), who later worked in Ikea, predated the Ikea concept.[24] Nevertheless, this particular polarity between Ikea and NK emerged on several occasions when I was directed to certain upper middle-class locations where I could find people with 'opinions' about design. Liv continued, 'If you wear furs, you don't shop in Ikea'.

From one perspective, then, Ikea merchandise popularises a common icon of cultural capital, transmogrifying elitist design into an affordable variant. References to the mass production of otherwise elite goods is pursuant with Ingvar Kamprad's descriptions of the store, whereby all social strata should have access to items that were previously beyond the reach of those on limited means. This theme is conventionally bolstered through the uniforms donned by managerial and floor staff, by the informal personal style of Kamprad himself and by the slogans posted on the Ikea web page to the production of mid-range, inexpensive goods. Unbeknownst to herself, a friend, Annika echoed a comment made in a Government Official Report dedicated to design. In this booklet new production methods and synthetic materials developed since the 1960s are pinpointed as advancing the cause of democratic potential through mass production and standardisation, examples of which are identified in large retailers such as Ikea and H&M (Ljungh et al 2000:75). For Annika Ikea represents the aspiration that everyone should be able to afford to furnish their homes to a nice albeit standard level: 'It is like H&M. Everyone should be able to have nice stuff, no matter what they earn'.

Take Elin, for example. Elin is a marketing professional and mother of one who lives in a detached house in a salubrious suburb of northern Stockholm. When we first met, she commented with a smile that the distribution of the catalogue is 'almost a public service – almost'. Later, she extolled the benefits of Ikea, underlining the pride she feels when overseas. In positing Ikea as 'almost a public service', Elin is nevertheless cognisant that her impressions are influenced by professional marketing strategies. In fact, she comments on the irony of her own experiences in light of this awareness.

Elin: Ikea represents family or family values, economics. Healthy values, non-capitalism, which is ironic for such a multi-billion-dollar company.
Pauline: How do they do that?
Elin: I think in almost everything they do by focusing on how important it is not to be expensive and how important it is for you to make a good deal.

Ingvar Kamprad is very, very important or has understood the importance of taking on the role of the cheap Smålänning, and that has a major connection with how Swedish people view Ikea. He flies tourist class, he drives an old Volvo and, of course, he lives in Switzerland and has a great big mansion – but that is not what we see.

A constellation of associations hinges on Elin's perceptions of Ingvar Kamprad's own upbringing, a background that is not unlike her own parents'. They would have similar views to those publicly endorsed by Kamprad.

Elin: I dunno. It is changing. I think where I come from, my parents are very much like Kamprad in quite a few ways, which is, even if you have money, you don't just spend it, you don't just spend to spend. Money – a dime is a dime – and if something is working, you don't just throw it away. And also you care for your stuff. You take good care of your car, house, clothes.

Issues of income and resources are thus played out in subtle and unexpected ways. Walking through the wooded landscape to her neighbour's house later that evening, Elin is equivocal in the placement of herself in this schema, aware that she doesn't aspire to the thriftiness of her parents' generation nor to the extreme spendthrift lifestyles that she perceives as characteristic of the current Stockholm scene. When we arrive, the home owners Martin and Cecilia joke that he occupies a high-ranking professional position in an international firm, while she has returned to third-level education and relative poverty. During the evening, Martin mentions that his earning ability ranks in the 'top thirty per cent' of earners in the country but takes pride in the fact that he doesn't 'flaunt it' like some people you might see around the fashionable upmarket square Stureplan. Not flaunting it is professed with pride, although it was hard not to notice the comfortable detached house in the salubrious suburbs and the two fashionable family cars. We sat on an Ikea sofa in their kitchen, and later, they showed me around their living room, furnished with Ikea shelving on which the television stands. Martin and Cecilia are also keen to convey that they 'love' Ikea and that 'Kamprad is a great guy'. During the evening, the couple did elaborate on the difficulties that arise from the sheer ubiquity of Ikea products. Planning a new kitchen, they cautioned, that is kitted out entirely from Ikea might not be advisable because 'it should be done right, if you have the money'.

The impact of ubiquity

Speaking to householders, many people mentioned the importance of striking a balance between the Ikea merchandise that one foregrounds in one's home and the display of uniqueness against that background. Of course, class and access to financial resources were highly significant in shaping this dynamic. Many middle-class professionals opined that although Ikea provided a good reliable standard, one shouldn't have too many large, bulky items from Ikea for fear of being perceived as socially sterile or unable to exhibit personal, individualised expression. One middle-aged, middle-class architect named Emil told me that, whereas it would be somewhat embarrassing to be seen shopping in Ikea in the 1980s, now it was okay. People now associated Ikea with reliable, good design rather than with flat-pack arriving with too few screws or missing pieces he added. The emphasis on design, albeit not cutting-edge design, was described as a kind of quality assurance and a marked departure from earlier Ikea products. Whereas some householders proudly presented their living rooms, kitchens or bedrooms as designed by in-house interior designers and kitted-out in Ikea, it was more common for this to be done in a slightly apologetic tone. One young woman, who worked as a cleaner and recently returned to Sweden after a stint abroad, showed me her new apartment furnished wholly in Ikea furniture and explained that she just couldn't justify spending large amounts in alternative venues. Again, another young professional couple who both work in marketing commented that it would be okay to have a room entirely fitted out with Ikea furniture so long as there was a framed image from an Ikea catalogue which mirrored the decorative layout of the room, thus turning the whole interior into an ironic parody.

Liv's reference to individuals with 'opinions' about design or wearing furs was surprisingly often made.[25] For her democratic design refers not only to aspiration of a common standard of living but also to active improvement and the rising up of working-class homes to a level that is on par with a broad middle-class base. Looking through the catalogue with me, Liv points to a few of the traditional pieces and makes comparisons between Ikea 'lifting up' or improving basic standards for most people and the nineteenth century *allmoge* style representing well-off farmers whose standard of living is now within reach. Such is the pervasiveness of this theme, that avoidance of Ikea products is pitched as requiring active effort, the motivations for which were described to me, negatively, in class terms.

Managing ubiquity: Anders and Mia

Anders and Mia were a couple in their twenties when we first met. Anders was twenty-six, and Mia was a few years his junior. They rented a small two-bedroom apartment in a block in Stockholm's southern suburbs. They had two small children – a two-and-a-half-year-old boy and a two-month-old girl. Mia was on maternity leave but anticipating a return to her studies after her leave, and Anders worked as a mid-level manager in telecommunications. The couple describe themselves as typical Ikea consumers, meaning they are young, have infant children and are living on a tight budget. When we met, they had lived in their present apartment for two years and were gradually decorating it. There were rumours that the block might undergo *ombildning*, meaning that it could be bought out by a cooperative of residents. If so, they were enthusiastic in their plans to work on it, but in the meantime, as renters, there was no scope or incentive to accomplish more than interior decoration. In either case, they pointed out, the children shared a bedroom, and that couldn't continue forever.

Standardisation, democracy and equality

In their ongoing decorative project, Anders and Mia visit Ikea about once or twice a month. Previously, they had an Ikea store card and credit cards and ran them up to the maximum, purchasing large furniture for their apartment. The moment came, however, when they decided to face the spectre of rising debt head-on and cut up all their cards. Anders tells me he was very 'anti-Ikea' until he and Mia had children and set up home together. Now he enjoys DIY and planning for the future. When I met them, they were attempting to minimise their financial outgoings and decided to be inventive in decorating their apartment, buying an Ikea kitchen worktop (diskbänk) to use as a floor for their balcony. They tried alternative large furnishing retailers, but in the end, keep returning to Ikea Kungens Kurva when making significant purchases. All the same, they were determined to purchase their sofa in a different store. The core problem for them is negotiating their preference for Ikea goods and the aesthetic it incorporates without 'our home looking like nine million other people's homes'. To counter this, they 'tried to keep the front room a bit Ikea-free at least so that it looks a bit different', Mia explained. In the extended quote that follows, they detail how this works on a daily level.

Anders: That depends, actually . . . as I said, some of our closest friends have gone and bought things after seeing them in our house. Then you almost get a bit . . . annoyed, you know.

Mia: There is plenty of stuff in Ikea.

Anders: So you feel like 'what the hell'. I mean, it's one thing if you're in someone's house who you've never met before and probably won't meet again, like a friend of a friend, but if it's a close friend who you spend a lot of time with and I see something nice, then I'm hardly gonna run off to Ikea the first thing and buy the exact same. Because we will most certainly spend more time with them. And you might then say, 'Oh, nice things!' kind of sarcastic. 'Nice shelf. Where did you get that idea?'

Mia: The last time I was over my friend's house, I said, 'It almost feels like coming home to our house'. Coz they've bought the same drawer, the same bed and . . . it was all exactly the same! They could at least have bought a different bed.

Pauline: And what did they say to that?

Mia: 'Oh, really?' It would have been OK with me, buying the same bed, but now they've gone and bought practically everything the same. Even the bathroom stuff. There is plenty of bathroom stuff there.

Anders: The lamp as well.

Mia: And the hat shelf in the hallway. We hadn't even bought that from Ikea.

Pauline: You got it somewhere else?

Anders: Yes, but they went out to get the same anyway . . . Damnit (laughs). It's kind of bittersweet, you know. You get offended, and at the same time, you're thinking, 'Hmm, they think our stuff is really nice!' (laughs)

Mia: It would have been enough with them saying our stuff was nice.

Anders: Or I could have said, 'If you're looking for some advice, then one hundred kronor an hour!' You already know the risk when buying something from Ikea. It's not worth moping about, but when it's a close friend who has so obviously gone to get the same after seeing it here, then that's annoying. But then again, it might happen that it's pure coincidence, but in this case, it's quite a lot of stuff . . . so that's suspicious.
Mia: Well, that's what I mean, if it had been only the bed.
Anders: But I said that it was OK. He did ask first, after all.
Mia: And the rest of his place doesn't look like ours.
Anders: We were actually over to Ikea the other day, you know, and he was looking at the mirror we have in the hallway. That's from Ikea as well. He was standing there looking at it, and I said, 'No way, José! Don't even look at that one!' And he said, 'What? Is that the one you have?' and I said yes. So, he thought it was nice but didn't relate it to the fact that it was the exact same one we had. That happens as well.

Standardisation and equality: Ikea as aggregate practice

What is the effect of ubiquity? The 'manifestly standard' label that applies to Ikea goods, although largely positive and accessible, could similarly be a source of ambivalence if one's home seemed to stand on the wrong side of shifting ideas regarding proportion. The opinion that it is preferable not to possess 'too much' Ikea merchandise frequently emerged, and occasionally, the implications of correct proportions cropped up when conversation moved from a description of goods to a description of householders. One woman described visiting an apartment furnished completely in Ikea goods and described it as 'cold – just like the owner', whereas others remarked that homes decorated in Ikea or too explicitly or thoroughly 'designed' hides the personality of the resident, so that both place and person emerge as somehow lacking an unspecified but essential quality.

The topic of taste, although continuously avoided in interviews, often became a flashpoint for these contradictions: most householders I spoke to avoided nominating good or bad taste and were visibly uncomfortable doing so. In conversations, although design appeared uncontroversially a 'good thing', taste was much more personal, circumspect and potentially polemic. When inquiring about taste, I swiftly sensed an uncomfortable shifting in the chair, a vanishing smile and awkward silent moments that passed while respondents considered how to respond. Eventually, several recommended I look up magazines that showcase 'good design', while others suggested that if an interior looked 'too designed', then it could be considered 'bad taste'. Respondents baulked at the question because they said it implied hierarchy or judgement. Taste is a personal thing, I was informed. Other people might have different taste, but *good* taste implies *better*. One woman responded, 'You might as well ask me to say if my children look better than my friends' or neighbours' children'. Within the confines of these discussions, Ikea became the medium for a surprising version of class rebuttal in fieldwork in which products stood as shorthand for ordinary householders over social climbers. This implies that it is the avoidance of Ikea goods that requires active effort rather than their acquisition.

One idiom that captures these series of equivocations was to emphasise how Ikea goods are like clothing – transient and trend based, sites of potential but subject to individual expression. Seasonal fashions are now standard for furniture retailers like Ikea, and stores seasonally invoke the regeneration of homes through a sprucing up of the interior. Not only that, but Ikea family members receive magazines and emails advertising special offers, while the Kungens Kurva outlet hosts special public meetings to advise and educate consumers on decorative projects. One explanation for these convergences can be found in commercial trends that ally furniture and fashion. The transience of clothing is particularly well suited to an analysis of mobility, connecting as it does the intimate body with the public world (see Chapter 6). As such, in making these connections, participants are recalling, if not explicitly, contemporary marketing strategies (Leslie and Reimer 2003). There is certainly something to this assertion, but I also feel that this explanation does not quite capture the full resonance of this analogy. Another perspective, then, is afforded by shifting the lens to the analogy of clothing. In anthropologists Miller and Woodward's study of blue denim, they contrast the everydayness of blue denim with the more pervasive notions of cultural norms, or the normative (2011). Unlike the normative, which contains a moral evaluation and presages collective judgement in one way or another, the everyday is specifically neither good nor bad, distinguished nor common. It is ordinary, and the route to ordinary is through comfort, they suggest. Comfort in this sense is both an individual physical feeling and a social category. Wearing blue jeans enhances comfort in both senses because they are classless and attract no unwanted gaze. Jeans allow one to be 'unmarked', to relax into anonymity and merge with the crowd. This instance of ordinary represents the post-semiotic, Miller and Woodward (2011) contend, because jeans truly signify nothing in particular. They are not moral or immoral, inferior or superior, conformist or distinct. In other words, they participate in no sanction or discourse to render them subject to normative expectations. They don't specify gender or class or age but facilitate a relaxation into the state of not wishing to be anything in particular, including not particularly ordinary.

Following this argument, Ikea domestic utensils – scented candles, lamps and rugs – are not purchased as a demonstration of equality or solidarity. Like blue denim, people do not purchase Ikea goods to express their desire for equality, yet by virtue of their ubiquity and ordinariness, they do in some small measure render people more equal. Thus, jeans and Ikea goods can be viewed as the objectification of equality through use, the distinction hinged on the fact that they are *consequentially*, but not intentionally, moral. Salient here is the core concept of *lagom*, meaning just right or appropriate, which several research participants described as a cultural category that received widespread affiliation. As *lagom*, the value of moderation in all things is infused with moral sentiment and a distrust of excess, which finds contemporary expression in moderate consumption. A related expression found in consumption studies is the idea of 'commonness in which everybody – high and low – strive to be able to identify with the middle' (Kjeldgaard and Ostberg 2007: 184). The middle, then, as a consensus-driven focal point assumes an ideological valence because it allows seeming contradictions, such as strong state welfarism and open markets to coherently coexist. Of course, this should not imply that contradiction, hierarchy and distinction do not exist – they clearly do – but rather that 'they are less acknowledged at least ideologically and discursively' (Kjeldgaard and Ostberg 2007: 184). Isenhour comments on the considerable stress placed on consumption as the route to individual identity construction, neglecting the social and symbolic, the historically contingent ties that bind people together (2010: 464). Against this seeming consensus, however lie issues of proportion and fraught perspectives on 'how much is right'. Getting the correct balance was stressed so that moderation was valued not only in relation to consumption but also in terms of striking a balance between the aggregate behaviour and the singularised expression. One motivation for dressing down in jeans, Miller and Woodward (2007) suggest, derives from an anxiety surrounding standing out. Here, too, respondents noted the value of Ikea is that it represents a 'safe option'.

So far so good, but the analogy fails when one recalls that Ikea goods are identifiable in a way that blue denim is not - as Anders and Mia are painfully aware. Democratic design is more closely harnessed to a local social cartography because, when pressed, respondents aligned it with an aspiration to create a broad middle-class aesthetic, focussed on national competence and regional concerns rather than on international movements, such as Ikea's credentials in sustainability or development projects. As a case in point, Sommar et al attributes a distinct provence to 'Swedish equality' (svensk jämlikhet) as sourced in the ubiquity, the inexpensive price and the accessibility of goods from companies such as Ikea and H&M clothing retailer, explicitly framing equality as deriving from mass-produced commodities (1998: 133). By virtue of inexpensive mass production, the accessibility of Ikea products come to materialise a kind of equality. Significantly, however, participants who nominate comparisons between Ikea and clothing do not refer to any generic label but specifically name H&M, the well-known clothing retailer. H&M was established in post-war Sweden and offers a range of low-cost fashionable clothing for men, women and children. It is principally associated with youthful consumers, and its wares are frequently identifiable on the streets of Stockholm. H&M is similar to Ikea in that respondents claim it offers affordable goods at a reliable standard but is in no way exclusive. Both retailers are generally regarded as successful internationally because of their combination of a low-cost sales pitch merged with fairly reliable trendy design (see Garvey 2013). Both corporations moreover are valorised as positively mainstream and a fixture in daily life – one man described Ikea merchandise as follows: 'You have it from the time you are a baby, like mother's milk'. Often, this assertion is distinguished from Ikea abroad, which I'm told occupies a high status in some countries. In other words, although Ikea is highly valued in terms of social capital abroad, in Sweden, both stores are 'for everyone'. These comments closely mirror an interview with former Ikea CEO Anders Dahlvig, who put it thusly: 'In many countries our image is more a yuppie, niche, and intellectual type of brand. In Sweden it's a brand for everyone. In the UK the brand is pretty "hot." You do not see that in Sweden' (Dahlvig et al 2003: 34).

Fashion as investiture

There is, of course, another nuance that emerges from the similarities between clothing and Ikea goods, which springs from the ambivalences inherent in fashion. Simmel's (1957) commentary on fashion taught us to recognise it as a form of allegiance and transience, participatory of collective values whilst also a medium for singular emulation. But Simmel's identification was not entirely new. If one traces the word *fashion* to its origins in sixteenth-century Europe, then one can see that it referenced giving form to or the act of making as a process (Jones and Stallybrass 2000). This meaning was superseded with one closer to a contemporary usage in denoting constant, giddy change and came to underwrite the long-term polarity between inner depth and the trappings of constant, superficial change. Simultaneously, though, the double implication of fashion as investiture survives in implying clothing as the making of the person and as a public imprint or inscription recognisable to both the wearer and the observer (Jones and Stallybrass 2000: 2).

Because Ikea products are pretty instantly recognisable in public and private spaces, a marked absence of them often implied a stance regarding fiscal resources. Those who eschew Ikea completely, Cecilia told me, are demonstrating the clear indication of elitism over those who don't. This does not mean, of course, that the visible demonstrations of class and economic resources are not highly visible in an affluent country such as Sweden. Visitors to the metropolitan centre cannot but be struck by the conspicuous and elaborate display of wealth in the city palaces and theatres, indexes of a long-seated aristocracy, but also more generally the stylish high-street clothing and many yachts, particularly when set against the tradition of income equality that was a hallmark of twentieth-century Sweden. The public sphere of the city centre exudes a wealth that dissipates as one moves into the suburbs. Against this background of identifiable affluence, I was surprised to find the absence of Ikea products in private homes suggestive of class criticism. More generally, respondents reported that they struggled over choices such as whether one could have an Ikea sofa or dining table or possibly both. On the other hand, having too many Ikea purchases was described as being socially sterile and a marked inability to exhibit personal, individualised expression. The conflicted nuances of the aggregate that typifies Ikea consumption is placed in stark contrast with the more individualized consumption. 'Being for everyone' became a common refrain in my fieldwork but equally was one that I quickly came to realize was double-edged. Too much design, as with too much Ikea, becomes a burden, and finding the correct proportions requires a deft hand. These logics are frequently fraught as individuals strive to create or maintain a domestic unit that conforms to broad conventional expectations all the while cognisant of competing norms all the while striving towards a personal stamp. In sum then, while Ikea goods objectify a spirit level of mass production and equality, ambivalent awareness emerged in discussions of the correct proportion of Ikea goods in one's home. In fact, many respondents viewed the accumulation of some Ikea goods as so inevitable that avoiding it would involve active effort on their part. Having nothing from Ikea, therefore, paradoxically becomes the canvas for muted class rebuttal: only those 'high earners' or people who 'wear furs' would go to the effort of avoiding Ikea completely. This should not imply, however, that this perspective does not hold its own ambivalences. Beyond a mere contemplation of norms, or a valorisation of consensus, we see a personal conflict emerging through negotiation of Ikea products in the chapters to come. This leads to diverse strategies that householders undertake to negotiate tensions between aggregate trends and personal expression that valorise design as an amelioration to domestic upkeep and maintenance but assuage an impression of the home as a public object. With its ebb and flow, democratic design draws historical narratives, governmental, popular and corporate discourses and everyday materialities into its slipstream. Next we move from public spaces to the private practices and emotive territory manifested in everyday design and domestic material culture.

Notes

1. See 'Democratic Design: Design for Everyone', Inter IKEA Systems BV, accessed 08/28/17, http://www.ikea.com/ms/en_JP/this-is-ikea/democratic-design/, for a more recent example, and https://www.youtube.com/watch?v=Zr0c6tatjFc for a clip from the Democratic Design Days event in Älmhult, Sweden.
2. Ikea is a key UNICEF partner in India, and the IKEA Social Initiative was launched in 2005 to support IKEA's fight against child labour in the supply chain. (Angela Walker, 'In Rural India, IKEA Solar-Powered Lamps Light a Path for Girl Students', UNICEF, accessed 26/01/17, www.unicef.org/corporate_partners/india_53698.html.)
3. The *Economist* magazine awarded Sweden the accolade of 'most democratic country in the world' out of a possible 167 countries. Sweden ranked highest in an assessment of sixty indicators across five broad categories, including the electoral process, government functioning, political participation, political culture and civil liberties (Kekic 2007).
4. Throughout the late 1990s, Nordic governments focused notable emphasis on the significance of democracy for their populations and saw three democracy commissions set up to buck the trend of a sharp decrease in voting. The Swedish Democracy Commission was established in 1997, for instance, and in 1998, the commission received a supplementary directive asking it to explore the particular reasons for the declining electoral turnout. The post of Minister for Democracy was established by then-prime minster Göran Persson (Arter 2006: 155). The findings of the three commissions differed in all three countries, but the Swedish commission spoke of a weakened identification with traditional collectivist norms and a tendency towards a 'secularization of politics'. However, although voter turnout might be low, civic interest in politics had not declined but was transferred into other activities. Democracy is increasingly detached from political parties into social movements or subcultures and circulates in new fora, for example, self-help or neighbourhood action groups or organisations established to aid the bereaved or to promote particular social agendas or charitable causes (Arter 2006: 158–160).
5. 'About Us', IKEA Foundation, accessed 03/08/17, www.ikeafoundation.org/about-us/.
6. Anna Winston, 'IKEA to Live-Stream Democratic Design Day Talks with Designers', *Dezeen*, June 6, 2016, accessed 14/11/16, www.dezeen.com/2016/06/06/ikea-democratic-design-day-sweden-almhult-live-broadcast-video-news-design/.
7. 'Vi vet att vi i framtiden kan bli ett värdefullt bidrag till demokratiseringsprocessen, inte bara här hemma' (Torekull 1999: 160, translation by author).

8 Per Lundgren personal communication. Visiting Tillsammans, the Corporate Culture Centre in Älmhult in 2010, I encountered a black-and-white poster in the public conveniences that showed a dated photographic image of a young woman in a minidress strapping beds and chairs onto the roof of her car. The image was accompanied with the text, 'Over more than half a century the IKEA concept has become a social and cultural phenomenon. Some say that the IKEA Concept has meant more for the process of democratisation than many political measures put together. It is a story that all of us have contributed to. Our impact on design, society and everyday life has been the subject of many museum exhibitions'. Liljevalchs Konsthall, Stockholm 2009, International Design Museum, Munich, Germany 2009.
9 Democratic design is frequently valorised as the company's design philosophy, not least with the Democratic Design Day events held in Älmhult in Sweden in 2017. But even in the Swedish Ikea catalogue in 2008, there was repeated emphasis on 'democratic design', particularly on pages dedicated to Ikea designers, aligning the individual creative with a broad spectrum of unnamed individuals. Meanwhile, a journalist writing in the New Yorker reproduces Kamprad's claim that 'a well-known industrialist/politician once said that Ikea has had greater impact on the democratisation proves than many political measures combined' (Collins 2011: 206, see http://www.newyorker.com/magazine/2011/10/03/house-perfect).
10 Cabra and Nelson (2004: 25) as a case in point speak of Scandinavian commitment to democratic design for almost one hundred years, a commitment that is now typified in Ikea merchandise, they suggest.
11 Quoting Statens insatser för form och design. SOU 2000: 75, 190–191.
12 The linkage to home-grown designed goods and the egalitarian potential of mass production is not coincidental. Internationally, these ideas have their roots in early modernist discourse in which utopian aspirations were located in the beauty and generative potential of mass production (Mattsson 2010).
13 During fieldwork, shop advertisements for Design House Stockholm proclaimed 'Scandinavian design is a natural asset and we have decided to bring it to you'.
14 Garry Deakin, personal communication.
15 Kristin Djerf, 'Ikea Pratar Mångfaldi TV, Print och Radio', Dagens Media, August 15, 2008, accessed 03/08/17, www.dagensmedia.se/nyheter/article15910.ece.
16 'Desto mer krut har Ikea lagt ned på att uppdatera sin hemsida, där kunderna numera kan lägga upp egna filmer och bilder. En direktlänk till det digitala folkhemmet, alltså, där man helt ogenerat kan snoka runt i människors vardagsrum och, som det är tänkt, hitta inspiration till egna projekt' (Madestrand 2008; see also www.dn.se/kultur-noje/alla-olika-alla-lika).
17 Det finns en viss paradox mellan svenskhet och mångfald, men hela IKEA:s organisationskultur är fylld av paradoxer (my translation).
18 Madestrand, Bo:Visst, Ikea har inget ansvar, men använd då inte ordet demokrati i reklamen Publicerad 2012–10–02 09:07, accessed 05/01/14.
19 In 1957, the Home Research Institute (Hemmens Forskningsinstitut) was renamed the National Institute for Consumer Affairs, which is now the National Consumer Agency. In so doing, the issues of domestic organisation were broadened to incorporate domestic consumption. This agency now exists to provide advice and guidance to consumer-related issues, but since 1978, it has monitored and advised on the standard cost of living, recognising that social participation is based on individual access to goods.
20 Indeed, Leira, for example, makes an argument that Scandinavian frameworks of public and private are coloured by traditional social democratic political culture in which traditional public sphere intervention in the home results in different preconceptions of civic privacy (1992: 169).
21 Turner and Whitehead report, 'Most municipal housing companies have chosen to sell off all or parts of their housing stock to residents. Since the "grand restructuring" of housing, very few middle or lower-income earners have access to owner-occupied

houses sold on the regular housing market. New construction is also targeting higher-income households and the situation is exacerbated by a very tight private rental market. Now, increased demand has given rise to a black market for rental contracts' (2002: 209). Most municipal housing companies are now run as limited liability companies, and more and more municipalities have chosen to sell off all or parts of their housing stock. The state, however, has until recently prevented municipalities from selling off all their housing stock in order to keep a share of rental housing. With a smaller stock that comprises less-attractive properties, the Swedish housing market may come to resemble the Irish or UK housing markets more closely, with a social as opposed to a public housing sector (Turner and Whitehead 2002: 214).
22 During the decade following 2000, municipal companies were being sold off in several parts of the city, and the housing shortage was a problem during fieldwork. Generally, however, it is the most attractive part of the stock that is sold, in which case, the municipality is in danger of keeping the most unattractive part of the stock. These sharp increases have had the most profound influence on lower income households, especially as housing allowances have not kept pace (Turner and Whitehead 2002).
23 This choice is interesting, as when I presented a paper to an academic audience in the city, I was told that the 'actual' opposition is more likely Svensk Tenn, the high-end design store and workplace of famous designer Joseph Frank.
24 A key designer in Ikea, Erik Wørts co-created (with Elias Svedberg) NK's flat-pack Trivia range of furniture in 1943. The Trivia series required self-assembly at home, minimised packaging costs and can be seen as a predecessor of the Ikea concept.
25

References

Arter, David. 2006. *Democracy in Scandinavia: Consensual, Majoritarian or Mixed?* Manchester: Manchester University Press.
Aynsley, Jeremy. 1993. *Nationalism and Internationalism*. London: Victoria & Albert Museum.
Calhoun, Craig J. 2007. *Nations Matter: Culture, History, and the Cosmopolitan Dream*. London: Routledge.
Collins, Lauren. 2011. "House Perfect: Is the IKEA Ethos Comfy or Creepy?" *The New Yorker*, October 3, available online at http://www.newyorker.com/magazine/2011/10/03/house-perfect. accessed 3/08/16.
Christophers, Brett. 2013. "A Monstrous Hybrid: The Political Economy of Housing in Early Twenty-First Century Sweden." *New Political Economy* 18 (6): 885–911.
Dahlvig, Anders, Katarina Kling, and Ingela Goteman. 2003. "IKEA CEO Anders Dahlvig on International Growth and IKEA's Unique Corporate Culture and Brand Identity." *The Academy of Management Executive* 17 (1): 31–37.
DeFazio, Kimberly. 2004. "IKEA and Democracy as Furniture." *Nature, Society, and Thought* 17 (2): 143.
Fallan, Kjetil. 2012. *Scandinavian Design: Alternative Histories*. London: Berg.
Garsten, Christina and Kerstin Jacobsson. 2007. "Corporate Globalization, Civil Society and Post-Political Regulation – Whither Democracy." *Development Dialogue* 49: 143–158.
Garsten, Christina and Kerstin Jacobsson. 2012. "Post-Political Regulation: Soft Power and Post-Political Visions in Global Governance." *Critical Sociology* 39 (3): 421–437.
Garvey, Pauline. 2013. "'Ikea sofas are like H & M trousers': The Potential of Sensuous Signs." *Journal of Business Anthropology* 2 (1): 75–92.
Giddens, Anthony. 1991. *Modernity and Self-Identity: Self and Society in the Late Modern Age*. Cambridge: Polity Press.
Gregory, Judith. 2003. "'Scandinavian Approaches to Participatory Design." *International Journal of Engineering Education* 19 (1): 62–74.

Gullestad, Marianne. 1992. *The Art of Social Relations: Essays on Culture, Social Action and Everyday Life in Modern Norway, Scandinavian Library.* Oslo: Scandinavian University Press.

Gupta, Akhil and James Ferguson. 1997. *Culture, Power, Place: Explorations in Critical Anthropology.* Durham, NC: Duke University Press.

Halén, Widar and Kerstin Wickman. 2007. *Scandinavian Design Beyond the Myth: Fifty Years of Design From the Nordic Countries.* Stockholm: Arvinius förlag/Form förlag.

Isenhour, Cindy. 2010. "Building Sustainable Societies: A Swedish Case Study on the Limits of Reflexive Modernization." *American Ethnologist* 37 (3): 511–525.

Jones, Ann Rosalind, and Peter Stallybrass. 2000. *Renaissance Clothing and the Materials of Memory.* Cambridge: Cambridge University Press.

Kekic, Laza 2007. "The Economist Intelligence Unit's Index of Democracy", *The Economist*, available online at www.economist.com/media/pdf/DEMOCRACY_INDEX_2007_v3.pdf. accessed 03/08/17.

Kjeldgaard, Dannie and Jacob Ostberg. 2007. "Coffee Grounds and the Global Cup: Glocal Consumer Culture in Scandinavia." *Consumption, Markets and Culture* 10 (2): 175–187.

Krause-Jensen, Jakob. 2010. *Flexible Firm.* New York: Berghahn Books.

Leira, Arnlaug. 1992. *Welfare States and Working Mothers: The Scandinavian Experience.* Cambridge: Cambridge University Press.

Leslie, Deborah and Reimer, Suzanne. 2003. "Fashioning Furniture: Restructuring the Furniture Commodity Chain." *Area* 35 (4): 427–437.

Lindqvist, Ursula. 2009. "The Cultural Archive of the IKEA Store." *Space and Culture: International Journal of Social Spaces* 12 (1): 43–62.

Ljungh, Claes, Martin Sundelius, and Kerstin Wickman. 2000. "Statens Insatser för Form Och Design." Statens Offentliga Utredningar. Kulturdepartementet.

Londos, Eva and Göran Sandstedt. 2005. *Folklig disajn: ett bidrag till Designåret.* Jönköping: Jönköpings läns museum.

Lujanen, Martti, ed. 2004. *Housing and Housing Policy in the Nordic Countries.* Copenhagen: Nordic Council of Ministers.

Madestrand, Bo. 2008. "Alla olika, alla lika Ikea hyllar mångfalden i nya katalogen." *Dagens Nyheter.* Available online: www.dn.se/kultur-noje/alla-olika-alla-lika/, 2008/08/14, accessed 10/02/16.

Madestrand, Bo. 2012. "Visst, Ikea har inget ansvar, men använd då inte ordet demokrati i reklamen." *Dagens Nyheter.* Available online: www.dn.se/arkiv/kultur/bo-madestrand-visst-ikea-har-inget-ansvar-men-anvand-da/, 2012/10/02, accessed 05/01/14.

Malik, Nesrine. 2012. "No Women Please, We're Saudi Arabian Ikea." *The Guardian.* Available online: www.theguardian.com/commentisfree/2012/oct/02/no-women-saudi-arabian-ikea, accessed 04/04/17.

Mattsson, Helena. 2010. "Designing the Reasonable Consumer: Standardisation and Personalisation in Swedish Functionalism." In *Swedish Modernism: Architecture, Consumption and the Welfare State*, edited by Helena Mattsson and Sven-Olov Wallenstein. London: Black Dog Publishing.

Miller, Daniel and Sophie Woodward. 2011. *Blue Jeans: The Art of the Ordinary.* Berkeley: University of California Press.

Mouffe, Chantal. 2000. *The Democratic Paradox.* London and New York: Verso.

Mouffe, Chantal. 2005. *On the Political.* London: Routledge.

Paley, Julia. 2002. "Toward an Anthropology of Democracy." *Annual Review of Anthropology* 31: 469–496.

Rajak, Dinah. 2011. *In Good Company An Anatomy of Corporate Social Responsibility.* Palo Alto: Stanford University Press.

Cabra, Raul and Katherine Nelson. 2004. *New Scandinavian Design.* San Francisco: Chronicle Books.

Reimer, Suzanne and Deborah Leslie. 2008. "Design, National Imaginaries, and the Home Furnishings Commodity Chain." *Growth and Change* 39 (1): 144–171.
Simmel, Georg. 1957. "Fashion." *American Journal of Sociology* 62 (6): 541–558.
Sommar, Ingrid, Åke E. son Lindman, and Nina Ulmaja. 1998. *Stockholm Modern: En Guide Till Stans Design*. Stockholm: Wahlström & Widstrand.
Torekull, Bertil. 1999. *Leading by Design: The Ikea Story*. London and New York: Harper Collins.
Trägårdh, Lars. 2007. *State and Civil Society in Northern Europe: The Swedish Model Reconsidered*. New York: Berghahn Books.
Turner, Bengt and Christine M. E. Whitehead. 2002. "Reducing Housing Subsidy: Swedish Housing Policy in an International Context." *Urban Studies* 39 (2): 201–217.
Verdery, Catherine. 1996. *What Was Socialism, and What Comes Next?* Princeton, NJ: Princeton University Press.
Wigerfelt, Anders S. 2012. "Mångfald och svenskhet – en paradox inom Ikea." In *MIM Working Papers Series*, edited by Christian Fernández and Anders Hellström. Malmö: Malmö Institute for Studies of Migration, Diversity and Welfare.
Zetterlund, Christina. 2012. "Just Decoration? Ideology and Design in Early-Twentieth-Century Sweden." In *Scandinavian Design: Alternative Histories*, edited by Fallan Kjetil, 103–116. London: Berg Publishers.

5
STORAGE SOLUTIONS
Clutter and Containment

Arriving outside apartments in Stockholm, it happened on more than one occasion that I would hear a vacuum cleaner working inside. In such situations, I would linger, hesitant, my finger hovering a few millimetres from the bell while wondering what to do. The necessity to be punctual was frequently impressed upon me while living in Stockholm. I was reminded that lateness is generally considered bad manners, and I noticed that the web page dedicated to public transport in Stockholm planned journeys so that one arrived at a destination with several minutes to spare. But equally, it felt intrusive to interrupt the quick spruce up that was evidently happening inside, especially as I suspected it was due to my imminent arrival. When I entered, I would step into an interior devoid of dishes in the sink, stacked papers or books on tables, untidy knick-knacks or children's toys strewn in reception rooms. Over time, I realised that I was looking for some disorder, especially when visiting households with young children or more elderly individuals who would not, perhaps, have the inclination or energy for a rigorous clean. Consistently, in the majority of cases, in the apartments of singletons, couples, the elderly, parents with young children or students, I failed to find the filling of domestic surfaces that would be common in Irish houses where cloths adorn tables, wall-to-wall carpets are standard, mats sit on floors and ornaments and framed photographs occupy shelves. Where, in other words, domestic surfaces are generally filled.

Long after the conditions that launched architectural modernism have passed, the modern aesthetic continues to have widespread currency in Sweden and remains profoundly popular (Hilson 2008). In the lifestyle pages of the national press, iconographies picturing white-walled, light-filled, sparsely decorated rooms are common and underscore twentieth-century Scandinavian design as an object of value.[1] Here representations of style consist of an aesthetic that anyone can espouse, copy and perpetuate, thus condensing national competence as both a professional practice and as something inclusive and everyday. Indeed, although design literature privileges the former, it is in the latter – ordinary homes – where the Scandinavian modern is put into practice. There is a distinct spatial logic to this aesthetic: the moniker Scandinavian design was devised for a series of exhibitions in the 1950s that promoted a limited cluster of objects rather than representing the full variety of design works in Nordic countries. These carefully selected items chosen for showcasing were 'almost exclusively objects for the home conforming to a modernist notion of aesthetic quality' (Fallan 2012: 3).

But if the Scandinavian modern remains iconic of twentieth-century domestic modernity, then it is timely to look beyond the icon and consider how the organisation of possessions intercedes in social action (Keane 2003). Reaching across both time and space, the idiom of the modern confers a remarkably rigid set of aesthetic principles in the households of my respondents. Clearly, many households, especially those not occupied by young professionals in Stockholm apartments, do not conform to the clean white walls and uncluttered spaces of the strict modernist aesthetic. For this reason, Ahl et al refer to the myth of the perceived coalition between Swedish taste and modern form (Ahl et al 2002). Nevertheless, I found a striking congruence in descriptive tropes that tended to revolve around adjectives such as light, clean or, in Swedish, naked (naken) or simple (enkel). I noted a stark acceptance of the significance of these tropes in the naturalisation of tidiness, the easy acceptance that clutter must be combatted and the smooth transference of a tidy environment to the person who occupies it.[2]

The seemingly insignificant routines of decluttering are both profound and profoundly overlooked in popular conceptions of domesticity.[3] Householders I spoke to referred to clutter, meaning objects out of place, as a universal and self-evident problem and a contravention to an ideal domestic order. Closely associated with this ideal, respondents nominated with ease a series of qualities that constitute, for them, in broad-brush strokes, the Scandinavian style: clean lines; blond woods; white walls; a stripped-down timber, such as birch, pine or elm; and uncluttered surfaces. In my informants' homes, a general lack of large-patterned curtains and tablecloths and an absence of knick-knacks and wall-to-wall carpets was noticeable as were the multiple light sources, candles and window lamps. 'We decorate with light' a designer informed me when I visited Ikea head offices in Älmhult in 2010. 'The Norwegians spend most on lights but next is us', she continued. Indeed, many householders talked of Swedish style in terms of what it is not: unadorned, plain furnishings, natural woods, devoid of distracting decorative flourishes or busy patterns. This was most powerfully recognisable in unfilled surfaces, such as tables, windows and walls in Stockholm. While visiting homes, I found clear surfaces, such as television and coffee tables, striking; often, their emptiness underscored by an plant or orchid, suggesting to me that no spaces are random. Occasionally, wider sociopolitical and historical credentials of a pared-down look are made explicit in the literature: the ostensible innocence or neutrality of plainness is belied in the claim that domestic furniture was more plain in Sweden than in Denmark or Finland, and as a consequence, more 'democratic' (see Howe 1999).[4] Plainness here is not merely an absence of ornament but a visual shorthand for serial reproduction and mid-century accessibility-cum-consumer democracy (see Chapter 4).[5]

A significant player in the organisation of personal possessions and the maintenance of an uncluttered aesthetic is Ikea, where the benefits of storage solutions are prominently advertised. If one compares Ikea catalogues from the 1960s to those current today, then one can see that emphasis on storage has 'significantly increased' (Löfgren 2012: 115; see also Czarniawska and Löfgren 2012, 2013). Moreover, the number of individuals renting external storage space has seen a dramatic increase since the turn of the millennium, demonstrating the ever-mounting difficulties of coping with possessions in the home (Appelgren and Bohlin 2015). But it is also evident from a brief perusal of Ikea catalogues that idealised interiors are not strictly minimal. More often, Ikea goods are employed not to remove possessions per se but to remove the randomness of daily life, to carve up living spaces into individual activity zones. One may see signs in Ikea, Kungens Kurva suggesting that 'personal possessions require good storage', implying that possessions should have a designated place and can be returned there after use. 'No lazy spaces' and the promotion of good storage solutions combine the 'workshop' ethic of serious productive activity with the 'refuge' of quiet relaxation (Hartman 2007: 484), although clear distinctions between both are often largely illusory.

Mundane routines that maintain domestic order are integrally implicated in social 'modes of representational order', actively constituting visions of the good and/or modern home, even though they are 'highly local, mundane and material . . .' (Hetherington 2004: 159). Precisely because they are local, mundane and material, ideas and ideals of Swedish style are central to aesthetic orders (Miller 2009) but are instantiated in the most ordinary of things. Of course, just what constitutes clutter and how it is apprehended is socially diverse (see Daniels 2010). Consider Makovicky's analysis of Slovakian homes where 'a cozy cluttered' aesthetic is actively created through 'the jumble of plants, plastic flowers, decorative objects, and mementoes' (2007: 293) in which wooden surfaces are adorned with tablecloths, handmade textiles, vases and porcelain figures. Such touches, and particularly the predilection for textiles – 'the layer cake approach' – represents an aesthetic of accumulation here: years of experience are manifested in the accretion of layers that cover all available domestic surfaces (2007: 293). In Makovicky's example, household surfaces carry the material trace of experiences and presences by holding and framing miscellanea, leading to clear surfaces to be understood in alternative ways.[6] The surfaces of things then forcefully carry the animating trace of human presence, and how we conceive of surfaces corresponds to ideas of clean and dirty, presence and absence, actual use and potential practice as well as to personal benchmarks that enter into dialogue with these notions. Here we explore these issues by moving beyond the presentational logics of common living areas and follow possessions moving from primary reception rooms to peripheral storage cupboards, walk-in wardrobes, basement storage provision and commercial storage space. Possessions may build up in these locations and snag the smooth circulating paths that householders aspire to. From here, their potential for disruption may be tamed through expulsion as waste or exchanged on web-based sites. In focusing on homes in motion, I examine the pathways that objects occupy and the practices that Ikea furnishings facilitate. Moving beyond the illusory stasis of a minimal aesthetic I follow things as they progress to household cellars and storage spaces to the vibrant second-hand economy and impinge on the fluctuating housing market.

It is striking that in the face of profound shifts in housing policy, a rather static social imaginary of the Scandinavian modern persists. We will see how a minimal iconography is situated within the intimate rhythms of everyday life, not as a reflection of 'Swedish style' but as the site where it is explicitly produced. It is within such contexts that Ikea purchases are located, as everyday design, the virtually invisible complement to quotidian life. Through decluttering – meaning routine practices of organisation, ordering and placement – the personal is distinguished from the possession, the intimate is tamed and the messiness that erupts from actual living is distinguished from ordered, planned patterns of life. Discussion of clutter was tangential to descriptions of aesthetics rather than central to them. But in focusing on these practices, I contend that far from merely reflecting a 'modern' domestic style, strategies enlisted to contain clutter actively produce it. Because of this fluctuating material environment, the question to be posed is not what does this aesthetic signify, but what does it make possible (cf. Keane 2005)?

Storage solutions

Many households I visited were constant hives of activity, characterised by a continual striving to keep possessions organised. When strategies of order lapsed, personal possessions, albeit cherished, became burdensome and unruly. These 'troublesome things' (Daniels 2010: 157) require ongoing practices to keep them in check, and my respondents speak of the battle with clutter, or 'decluttering', in order to reinstate harmony in their homes. In conversations with householders, people often introduced the topic of containment: how to keep possessions in check and the necessity of rigorous vigilance to keep chaos at bay. Possessions must be ordered and placed, I was told, so that they don't randomly erupt into living spaces. Respondent discussion thus swiftly drifts from what constitutes the domestic aesthetic to how it may be accomplished, from decorative logics to practices, from 'blond woods, white walls' to the minutiae of personal possessions – the trouble with shoes, for example – and the practices of containment that must be imposed. Amidst the vigilance and the constant patrol of unruly possessions, several respondents voiced just how disquieting it is to have one's domestic space in disarray. Consistently, the disquiet that comes with clutter is described as not merely an annoyance but as linked to deep emotional disquiet. During fieldwork, the superiority of the clear surface was continually reiterated as an ideal by informants, close to 'Swedish style', and one that required constant maintenance. Removing unwanted presences is accomplished by maintaining a minimal home, keeping possessions in storage and excising 'excess'. But although Ikea showrooms demonstrate the benign benefits of successful storage, the image of order vanishes in the realisation that tidy homes, clear surfaces, ordered possessions and light and airy environments require countless hours of dedicated activity. In this respect, respondent allusion to the Scandinavian aesthetic not only entails continuous unseen work but also emotional commitment, investment in free time and personal finances that are masked in spic-and-span images.

The suppression of clutter

Visiting range strategist for Ikea in 2010, Lea Kumpulainen describes the Ikea style to me as essentially modernist, following twentieth-century Scandinavian design trends, adopted widely in Euro-America in the post-war period and generally 'for middle-class down'. In its current form, adapted by Ikea designers, there is still a pronounced espousal of clear surfaces and good storage as beneficial to domestic harmony and efficiency. Ikea furnishing aids householders in streamlining their homes in order to achieve functional comfort and thrifty design, she adds. Ikea storage facilitates the removal of stray, unwanted possessions that harbour the potential to haphazardly fill spaces, impede movement and interrupt the smooth running of the household. Storage is described by respondents as a bulwark against matter out of place (Douglas 2002), not only aiding the householder in impeding the constant movement of goods but also facilitating the fixing of personal possessions in allocated spaces.

This emphasis has an established history, one that mutually reinforces the benefits of maintaining matter in place but also in valorising the plain, unadorned surface. The latter is evident in the emphasis on light and airy surfaces of classic early modernism in which surface ornament was the 'abject which must be expelled' (Leslie and Reimer 2003: 296). Antagonism towards surface decoration extended to colour in which the 'white of whitewash' was regarded as 'absolute' and the 'eye of truth' (Le Corbusier 1987: 190 in Leslie and Reimer 2003: 296). The superiority and morality of clear surfaces infiltrated twentieth-century architecture, design and commentary, as found in thundering critiques of ornament. Starkly reminiscent of the argument entitled 'Ornament and Crime' written by cultural critic and architect Adolf Loos and published in 1910 is modernist architect Le Corbusier's pronouncement that 'trash is always abundantly decorated; the luxury object is well made, neat and clean, pure and healthy, and its bareness reveals the quality of its manufacture' (Le Corbusier 1987 [1925]: 87). For those in the early modern movement, the unadorned surface was value loaded as a material manifestation of social and aesthetic ideals. The capacity of surface colour to harbour the morally dubious and sullying traces of personhood persists, according to Michael Taussig, who describes surface ornament as a dangerous excess (2009). He contends that colour is a 'splurging thing, an unmanageable thing, like a prancing horse or a run in a stocking, something, this thing, this formless thing that we need to fence in with lines and marks, the boundary-riders of thought' (2009: 17). Colour is the other to refinement, Taussig contends, because colour carries the implication of surplus, of something unnecessary added to form. It is a surface that fills spaces, envelops and engulfs. Etymologically originating from the Latin *celare*, to conceal, the word *colour* springs from a meaning of duplicity. In the West, colour is maligned through association with the technicolour world of advertising and fashion or gaudy interiors or clothing, implying a lack of discretion or childlike sensibilities. Such chromophobia is explained as 'taste' as it survives generational change and shifting fashions. Taussig argues that more than a fad, chromophobia is profoundly corporeal, a technique of the body, habitually engrained (2009: 12).

The quality of unadorned surface and aesthetic of emptiness was central to the promotion of light-filled interiors and minimal furnishings that came to be a hallmark of early modernism. Although nineteenth-century bourgeois interiors could be defined through their profusion of possessions (Frykman and Löfgren 1983), the mid-twentieth century came to valorise an altogether different aesthetic defined through the streamlining of spaces and people. In Nordic countries, the starker, industrial look of the European international style was soon replaced with a 'softer' aesthetic that derived from craft traditions but that nonetheless allowed for the mass production and standardization of furniture.[7] Designer Bruno Mathsson, together with Carl Malmsten and Josef Frank, led in defining and disseminating Swedish versions of modern design, embracing the idea of 'furniture architecture' and espousing the benefits of light and humanistic design, which garnered broad popular appeal in the mid-twentieth century (cf. Robach 2002; Selkurt 2003; Sörlin 2002). Modernist designers were not necessarily path-breaking in espousing the sociopolitical and moral inferences of minimal interiors and light-flooded rooms. European colonial actors had already aligned metaphors of modernity with visuality, 'shedding light' on colonial populations (cf. Mrázek 2002). Architects within the modern movement were astute, however, in rendering utopian visions of equality and transparency in mundane, empirical contexts, thus capitalising on an already established vision of the 'stripped down bareness and simplicity of the vernacular home' (Arrhenius 2010: 140). In so doing, traditional domesticity was enlisted in the forward march towards future aspiration. The Scandinavian version of the international style called funkis was one expression of these ideals and had a profound influence on Swedish interiors and industrial design. Funkis (after funktionalism) was introduced to the broad public in the early twentieth century and was primarily favoured by an educated, professional elite, although international modernist styles later gained purchase within a national design vernacular. As part of this cultural package, Scandinavian furnishing came to be represented as modern but 'homely', more 'human' and less radical than the chrome and tubular steel designs of central Europe. Design originating in Nordic countries tended, moreover, to be associated with the unassuming quality and splendid ordinariness of the Scandinavian home. In a 1961 study of Scandinavian design, Ulf Hård claimed that functionalism never fully took root in Nordic interiors. Instead, 'The Scandinavian home is a little place where one quite naturally employs unpretentious means to bring comfort and warmth into the confining circle of the evening lamp' (1961: 13; see also Garvey *forthcoming*).[8]

Good housing

In designing for the control of clutter, the acquisitive potential of domestic consumption was not foreshortened but encouraged, which was strategically advantageous in the context of a post-war economic boom. International Scandinavian design exhibitions downplayed strict minimalism and instead illustrated how possessions could be stored in uncluttered modern settings.[9] Not only isolated artefacts but also the composite of the domestic environment and corresponding lifestyle was exhibited.[10] Social aspiration, in short, was on display, but as a didactic instrument, it soon found expression in a more common – and more inclusive – vernacular. Mid-century state agencies, cooperative bodies and corporate interests soon coalesced in interpolating efficient storage in perceptions of quality housing. By the 1960s, the planning and organisation of personal possessions, the provision of domestic equipment and adequate storage was firmly ingrained in housing policy and presented not as an aesthetic but as 'good housing'. This can be seen in the publication of the *Good Housing* booklets that were published by the Royal Board of Residential Housing (Kungliga Bostadsstyrelsen),[11] in publications produced by the Swedish Society for Art, Craft and Design, in consumer organisations and in private retailers. In a booklet dedicated to furniture advice published by the National Design Organisation, for example (Berglund and Engdahl 1961), precise measurements are given on the size of the standard wardrobe and how to make full use of space. Opening with an acknowledgement of the variety of storage vessels available in modern homes – dressers, wardrobes, cabinets, linen cupboards – it goes on to detail the categories of possessions that householders store – food, clothing, sleep and hygiene products, home care, leisure, reading, writing and decorations (1961: 158).[12] Continuing with the size of average cupboards, it explains how one might best make use of them by folding clothing items correctly and how to arrange furniture in order to maximise space in apartments.

In recent years, the requirement for good storage as a bulwark against small spaces has accelerated, and many people identify the shrinkage of domestic space as a pressing problem. Visiting Byggtänst, an agency that provides information on all aspects of construction, I was told that contemporary families with children, called the 'grey generation', are choosing to live in the city centre in preference to suburban life. This trend results in several consequences: instead of the traditional expectation that each child should have his or her own room, now two children might share. Also, new apartment blocks situated in city areas have car parking around the blocks – thus sacrificing green spaces – instead of built into basements, as one might find surrounding mid-century constructions. Affordable shops dedicated to household goods and storage were popular amongst students I spoke to who were setting up home for the first time.[13] Magazines such as those produced by the large housing cooperative HSB, called *Our Residence* (*Vår Bostad*), gives advice to its 535,000 members on how to maximise space or to create individualised bed or playrooms for children under the heading 'room for children' ('plats for barn') or 'own space' ('ett eget rum or egen vrå', issue 2, 2008). One issue, for example, detailed how one

FIGURE 5.1 Hooks are commonly used in the living spaces of my respondents. The ones pictured are secured to the underside of shelves to hang keys.

Source: Photo by author.

family divided their living room in two in order to allow their toddler to have his own play area. It itemised the cost of the shelving, storage, lighting and toys and added tips to other readers who might follow this example.

The material minutiae of storage practices

The term *possessions* camouflages the diversity, the quantity and the quality of things that one finds in a home, especially as in actuality these things are routinely and rigorously differentiated. Of course, ownership does not encapsulate all domestic things, particularly when renting, borrowing, swapping and sharing economies are on the rise (Belk 2010, 2014). In the context of contemporary domestic retail, things are moved on, circulated, disposed of or exchanged within an ever-lessening time frame. But what is clutter if not the personal detritus of intimate daily life? What we call clutter provides the proof of intimate life and often bodily presence, one that is nevertheless monitored. In addition to the circulatory passages that things undergo when they are expelled from the home are the parallel practices that adjudicate how far the personal or intimate may infringe on domestic space.

Within the homes I visited, a series of storage practices spatially and temporally fix the transience of personal possessions.[14] Starting with the most transient are the surfaces of coffee tables, kitchen tables and worktops on which objects circulate most frequently. Cups, dishes, reading material, food and so on are deposited for

FIGURE 5.2 Light and airy homes are created through storage practices.
Source: Photo by author.

short periods before being removed, cleaned, stored or disposed of. Likewise, relatively unobtrusive hooks are ubiquitous in hallways, on kitchen and bathroom walls and in bedroom closets. Hooks cater to easy access and the frequent circulation of things and are found near the loci of shared activities. They specify the occupants of households, cater to and prompt certain activities. The kitchen may have lines of hooks for hanging tea towels, dishcloths or brushes, while in hallways, one often notices a variety of hooks inside the door. Above them, I often saw shelving that held hats, scarves and outdoor equipment. One woman showed me a small Ikea hook that screws into the underside of a hallway shelf to store, yet conceal, house keys. Inspecting her many hooks, she questions why they are so few in other places: 'Why don't you have more hooks for stuff in Ireland – or pegs – as you call them?' It was true. I had encountered the range and frequency of inexpensive hooks in city-centre department stores as striking. I had delighted in their canny usefulness and wondered why hooks were not used more in Dublin.

Storage facilities such as these are not intended to activate memory or to afford long-term abeyance but to participate in a moral evaluation of how homes, possessions and people should be organised. Hooks define the limits of participation. In bathrooms, there are frequently an array of hooks for different functions: hooks for hand towels, hooks for bath sheets, hooks for residents and hooks with 'guests' labelled on them. The hook represents periodic action, meaning short time frames because of related activities (see Drazin and Frohlich 2007: 61). In hallways, their contents tend to be seasonal, while in bathrooms, their contents can change on a

FIGURE 5.3 Storage cages in the basement of some apartment blocks.
Source: Photo by author.

daily or weekly basis. Hooks designate members of the household. For example, hooks are frequently positioned as level with child height to actively encourage children to hang up their own coats, a practice that is underscored in childcare centres in order to promote the values of self-sufficiency and independence. Following a comparable function, most people have shoe shelves or shoe cupboards just inside their front doors, often adjacent to full-length mirrors. One woman who I call Maya had a light, white plastic Ikea wall hanging with shoe-size crevices in which to keep her footwear. Taking up much of the end wall, the white synthetic sheen was very visible as one approached the door and gave the impression of a wall of shiny shoes, which she didn't like. It was picked up on a whim in Ikea and ugly, she conceded. But her live-in boyfriend was 'used to it now', and eventually, she decided that its function was too important to do without.

Possessions that are a little less transient can be placed elsewhere, including in kitchens cupboards, living-room shelving and low tables and drawers that hold television sets and music collections. Shelving in bedrooms becomes the repository of the detritus of day-to-day activities, such as hand mirrors, reading matter, household documents and other items that are required to be close at hand but do not have a defined place. Equally for transient use are the dedicated rooms for prams and buggy storage on ground floors of apartment blocks, the walk-in cupboards in bedrooms and hallways or the individualised storage rooms on ground or basement floors. Here seasonal items such as clothes or sportswear might be placed. Others are placed for mid-term storage in floor-to-ceiling wardrobes or shelving. One

FIGURE 5.4 Storage cupboards are common in apartment hallways.

Source: Photo by author

woman explained that her family has so many weather-related clothes, shoes and toys that it would not be possible to have them in cupboards inside the door.

Finally, a long-term conduit for disposal is the basement cages or walk-in wardrobes in apartment blocks, attics in houses or other storage areas that are common in Stockholm. In one apartment block I visited, there was an labyrinth of small hallways that ran under the building lined with storage cages. These cages were filled to the brim with furniture, clothing, old books and sports- or child-related paraphernalia. Cages such as these provided long-term or seasonal staging posts for many of my informants who managed their goods through a process of occasional retrieval or lengthy abeyance. In the long term, some possessions acquire a latency, kept in the anticipation that they will accrue a personal or financial value at some later time.

The 'index of solidarity' for the home is 'not the stoutness of the enclosing walls but the complexity of coordination' (Douglas 1991: 306). People who devote effort to patrolling and maintaining the home on an individual or collective level through the coordination of tasks and activities, the allotment of resources and the consideration of stakes and claims testify that there is a lot to lose if such activities unravel. Storage is a practice in complex coordination that gives name to future planning and the calculation of potential: what is valuable now, and what shall we keep until later (cf. Douglas 1991)? Not only do storage cupboards store clothes and personal items but also rooms store people. We designate certain rooms for children or for adults, for daytime or evening use. Equally, there are clear temporal and spatial aspects to the categorisation of possessions. Designated spaces, such as cupboards, wardrobes and storage areas, spatially cater to an alternative temporal, spatial, individual or collective calculation. But the 'complex coordination' apparent in my respondents' homes is never static, and the possessions that are stored are rarely done so in the expectation of permanence. On the contrary, the majority of storage equipment in the home, from small hooks to large walk-in wardrobes, is so placed to allow for circulating rather than fixed things.

Storage allows for the easy movement of people and things to circulate along established pathways within the home and along extra domestic routes. The home, from this perspective, appears more as one node within a network of circulating people and things than as a fixed, bounded entity. Clutter snags these networks and impedes movement, whereas storage clears pathways and facilitates circulation. Tensions may arise from clutter, representing obstructed movement or jarring temporal frames, where circulation happens more quickly or slowly than expected. This was evident when I met Marit, for example. Marit is a skilled collector of mid-twentieth-century furniture but had more furnishings than she could use or display. Her interior was striking not the least because her sofa matched her walls in a deep red colour, a marked difference from the conventional white that was typical of the homes I visited. But it was also clear that Marit indulged her interest in the knowledge that her home differed from many of her friends and neighbours. Normally, she does not shop in Ikea except for small things like 'wrapping paper, candles, washing-up brushes and no furniture items', with the exception of storage items such as the Billy bookcases she purchased a few years beforehand and describes as 'the classic Billy'.

Marit purchased the majority of her furnishings in auctions and seeks out mid-twentieth-century design items, stating that she would always look to auctioned items for signature goods but goes to Ikea for 'modern things'. As we sit on her sofa and drink coffee, she tells me that the sofa is one of a pair: she found such good value several years ago that she bought two sofas of the same 1950s type but lent one to an aunt. Now she acknowledges that she has all the furniture she needs but cannot resist attending auctions and occasionally still purchases. She gets a thrill from auctions, but consequently, she has a storage space in the basement that is 'full of coffee tables'. Marit identifies self-expression through home as the reason why she claims one should endeavour not to mimic the Ikea catalogue at home. She explains:

> I liked that it has been used before and that it has a history to it. For pottery and things, I am very interested in local production, the same with furniture. If it is Scandinavian, then I like it better, but mostly it is the design. I like that it is not that common. You can get your own style, and it doesn't look like everyone else's living room. That is something that people really don't like: 'Oh, we don't want our living room to look like it has come out of the Ikea catalogue'.

Marit: You want to have everything very neat before you invite someone over. It is not everyday with laundry all over. It has to be really tidy. It is silly in a way, but eh, it is just you are afraid of what people might think: 'Oh, Marit is a messy person'.
Pauline: And that is bad?
Marit: Yes, it is really bad.

Emma, similarly, told me it is a 'big thing' for her husband to maintain order over their possessions, especially when they lived in a small apartment, and he constantly battled with their stuff. 'We needed to hide a few things, like with lots of drawers: How do we put away things, and how do we organise it all?' Speaking about the storage inside their front door, she described the ongoing discussion they were embroiled in to manage their footwear.

Emma: Shoes, shoes, shoes, like I said. You should really declutter. The entrance was a really big, big thing. I really never allowed cupboards; they look ridiculous. So we left them on a shoe shelf.
Pauline: That was OK with him?
Emma: It was, and we had it. We didn't keep out the twenty pairs; we put some away in the attic. That was very important to him, and putting hooks everywhere, or pegs, as you say in Ireland. It is important so that you can organise and buy drawers to get things put away, to systemise.

Emma describes the result of her husband's labour as 'to make him happy'. Spending a Saturday clearing and tidying the garage will not be evident to anyone save himself and his family. Equally, because the family is in the process of moving into the house, she glances around to illustrate that the couple is not anxious about being seen to be tidy. The point is not tidiness as such, she qualifies. 'It is his relief. He knows there is a place where everything belongs'.

> You don't have to spend time searching for things when you need to go away. It was a big joy for him to organize the garage the other weekend, and he is not a handy man. But to make it nice and tidy, and he would have lot shelves there. He spent a whole Saturday doing it. First, we had a problem – we had a leakage – but after that, he happily spent it in there.

Home staging/the home as stage: 'We want to enjoy the emptiness!'

Khaled, a thirty-four-year-old father-of-two, had recently moved into a new house in a southern Stockholm suburb when I met him. He was self-employed and had two employees in his small but thriving business. He and his wife, Nina, and their two small children (aged three and one) were in the process of settling in when I visited them, and they still had not decided on how to organise their home. The house is spacious, covering 360 m2 in total, 175 m2 of which is reception rooms and bedrooms. There are large storage rooms in the basement that are partly filled, one of which adjoins a large garage. Their large living room is surrounded by floor-to-ceiling windows that look out onto neighbouring houses and green space. Khaled and his family previously lived in a bostadsrätt apartment. Bostadsrätt is a property form that originated in the cooperative movement of the early twentieth century. Not purely owner-occupied, it describes a situation in which the occupier of a unit (generally an apartment) is a shareholder of a cooperative that owns the unit, along with several others (generally the block of apartments). For a fee, the resident acquires shares in the co-op and has the right to live in the apartment for an unlimited amount of time, or alternatively, to sell this right to a new resident or shareholder (Christophers 2013: 889). In the run-up to the sale of their apartment, their estate agent handed Khaled a leaflet that advised property owners on how to style their homes for the marketplace. The couple followed the guidelines and packed away the leaflet for future consultation. In presenting their home for viewers, the family was cautioned not to have anything on the floor, to clear clutter and to hide personal possessions. Toothbrushes and all intimate items should be hidden, while reception room tables should be devoid of any traces of personality, except perhaps with a vase with fresh flowers.

Khaled was outspoken in his wishes to maintain an uncluttered aesthetic, especially having acquired a spacious home. 'One must be very structured', he tells me. One must have smart storage spaces for things that are 'actually important'. In keeping with a common idiom of efficiency as an explanation for the importance of ordering domestic possessions, Khaled described a similar ideal:

> You spend very little time and effort reaching for the things you need. For example, if you want to vacuum this room, then you want it to be easy, right? You want space, you want it to be easy to get around the TV and the cable. You don't want the clutter to suck up the dirt. That is one way to see it, and another way to see it is that you want to be able to find things you are looking for. A cluttery place hides so many things. It is aesthetic, too, to have less things. I think it is obvious: people like that. It is la mode. I think it is la mode.

Khaled was born in the Middle East, but his family moved to Sweden when he was one year old. His decorative choices reflect this dual influence on his life. In certain circumstances, he enjoys mainstream interior decoration, but at others he likes to mix it with culturally diverse preferences, such as sitting on cushions on the floor in a manner that is more in keeping with the body and feng shui, he tells me.[15] On this occasion as we sit in their living room, the couple speak of their hopes to integrate both, one corner with low tables and cushions, while another will house their two brand-new brown leatherette sofas from Ikea with matching coffee tables, the translucent packaging material of which was still strewn on the floor when I arrived.

Khaled first saw the sofas in a pub, and a friend recognised them from Ikea. They represented a new style, one that was not widely known. He came home, looked it up in the catalogue and later showed Nina. When they went to see it in Kungens Kurva, Nina liked them immediately, and within ten seconds, their decision was made. Nevertheless, Khaled doubts he will immediately identify his sofas as sourced from Ikea when friends start to visit: 'My feeling now is that I don't want to tell them that I bought them at Ikea, unless they ask, of course, but I consider it, me and my friends, we consider it not exclusive, or fantasy-full, imaginative: "Oh, so you bought it from Ikea. That was not hard enough"'.

The couple is not confined by limited domestic space and enjoys large storage rooms in the basement of their house. However, the control and circulation of their possessions is a pressing problem. In anticipation of their move, they miscalculated how large their new living room would be. Now they have a problem because they also purchased the sofas that were already in the house from the prior owner. 'We didn't plan to buy them, but we bought them to get rid of him' he said, assuming they had plenty of space.

> We thought we would have separate seating groups, and we bought these just weeks ago thinking that the room was a bit bigger, and now it feels like one sofa too many. We are trying to fit them so that we can have two groups.

In addition, they wished to have an area of the floor for cushions and sitting and lounging, which Nina describes as Chinese style, but find now that one group of sofas must go into a large hold-all room downstairs that has no specified function other than storage.

From an initial move aimed at maximising space and enjoying a minimal life, they find that securing this ideal, is a task that requires constant negotiation and a significant financial output. 'From the beginning, we thought we had enough space to have two sofa groups, and it would be a relaxed setting, but it is not, so we are back to the beginning. We don't want this cluttery living'. He continued:

Khaled: I feel sick when I ... when my way is cluttered with stuff. So, I feel this is good for modern people who have so many things to think about. You want your home to be nice and easy. You have to have storage for this. I mean, it is a luxury way of living, and in order to be able to do that, you have to have places, other places ... I can give you an example. To be able to do this styling of our flat, which we sold, we weren't able to keep everything inside the flat. And our storage rooms in the attic and in the cellar were full. What we did was to hire a self-storage room just for this ... styling, so we paid like five hundred kronor extra a month. To be able to have this less ... less living ... it takes effort, and it costs. That is how I see it. But other people might see it as 'Why didn't you get rid of the stuff, throw it away?' But we didn't.

Pauline: What will you do with the stuff?

Khaled: We will sort it out when we have time. I will slowly go through everything we have and do the normal sorting procedure: De we need this stuff, should we keep it, should we throw, should we sell?

Pauline: And is this for furnishing?

Khaled: It is everything, everything. And we should make it a routine also. Do it one time a year. Just everything ... If we buy something new, then we have to get rid of something old. So one thing in, one thing out, to be able to keep this way of living ... We are realising we brought with us too much stuff, too much garbage. We didn't know we had so much garbage with us. We are aiming with living with less stuff. Less is more, you know. We are heading for that, which is why we bought a house with space, and with less stuff, we want to enjoy the emptiness.

Waste and its placement is an expression of ordering practice. Arriving at order out of chaos is an expression that many informants professed as significant in helping them feel at home, thus signalling an emotional territory that was frequently fraught with contradictory impulses that individuals found difficult to articulate. One woman, who I call Ursula, referred to the 'lightness' of Swedish style as opposed to the 'heaviness' of US rustic styles, where she had lived previously. Both light and heavy in this example describe a material aesthetic as well as an emotional state (Garvey 2013). Khaled identifies the necessity of order and placement as expressive of modern living. The modern home for him required acquisition, but paradoxically, the evidence of that acquisition must be continually monitored, evaluated and in large part hidden. New sofas from Ikea in addition to scatter cushions on the floor pertain to the transnational cosmopolitan style that Khaled aims to achieve. Against this, he considers his appreciation of modern domesticity as springing from his experiences growing up in concert with the images he sees on television shows and in expos and newspaper supplements. His response to these influences is to keep some things in storage, awaiting small incremental inclusion or large-scale expulsions, and in so doing, acquire authority over their possessions. Greater efficiency is nominated as the expected outcome of such ordering techniques in which burdensome possessions threaten the smooth running of the household and represent the potential for disarray erupting onto the cleared surfaces of the main living areas.

In the example of Khaled and Nina, one can juxtapose the lived realities of the indexical emptiness portrayed in images of light-filled, airy homes in property supplements with an ongoing struggle with brute materiality. What we do with things, what we make present and absent, is part of the totality of consumption. Relationships that are internal to the household or part of extra-domestic relations are enacted around 'what is there but sometimes also around the *presence* of what is not' (Hetherington 2004: 159, emphasis in original). Departing from ideas of fixity, we see the productive capacity that mobile things incur. The creation of specific absences – tidying away shoes, picking up laundry – as well as presences are evocative in forging connections between oneself and others, although complete absence, Kevin Hetherington reminds us, is an illusion (2004). Nothing is totally removed, just placed elsewhere. What is more, the placement of possessions is a practice in removing or taming their agency. When this has not worked effectively, we encounter their presence as transgressive, dirty or just plain wrong. Effective movement of clutter therefore neutralises its power to confront us. Because of its mundanity, however, combatting clutter may be regarded as self-evident, which goes some way to explain why my respondents emphasized correct procedures but also why such procedures were rarely explicitly volunteered. For Khaled and Nina, like many others, this enjoyment of the 'emptiness' not only applies to market rationalisations but also is carried through in how they wish to maintain a stress-reducing and efficient inner landscape. Conforming to the ideology of home as a bastion for individuality and intimacy, for unique expression and singularisation, it is nevertheless striking that it is here that the detritus of intimate routines is most rigorously patrolled.

Emotional economies, colourful environments, animated surfaces

More than mere matter out of place, anthropological scholarship has attended to the ways in which surfaces can be animated with the trace of humans in either positive or negative ways. Diana Young's study of UK estate agents, for example, examines the promotion of whiteness and so-called neutrality in interiors to bolster a feeling of spaciousness and to downplay the animating trace of lives lived (2004). Referring to earlier, seminal works in anthropology such as the circulation of shell valuables (Malinowski 1922), Young refers to the patina that accrues to objects through use and exchange, how colour and surface texture carry animating presences, ascribing identity and personhood in immediate and compelling ways. Properties for sale, she finds, ideally showcase a 'blank canvas' (2004: 10), which is perceived as clean and devoid of traces of people as found in dirt, scuff marks or perceived 'brash' forms of decoration. In the housing market, property is less likely to sell when it is not presented in show-house style, when traces of previous persons have not be adequately removed. Not only a UK phenomenon, a visual iconography showcasing a minimal aesthetic is bolstered in Swedish property pages of broadsheet media (*Dagens Nyheter, Svenska Dagbladet*) and popular interior decoration magazines (*Sköna Hem*). In these spreads, domestic interiors are presented as a fait accompli, a self-evident aesthetic logic that is ordered and presented in finished form. Here hints of lives and personalities that were housed in these interiors are largely eradicated.[16] Apartments or houses, then, that are too decorated or where there are smudges or busy patterns on the walls impede the flow of market and slow down its potential for sale. The blankness of the neutral space is snagged on the indices of personality and deemed less attractive. Cleanliness therefore does not only refer to dirt but also relates to the 'integrity of the surface and to the absence of traces of other people's lives' (Young 2004: 9, in Buchli 2013). This is negatively valued in the housing market because it is difficult to obviate the presence of people from surface interiors. Young notes there is a moral dimension also where the eradication of previous owners and personalities is taken as indication of 'good quality', indicating to buyers that a property is looked after.[17]

White-painted interiors conform to the 'simplicity' of the twentieth-century design aesthetic and again, the spread of light was a metaphor for Ikea's reach to myriad global homes. Just think, then-marketing manager Nils Larsson said to me during our meeting in 2008, of those houses with a single light bulb hanging from the ceiling. This is the image he conjures and leaves hanging in the silence that follows. I am expected to understand what is wrong with this scenario. For my respondents, lightness tended to the praised as a sought-after quality, while light woods were described by research participants as having a Nordic provenance and indexical of the Scandinavian aesthetic, along with clean lines, simple furnishings, uncluttered surfaces and unimpeded daylight. Similarly replacing any hint of 'dark and gloomy' is the 'clean, simple and fit for purpose, as well as light and airy' that is advanced by the Ikea corporation in global stores as iconically Swedish (Kristoffersson 2014: 60).[18] Keane (2005) reminds us however that the saliency of certain qualities is instrumental to how we appreciate and comprehend the object world. Icons such as the Swedish modern are composed of material forms and sensuous qualities that are situated within a world of action and consequences, open to the vicissitudes of convention, challenge or change. Instead of fixed aesthetic forms new arrangements arise out of seemingly insignificant physical qualities and we see just that in the millennial trend that celebrates colour in domestic interiors, thereby disrupting any simple descriptive trope regarding Scandinavian style. Instead of emanating from state agencies or civil collectives as in the past, it is the media, commercial advertising and public expos that individuals cite as sources of new aesthetic trends. One woman, echoing several others, pinpointed the 1990s as the 'beginning' of a raft of televisions programmes that focussed on interior decoration. As Pia, a forty-five-year-old mother of two, said:

> In the last years, there has been more interest in taking care of your home and buying nice sofas and design and making your home look nice. Special magazines are doing really well, people are buying them. The last ten or fifteen years, maybe, not more, I think.

Television programmes highlighted the benefits that could be accomplished by amateur enthusiasts through sprucing up tired surfaces or mixing and matching new furniture items with older antiques. And increasingly one encounters the exhortation to 'forget white walls. Now we want wallpaper with a textile feel or that looks like hard materials – stone, wood, metal or mosaic' on the lifestyle pages of same broadsheet newspapers that otherwise celebrate the simplicity of light and airy homes.[19] In contrast to Taussig's description of colour as defilement therefore comes the mounting valorisation of colour as a prominent vehicle for emotional expression amongst mainstream retailers and design practitioners.[20] The use of colour to animate domestic interiors was evident at the launch of the 2008 issue of the Ikea catalogue when Ikea's marketing manager, Nils Larsson, championed 'throwing out minimalism' in favour of a more vibrant, colour-infused aesthetic. The evocation of colour was explicitly linked to sentiment and celebrated as a new home-interior trend, heralded as something of a departure from the past.[21] Ikea managers have attested to the long-term prominence of bright primary colours in Ikea furnishings so that recent trends have been described to me as going back to roots. Equally doubtless, however, is the contemporary twinning of colour and emotion – what colours feel like, how they alter mood, as well as the exhortations that colour can uniquely be harnessed in 'self-expression'.

Relevant here is current marketing strategy in which colour increasingly carries the positive inflection of authentic 'deep' emotion as opposed to cool abstract rationality (Malefyt 2007, 2003), part and parcel of turn of the millennial trends in commerce that recruit colour and sensation in selling positive experiences and products (Howes 2003, 2005). By spring 2012, Inter IKEA Systems BV magazine *Live* exhorts readers on its cover to 'Pick a Colour: The Ones That Make You Happy Are Always in Style!' while the cover image shows two blond children at an outdoor red polka dot-covered table, seated on red chairs against a green background. On the opening pages of the magazine, *Live* editor, Lotta Brandt, recommends that householders 'dare to try new things . . . Be inspired to play with textiles, experiment with colours and organise your home so it's a better fit for how you live'. One of the ways to accomplish this is to be playful, personalise the home and express yourself.[22] This emphasis can be found in many global corporations, but Löfgren points out that the particular flavour of informality, the focus on erasing

122 Storage solutions

FIGURE 5.5 Displays of Scandinavian design in the National Museum in Stockholm.
Source: Photo by author.

traditional rules and the particular emphasis on spontaneity had a specific resonance within Sweden (Löfgren 2005: 19). Previous distinctions between public and private, work and home, were thus actively undermined at a time when consumption patterns moved away from durable goods and towards experiences (Wikström 1997 in Isenhour 2010).[23]

We see this trend again in centres of cultural production. In the substantial, empty white-walled rooms dedicated to Swedish design in Stockholm's National Museum, one finds extensive plinths filled with chairs and tables that demonstrate the Swedish design tradition. To foreclose any ambiguity, there are informative posters attached to columns that announce 'The 1900s – The Century of Design!' Here items of domestic furniture stand as indexes of a national design tradition, including an Ikea chest of drawers and a small Lack table alongside postmodern examples such as Bohlin's concrete chair. The furniture items are combined with informative descriptions that document a national progression from 1900 to 2000. Documenting the linear trajectory, the visitor is informed that 'simple forms, natural materials, light-coloured woods and straight lines dominated the picture of Swedish design' during the 1990s. This pervasive iconography is disrupted at the close of the century, however, when we are told that more 'expressive forms' have come to the fore. Now, the twenty-first century is marked by 'luxuriant forms and bold colours, sometimes alluding to kitsch, maybe seen as a reaction to the light

FIGURE 5.6 An Ikea product as index of Swedish design in the National Museum in Stockholm. The red table is an Ikea Lack table.

Source: Photo by author.

austere neosimplicity'. Emotion, kitsch and expression executed through colour, affect and irony is counterpoised against the 'neominimalism' or 'neofunctionalism' of the early years of the 1990s. Designers are asking 'new questions about function and the selection of material', the visitor is informed. Nestled amongst more high-cost, high-profile pieces sits the scarlet particle board of the Ikea Lack table, which strikes me as an odd choice to represent Ikea design. Its scarlet colour is eye-catching amongst the mainly wood hues and neutral tones of the objects around it. Instead of something from the Stockholm range that pledges 'top quality', 'smart craftsmanship' and 'design in every detail'[24] is the most humble and inexpensive of items, retailing for around 99 SEK (€10). Instead of a show-stopper, the Lack accentuates the ordinary but also stands as an index of a century-long design trajectory.

What does Swedish style make possible?

If twentieth-century Sweden is characterised by an aesthetic, then it is the Nordic variant of the modernist movement in architecture and design (see Hilson 2008). During this century, the home has come to occupy the bastion of privacy, of personal expression and individual identification. Nevertheless, while any individual home is the site for unique expression and value judgement, through the framework of the Scandinavian aesthetic, a national conversation of long standing is entered into. In this chapter, I have traced the diverse expressions of the modern in corporate, domestic and state sectors and it should be clear that in acknowledging the narrative of a Swedish style, it is a mistake to look for total consistency behind the semantics of this idiom. In referencing this aesthetic, householders are not making strict reference to a clearly defined materiality but instead are pointing to an idealised and unchanging vision of domesticity that has a distinct national provenance. This idealisation is entirely in keeping with the utopian pretensions of early modernism and with the diversity that has always existed in actual homes.

The valorisation of colour represents a novel route by which commercial actors attempt to conscript sentiment and channel it through a narrow decorative palette. But while the trends that transpose colour and emotion are variously successful, much more pervasive was the expectation that the home is the site for personal expression. In the past, there has been emphasis on the social sameness created through 'aesthetic fostering' and informing the population 'how they should decorate and live in their homes' (Ekström 2010: 522; see also Robach 2002). Within this framework, the legacy of a totalising domestic environment of the twentieth-century modern movement stands in stark contrast to the diversity that characterises households today (Hirdman 1992, 2013).

However, although the totalising modern movement does appear a stark contrast to contemporary pluralism, some overarching convergences in approaches to interior decoration are also apparent.[25] Respondents report that the 1990s marks the beginning of a raft of interior decoration programmes that valorised the creative upkeep of the home and the decorative potential of the interior. What individuals called Swedish style is actively created through such ordinary household routines, it is objectified in the materials and arrangements of furniture, in the spaces between objects and in the practices that surrounded these pieces. But what is significant here is that the ideal of Swedish style as light and airy remains remarkably static in the face of continuous material mobility within the domestic interior as well as in a shifting housing market outside.

Iconographies of the modern are always embodied in physical form and therefore open to the vagaries of interpretation and change. In recent years, and as part of an international phenomenon, colour and sentiment have been foregrounded in design activities, centres of cultural production and commerce. It is not surprising, therefore, that the ubiquity of the minimal aesthetic has been described as a 'myth' (Ahl et al 2002). The core objective of this chapter however is to illustrate that diversity in practice does not preclude an abiding commitment to an established and idealised form. Descriptions of this form were surprisingly uniform by respondents of all ages, a consistency that overarched the diversity of their actual domestic arrangements. For my respondents, and compared to their parents' generation, housing is more fluid both in structure and in decoration than ever before. With that, one finds a richer variety of decorative schemes and tastes, new avenues to acquire furniture and less fixed authority as to what is right. A high investment in time and energy is required to secure a home that fits one's private and public profile. When research respondents spoke to me of Swedish style or the Scandinavian modern, it was often as a timeless, stable category, immutable to the upheavals that were implicated in the shifting terrain of housing since the turn of the millennium.[26] Aesthetic orders such as Swedish style provide a visual shorthand for the stability of the past that masks the disruption occasioned by the shifting, unpredictable realities of contemporary housing in Stockholm.

Notes

1 For example, see http://www.skandiamaklarna.se and https://www.instagram.com/skandiamaklarna/ accessed 08/06/17
2 For example, one respondent suggested, 'I tidy for myself, but I also don't want work colleagues visiting and inspecting everything. I don't want them to say, "Anna is not a tidy person"'.
3 This was particularly emphasised in the homes of young and middle-aged, middle-class professionals where muted colours, unpatterned furniture, relatively few tablecloths and random personal possessions were evident in living areas. In homes such as these, traces of children – outside of bedrooms – were restricted to boxes of toys stacked neatly in living room corners.
4 Howe comments that by virtue of the simplicity and plainness of Swedish domestic furniture, it was more democratic. Because Sweden was industrialised later than Denmark it availed of the opportunity to invest in more automated work practices and serial production on a mass scale. (1999).
5 Leading us to question if this form of mass production is perceived as a material avatar of the combined processes of liberal capitalism and universalist welfare.
6 Grant McCracken (1989) writes about the sparseness of the minimal aesthetic as sterile, forbidding and 'Scandinavian', suggesting that empty surfaces are somehow less animated or peopled than cluttered ones.
7 Scandinavian design departed from its European counterparts also in incorporating pale woods, such as pine, spruce and birch, and natural materials, including oxhide, jute or linen-based fabrics (Howe 1999). The use of laminated woods and organic forms was pioneered in the 1930s by designer Bruno Mathsson and replaced the tubular steel popular in the German Bauhaus.
8 Interestingly, one catches a glimpse of this transition in early Ikea catalogues. Catalogues from 1951 to 1954 show a rapid transition from interiors with ornate suites called 'Oak furniture in renaissance style' (*Ekmöbel i renässansstil* 1951: 33), 'Luxury Rococo Bureau' (*Rococobyrå i Lyxutförande* 1953) or 'Model Oxford – an Aristocrat among Furniture' (*Modell Oxford – En aristokrat bland möbler* 1953: 58). By 1954, however, one can find a style entitled Louis XVI alongside an exhortation that 'modern people with good taste choose Ikea' in the same catalogue (1954: 33). The disjuncture in range is stark, with pronounced differences in the naming of furniture and also in the atmosphere of the rooms: sideboards give way to bookcases, and furniture advertised in 'the modern style' promotes rational and function qualities, such as a chair model named 'Art' fashioned for 'anatomically correct rest' (*Fåtölj Art för anatomiskt rikig vila*,1953: 23). 'Moderna människor med god smak väljer sin bosättning hos Ikéa' (1954: 55). See also 'Modell Exita: Exklusiv sovrumsmöbel i modern stil' (1954: 55).
9 Such as the groundbreaking Design in Scandinavia exhibition (1954–1957) that downplayed strict minimalism, instead allowing for the possibility of possessions in uncluttered modern settings. Upwardly mobile professionals could acquire an interior decor that conformed to elite trends, but these trends rapidly infiltrated mainstream markets.

10 In the 1950s, the launch of Scandinavian design on the American market was poised as a deliberate play on democratic credentials involving a distancing from the stark austerity of the international style.
11 Published shortly before the Million Homes Programme was launched in which a million dwellings would be built over the following decade and which interior organisation is planned to a high degree of detail.
12 Opening with the statement that 'our modern housing is equipped with dressers, wardrobes, cleaning cabinets and often with a linen cupboard. But these cabinets cannot accommodate all our items. The table shows what most of us have to keep in the apartment.' 'Våra moderna bostäder utrustas vanligen med köksskåp, garderober, städskåp och ofta med linneskåp. Men dessa skåp rymmer inte alla våra föremål. Tabellen visar vad de flesta av oss har att förvara i lägenheten' (1961: 158). The author goes on to detail the categories of things that householders store (meals, clothing, sleep and hygiene products as well as home care, leisure, reading and writing materials and decorations ('måltider, beklädnad, sömn, hygien, kläd-o-bostadsvård, fritid, lästning och skrivning och pynt').
13 One such store called Granit, retailed empty poufs that can be filled with clean bed linen and towels while also functioning as footrests.
14 See Drazin and Frohlich 2007 for inspiration for this section.
15 Feng shui is a philosophical system of harmonizing people with their environment which is derived from China.
16 I suggest the designation of clutter often refers to the most personal of possessions, those items that are close to the body, such as clothing, shoes, hairbrushes, make-up and so on. I focus on the importance of storage, the aesthetics of clear surfaces and the requirement to declutter as part of this aesthetic, generally acknowledged by my respondents as a 'good thing', as a value-laden or normative goal (Miller 2009: 19; see also Hosein 2009).
17 Laurence Douny (2007, in Buchli 2013), in contrast, touches on a similar point from an alternative perspective and problematises the category of clean amongst the Dogon in Mali, where dirt indexes life and prosperity. Sooty walls attest to the house fire and the vitality of the household. Touching walls by family members or visitors and leaving traces of dirt that accumulates at these points testifies to the vitality of people in the household and provides ontological security to those at home (Douny 2007: 315, in Buchli 2013: 126). These enlivening smudges 'fix' people to surface interiors. However, anthropologists have also acknowledged the opposite argument in which presences may be most marked by empty space (Bille et al 2010; Buchli and Lucas 2001; Gregson et al 2007; Hetherington 2004).
18 Internationally 'modern' design has witnessed a resurgence in home-furnishings retail since the 1990s (Leslie and Reimer 2003), and aesthetic qualities such as 'light and airy' feature strongly.
19 Glöm vita väggar. Nu vill vi ha tapeter med textil känsla, eller som ser ut som hårda material – sten, trä, metall eller mosaik, my translation. Published in Dagens Nyheter, March 1, 2014, available online at www.dn.se/bostad/murrigt-metalligt-och-mer-monster/ accessed 01/05/15.
20 Notwithstanding some continuities, we also see a twenty-first-century shift in which colour, decoration and transience are increasingly introduced into the modern repertoire. For example, Ikea's modern range is eclectic, combining modern, 'clean-lines' with traditional elements, such as the 1990s reproductions of Gustavian style, a neoclassical range developed in concert with the National Museum in Stockholm and the Swedish National Heritage Board (Kristoffersson 2014: 65). More forcefully still is the forceful introduction of colour.
21 Elsewhere, I have argued that lightness as an idiom weaves the social and material into one tapestry (Garvey 2013). Lightness does not only imply lack of clutter but also refers to sheen, weight, colour, form, degree of ornamentation or even the absence of objects. Lightness is emotive: several respondents countered that not only clutter but also vibrant pattern can induce a feeling of physical discomfort. Since the turn of the millennium and adding a new trend to previous modern styles, international retail trends recruit colour

and sensation in selling products (Howes 2005; Malefyt 2012). Not only colour but also a heady mix of artificial smells, tastes or sounds are enlisted in contemporary marketing. The pursuance of a full register of senses has been enlisted in the hope that shoppers will respond to commercial products in more profound ways (see Chapter 2).

22 Howes, for example, charts the 'sea-change in the sensual logic of capitalism' in the 1990s, when global companies began to expand their repertoire of trademarked logos to include smells, tastes and sounds. A new, aesthetically charged revisioning of the visual and tactile qualities of things is cast as the route to people's feelings and evaluations of products. His emphasis is linked to the so-called experience economy, the late twentieth-century turn to promoting experience as a a primary idiom of contemporary branding practices (see Chapter 2). As part of a 'cult of the informal', a trend towards dismantling traditional hierarchies emerged across a spectrum of industries from biotechnology to cultural centres, while the performative and emotive dimensions of branding were embraced in commercial enterprise. This emphasis can be found in many global corporations, but Löfgren points out that the particular flavour of informality, the focus on erasing traditional rules and the particular emphasis on spontaneity had a specific resonance within Sweden such that the concept of the experience economy was adopted 'both faster and stronger in Sweden than in most other European countries' (Löfgren 2005: 19, see also Löfgren 2013).

23 Not merely a retail strategy, a shift towards colour and affect is discernible in design circles, commercial centres and home decoration exhibitions in Stockholm. This sales pitch has wide appeal, reminding us of the Casa Cor exhibition we encountered in Chapter 3. Casa Cor means House of Colour.

24 'Stockholm', Inter IKEA Systems BV, accessed 03/08/17. www.ikea.com/ie/en/collections/stockholm/.

25 It is worth noting, though, that in tandem with emphasis on the experience economy, and on the constant valorisation of positive experiences in late 1990s, came resistance by individuals who encountered a standardisation of experience or emotion in standard commercial transactions (Löfgren 2013). People detached themselves from commodification processes, he suggests, or invoked irony to resist an ever-advancement of emotions in the marketplace.

26 Although modernist strictures possess 'a certain affinity with totalising social theories that attempt to fit all cultural forms into a particular pattern, mould or trajectory' (Attfield 2000: 171), the legacy of modernism ultimately remains ambiguous.

References

Ahl, Zandra, Emma Olsson, and Anna Kleberg. 2002. *Svensk smak: myter om den moderna formen*. Stockholm: Ordfront.

Appelgren, Staffan and Anna Bohlin. 2015. "Growing in Motion: The Circulation of Used Things on Second-Hand Markets." *Culture Unbound: Journal of Current Cultural Research* 7 (1): 143–168.

Arrhenius, Thordis. 2010. "The Vernacular on Display: Skansen Open-Air Museum in 1930s Stockholm'." In *Swedish Modernism: Architecture, Consumption, and the Welfare State*, edited by Helena Mattsson and Sven-Olov Wallenstein. London: Black Dog Publishing.

Attfield, Judy. 2000. *Wild Things: The Material Culture of Everyday Life*. Oxford: Berg.

Belk, Russell. 2010. "Sharing." *Journal of Consumer Research* 36 (5): 715–734.

Belk, Russell. 2014. "You Are What You Can Access: Sharing and Collaborative Consumption Online." *Journal of Business Research* 67 (8): 1595–1600.

Berglund, Erik and Sten Engdahl. 1961. "Möbelråd." *Form*: 221.

Bille, Mikkel, Frida Hastrup, and Tim Flohr Sørensen. 2010. *An Anthropology of Absence*. New York: Springer.

Buchli, Victor. 2013. *An Anthropology of Architecture*. London: Bloomsbury.

Buchli, Victor and Gavin Lucas. 2001. *Archaeologies of the Contemporary Past*. New York: Routledge.
Christophers, Brett. 2013. "A Monstrous Hybrid: The Political Economy of Housing in Early Twenty-First Century Sweden." *New Political Economy* 18 (6): 885–911.
Czarniawska, Barbara and Orvar Löfgren. 2012. *Managing Overflow in Affluent Societies*. New York: Routledge.
Czarniawska, Barbara and Orvar Löfgren. 2013. *Coping With Excess: How Organizations, Communities and Individuals Manage Overflows*. Cheltenham: Edward Elgar.
Daniels, Inge. 2010. *The Japanese House: Material Culture in the Modern Home*. Oxford: Berg.
Douglas, Mary. 1991. "The Idea of a Home: A Kind of Space." *Social Research* 58 (1): 287–307.
Douglas, Mary. 2002 [1966]. *Purity and Danger: An Analysis of Concepts of Pollution and Taboo*. London: Routledge.
Douny, Laurence. 2007. "The Materiality of Domestic Waste: The Recycled Cosmology of the Dogon of Mali." *Journal of Material Culture* 12 (3): 309–331.
Drazin, Adam and David Frohlich. 2007. "Good Intentions: Remembering Through Framing Photographs in English Homes." *Ethnos* 72 (1): 51–76.
Ekström, Karin M. 2010. *Consumer Behaviour: A Nordic Perspective*. Lund: Studentlitteratur.
Fallan, Kjetil. 2012. *Scandinavian Design: Alternative Histories*. London: Berg.
Frykman, Jonas and Orvar Löfgren. 1983. *Culture Builders: A Historical Anthropology of Middle-Class Life*. New Brunswick: Rutgers University Press.
Garvey, Pauline. 2013. "'Ikea sofas are like H&M trousers': The Potential of Sensuous Signs." *Journal of Business Anthropology* 2 (1): 75–92.
Garvey, Pauline. Forthcoming. "Consuming Ikea and Inspiration as Material Form." In *Design Anthropology: Object Cultures in Transition,* edited by Alison J. Clarke. London, Oxford, New York, New Delhi, and Sydney: Bloomsbury.
Gregson, Nicky, Alan Metcalfe, and Louise Crewe. 2007. "Moving Things Along: The Conduits and Practices of Divestment in Consumption." *Transactions of the Institute of British Geographers* 32 (2): 187–200.
Hård af Segerstad, Ulf. 1961. *Scandinavian Design*. London: Studio.
Hartman, Tod. 2007. "The Ikeaization of France." *Public Culture* 19 (3): 483–498.
Hetherington, Kevin. 2004. "Secondhandedness: Consumption, Disposal, and Absent Presence." *Environment and Planning D: Society and Space* 22 (1): 157–173.
Hilson, Mary. 2008. *The Nordic Model: Scandinavia Since 1945*. London: Reaktion.
Hirdman, Yvonne. 1992. "Utopia in Everyday Life – Problems and Background." *International Journal of Political Economy* 22 (2): 5–19.
Hirdman, Yvonne. 2013. *Sveriges Historia 1920–1965*. Johanneshov: TPB.
Hosein, Gabrielle. 2009. "Food, Family, Art and God: Aesthetic Authority in Public Life in Trinidad." In *Anthropology and the Individual: A Material Culture Perspective,* edited by Daniel Miller. Oxford and New York: Berg.
Howe, Susan. 1999. "Untangling the Scandinavian Blonde: Modernity and the IKEA PS Range Catalogue 1995." *Scandinavian Journal of Design History* 9: 94–105.
Howes, David. 2003. *Sensual Relations: Engaging the Senses in Culture and Social Theory*. Ann Arbor: University of Michigan Press.
Howes, David. 2005. *Empire of the Senses: The Sensual Culture Reader*. Oxford: Berg.
IKEA Catalogue. 1951. Älmhult: IKEA Communications AB.
IKEA Catalogue. 1953. Älmhult: IKEA Communications AB.
IKEA Catalogue. 1954. Älmhult: IKEA Communications AB.
Isenhour, Cindy. 2010. "Building Sustainable Societies: A Swedish Case Study on the Limits of Reflexive Modernization." *American Ethnologist* 37 (3): 511–525.

Keane, Webb. 2003. "Semiotics and the Social Analysis of Material Things." *Language & Communication* 23 (3): 409–425.
Keane, Webb. 2005. "The Hazards of New Clothes: What Signs Make Possible." In *The Art of Clothing: A Pacific Experience*, edited by Susanne Küchler and Graeme Were, 1–16. London: University College London Press.
Kristoffersson, Sara. 2014. *Design by IKEA: A Cultural History*. London: Bloomsbury.
Le Corbusier. 1987 [1925]. *The Decorative Art of Today*. Translated by James Dunnett. London: Architectural Press.
Leslie, Deborah and Suzanne Reimer. 2003a. "Gender, Modern Design, and Home Consumption." Environment and Planning D: Society and Space 21: 293–316.
Löfgren, Orvar. 2005. "Cultural Alchemy: Translating the Experience Economy Into Scandinavian." In *Global Ideas: How Ideas, Objects and Practices Travel in the Global Economy*, edited by Barbara Czarniawska and Guje Sevón, 15–29. Malmö: Liber and Copenhagen Business School Press.
Löfgren, Orvar. 2012. "It's Simply Too Much: Coping With Domestic Overflow." In *Managing Overflow in Affluent Societies*, edited by Barbara Czarniawska and Orvar Löfgren, 101–124. London and New York: Routledge.
Löfgren, Orvar. 2013. "Changing Emotional Economies: The Case of Sweden 1970–2010," *Culture and Organization*, 19 (4): 283–296.
Makovicky, Nicolette. 2007. "Closet and Cabinet: Clutter as Cosmology." *Home Cultures* 4 (3): 287–309.
Malefyt, Timothy Dwight de Waal and Brian Moeran. 2003. *Advertising Cultures*. Oxford: Berg.
Malefyt, Timothy Dwight de Waal. 2007. "From Rational Calculation to Sensual Experience: The Marketing of Emotions in Advertising." In *The Emotions: A Cultural Reader*, edited by Helena Wulff, 321–338. Oxford: Berg.
Malefyt, Timothy Dwight de Waal. 2012. "Touching Consumers: Engaging the Senses in Consumption." *The Senses and Society* 7 (3): 350–355.
Malinowski, Bronislaw. 1922. *Argonauts of the Western Pacific: An Account of Native Enterprise and Adventure in the Archipelagoes of Melanesian New Guinea*. London: Routledge and Kegan Paul.
Mrázek, Rudolf. 2002. *Engineers of Happy Land: Technology and Nationalism in a Colony*. Princeton: Princeton University Press.
McCracken, Grant, ed. 1989. "'Homeyness': A Cultural Account of One Constellation of Consumer Goods and Meanings." In *Interpretive Consumer Research*, edited by Elizabeth C. Hirschman. Provo, UT: Association for Consumer Research.
Miller, Daniel. 2009. *Anthropology and the Individual a Material Culture Perspective*. Oxford: Berg.
Robach, Cilla. 2002. "Design for Modern People." In *Utopia and Reality: Modernity in Sweden, 1900–1960*, edited by Cecilia Widenheim, 186–201. New Haven: Yale University Press.
Selkurt, Claire. 2003. "Design for a Democracy: Scandinavian Design in Postwar America." In *Scandinavian Design: Beyond the Myth: Fifty Years of Design From the Nordic Countries*, edited by W. Halén and K. Wickman, 59–66. Stockholm: Arvinius.
Sörlin, Sverker. 2002. "Prophets and Deniers: The Idea of Modernity in Swedish Tradition." In *Utopia and Reality: Modernity in Sweden 1900–1960*, edited by Cecilia Widenheim and Eva Rudberg, 16–25. New Haven: Yale University Press.
Taussig, Michael T. 2009. *What Color Is the Sacred?* Chicago, IL: University of Chicago Press.
Wikström, Solveig R. 1997. "The Changing Consumer in Sweden." *International Journal of Marketing* 14: 261–274.
Young, Diana J. B. 2004. "The Material Value of Color: The Estate Agent's Tale." *Home Cultures* 1 (1): 5–22.

6

STILL LIFE?

Circulation, emotion and mobility

At the exit of the Ikea store in Älmhult, I noticed this sign:

> Goodbye, come again soon. Come when it suits you! Dream in peace and quiet or mingle with the other home-decor lovers.[1]

If one accepts the Ikea slogan that home 'is the most important place in the world', what burden does this bring? Normative domesticity, according to my respondents, entails an expectation that, one way or another, the particularity of household residents is stamped on the otherwise common. But self-expression is not only deliberate and coherent but also often conflicted and fraught. Although respondents speak at length of the necessity to 'feel at home', the requirement for self-expression holds ambivalent, uncertain qualities and is composed of a series of practices rather than finished forms. Carrying the heavy symbolic weight of specific lives and identities, personal possessions place individual households within national frameworks and global movements but also puncture the broader project of domestic imagination with personalised forms of participation. At this juncture mobility or change may be actively employed to open up an ontological space that facilitates creative play with self-image or come to terms with 'layers of fractured experience' (Garvey 2001: 66, Norris 2008, Buchli 2013). Often, it is through a 'series of incremental and temporary performances' that respondents consider self and other (Norris 2008: 416), that work to challenge commercial trends, disrupt domestic norms or heighten desired for emotive states. In the midst of pronouncements on the benefits of shimmering colours and mood, playfulness and expression within commercial circles, there is another aspect of emotion that emerged with force during fieldwork.

A key word here is fluidity. Late twentieth-century interior decoration in Sweden implied an entangled practice of self, family and home construction (Löfgren 1994) but one that too often suggests purposive stasis over haphazard mobility, privacy to the exclusion of public and fixed male and female roles. Now, with greater fluidity of home-based identities and gender roles comes a reimagining of normative domestic models previously defined through immutable material arrangements. Captured in terms such as the domestic *sphere* is a territorialization of familial relations a bolster to the ideology of a discrete, self-contained entity. Instead I adopt the term 'domestic nexus' to capture both the cross-cutting influences and the myriad ways in which the architectural form houses conflicting dispositions.

Taking mobility and transition as my cue, I continue to move inwards from the lively public spaces of Ikea showrooms and advertising campaigns to follow the people and things that traverse discrete boundaries of public and private, collective and intimate that are formative of emotional states, gender roles and domestic ontologies. The background for this chapter lies in several research participants reporting that visiting Ikea in Kungens Kurva assumes heightened emotional impact for those experiencing difficult transitions. Often, an emotive response is evoked through the active dialectical tension that arises from the oscillation between actual homes and domestic effigies found in Ikea, where showrooms evoke the feeling of alternative homes replete with householders engaged in the lively pursuit of domestic acquisition. Home can present an extraordinary burden to individuals who find themselves bereft of the nurturing relationships that characterise domestic ideologies, which may be alleviated or heightened through engagement with the animated hum and engaged practices that characterise Ikea showrooms. Contemplating the emotional fault lines that underscore the micro-routines of everyday life, therefore, is not merely a question of physical heft. Some householders find emancipation in things that carry no historical or personal weight, and both male and female respondents turn to Ikea furnishings to mark or measure a sense of fixity in their own lives (Garvey 2013).

Circular Ikea and informal markets

In contrast to perceptions of domestic stasis, the flat-pack furniture trade is often characterised by planned obsolescence, suggesting a relentless maelstrom of consumables that arrive in homes, whirl and settle for short spells until eventually cast out as fads change. Seasonal fashions now characterise furniture retail in ways that were unprecedented for much of the twentieth century, and 'lifestyle' or 'lifestyle retailing' gives name to this contemporary trend. Ikea is occasionally described as a harbinger of this retail trend because it is explicitly lifestyle oriented, trend conscious and promotes a vision of furniture as disposable. The acceleration of furniture production and consumption in keeping with seasonal fashions is relatively recent, however (see Reimer and Leslie 2003b: 434; see also Garvey 2013; Wickman 1995). For much of the twentieth century, furniture shopping was infrequent. Even by the turn of the millennium, Ikea's North American market research found that the average householder changed furniture only one and a half times over a lifetime (Coppola 2002, in Leslie and Reimer 2003b). Enhanced by global neo-liberal economic policies, this situation has intensified in Europe and North America with a dramatic increase in the turnover of the furniture trade, a shift Leslie and Reimer call the 'era of Ikea' (Leslie and Reimer 2003b: 436). As if to copper-fasten this millennial circuit of ever-mobile goods, ideas, services and people, recent economic models emphasise the 'circular economy'. This idiom describes an emerging economic model that seeks to generate capital through diverse actions, including recycling scarce materials, generating capital from waste and displacing long-term ownership of goods with ephemeral rental instead (see Crang et al 2013; Gregson 2013, 2015; Gregson et al 2007). For example, furniture and household goods found in the buy-and-sell of flea markets are not only becoming ever-more mainstream but also are bolstered by corporate, governmental and supranational initiatives that valorise actions that come under the rubric of recycling or sustainable consumption (Isenhour 2010a, 2010b).

The circular economy purports to challenge traditional economic models of production, consumption and disposal in order to foster new ways of dealing with dwindling natural resources, replacing the idea of the market as a monolithic entity with the 'messy world of circular *economies*' in which what was once considered waste is now deemed a resource (Gregson et al 2015: 220). Recently, members of Ikea's sustainability team have claimed that the circular model provides one remedy for 'peak stuff', meaning that mounting global consumption is set against a background of finite natural resources.[2] Policies that advance better sustainability of these same scarce resources underpin a series of Ikea production initiatives and branding strategies that lead, according to members of the Ikea management team, to new opportunities, new resources and new forms of capital.

Of course, parallel to efforts to minimise the depletion of the world's resources is the ever-shifting territory of global domesticity. Attending a Global Furniture Forum organised by Ikea in Ballymun in Dublin in February 2016, then-deputy range strategist Leoni Hoskins presented 'Circular Ikea' to the assembled staff and audience, mentioning key products that owe their success to the fluidity that marks contemporary housing.[3] 'Change more, consume less' was one phrase that was reiterated during the workshop. Design disasters, we were told, can lead to exciting new possibilities. Taking an example of a small metal trolley on wheels called the Råskog, Hoskins detailed its staggering success on the international furniture market. When the steel, epoxy powder-coated trolley was first designed and presented to the Product Council in Älmhult, there was some appreciation that it would contribute to interior living, that its wheels would allow movement between diverse rooms and activities. The three trays allow it to carry vegetables, for example, or small personal items, while the wheels mean it can be used throughout the household and is small enough to fit into tight spaces.[4] Internationally, the Råskog sells each week close to what it was imagined by the Product Council it would sell in total.[5] Gazing on this unexceptional wheeled trolley, the point was made. In addition to the scarcity of environmental resources is the fact of ever-shrinking living environments.

At a time of reduced apartment sizes internationally and highly mobile populations, it is not surprising that large corporations such as Ikea valorise the freedom that comes with mobility. In February 2017, just as this publication was preparing to go to press, a particular PS range was launched that celebrated fluid lifestyles. On its web page, it praised, 'Things you can easily pick up and move – within a room or from home to home. And furniture that frees you up instead of weighing you down'. Other designers on the web page commented on the number of times they have themselves moved and the necessities this incurred, including the practicality of foldable tables and sofa for those living in 'small spaces'. Internationally, the requirement for mobile devices to allow householders to do different things in the same place is becoming ever-more acute.[6]

Flea markets, mixing and matching

Against the background of circular markets is a lively marketplace retailing second-hand, vintage, antique and recycled furniture and consumables. Many respondents refer to the inclusion of items of furniture that carry a personal or family history as an aspiration in the successful completion of a personal environment. What people described as 'mixing and matching' does not necessarily demand inherited goods, and young respondents (students or young married couples in their twenties and thirties) described the singularised, offbeat finds they uncovered in skips and cellar dumpsters. Although heirlooms can be accumulated over a lifetime and passed between generations, other people delight in what may be uncovered in skips and apartment basements or purchased in metropolitan flea markets. In so doing, most respondents claimed that Ikea furniture should be mixed and matched with family heirlooms or quirky finds, providing contrast to the perceived mainstream.

The vibrant popularity of flea markets, swapping and vintage goods is very visible in Stockholm. I found it striking just how often I encountered posters on the notice boards in public parks advertising children's clothing swaps or informal exchanges of household utensils in apartment block cellars. The popularity of these, plus the growing enlargement of Internet-based sites and Internet communities where objects are exchanged, traded or swapped is such that it has not escaped attention from popular media and academia. High-street retailers, particularly in the clothing and electronic sectors, are encouraging consumers to return used items for recycling, while second-hand shops – pitched as vintage or retro – are increasingly visible in city centres. The second-hand market for branded goods meanwhile is becoming so mainstream that brand strategists are increasingly obliged to incorporate this market into their brand planning (Clarke 2010). Indeed, clothes swapping is so popular that a dedicated web page exists detailing such exchange events around the country (Klädbytardag, in Appelgren and Bohlin 2015: 152).

Furniture advertised in flea markets increasingly celebrate the accreted history of previous owners as they move from person to person and accrue a 'cumulative identity' over time (Weiner 1992: 32–33). Recycled goods retain the rich tapestry of previous lives in the wear and tear, faded colour and stretched fabric that carries past social biographies on the surfaces of things. This surface detail, signalling previous use, has been viewed negatively in the past, but now a new trend is on the rise. Instead of the placement of things within conduits of disposal as a way to neutralise their value, what we see is the opposite and some Swedish traders, Appelgren and Bohlin report, highlight the previous lives of goods and celebrate those details that materially adhere and socially mark them. Now, second-hand furniture might carry labels detailing where they come from or who previously owned them and are pitched as on an onward progression to the next home. One respondent, who I call Siri, is somewhat typical in perceiving a distinct quality conferred on objects by virtue of their circulation and accumulated social biography. Siri was a forty-two-year-old security guard who I met one quiet morning in Ikea when I was distributing research leaflets to a slow but steady stream of shoppers. She lived alone, renting a small one-bedroom apartment in a lively part of the city that was home to a street market that stretched along the waterfront. Accepting its minimal dimensions for the apartment's central location, her sparsely furnished apartment consisted of a living room with a tiny bedroom off the kitchen, which had just enough room for a small single bed. As we talked, she enthused about her armchair and bookcase, both mid-twentieth century and Scandinavian in origin. Her avid interest in classic modernist furniture sprung from its 'clean and modern' look, 'less sharp than later pieces that are all squares and right angles', which was both inspired and fed by frequent visits to metropolitan flea markets. Siri had relocated several times in the previous ten years, which she remarked vaguely was 'not very unusual in my circle'. She rented her first apartment in her late twenties after several years in a housing queue. She was lucky, because although she was not at top of the list, she accepted an offered apartment before seeing it and could move in straight away, thereby allowing her to jump the queue. She worked part time and had a limited budget and so used her spare time to explore the city flea markets (loppmarknader) before they became trendy. She attributes the fashion for old stuff, antiques and second-hand goods to television programmes that turned their focus to antique shows and designed homes in the 1990s. From this decade, a discernible shift in clientele was apparent as middle-class householders started to turn up: 'Then it was okay for people to go', she said.

Visiting flea markets encouraged Siri to acquaint herself with 'old furniture', such as classic twentieth-century pieces that could still be found there. She calculated that purchasing second hand would cost the same as buying new but would yield 'much better quality'. Living alone and without the resources that one might normally need to collect fashionable furniture or even a car for transport, she scoured second-hand venues and found some bargains. For her living-dining room, Siri bought a new sofa from Ikea but sourced the rest in various metropolitan flea markets, and she is particularly pleased with a vibrant orange-painted wooden wardrobe that she purchased for 400 SEK (€42, approximately) that she describes as 'lots of fun' and that she had originally intended repainting. In contrast to her avid interest in these sites, Siri describes Ikea goods as a kind of provisioning, a mainstay that provides all the incidentals that are not afforded by her constant exploration of informal sales and out-of-the-way markets. She enjoys purchasing in Ikea Kungens Kurva because it is cheap, reliable and part of her 'upbringing', where one can find 'standard fare'. She says, 'Yes, you grew up with it, more or less' and has sourced all her kitchen utensils there.

If Siri chooses the classic modern style to represent her stylistic preferences, then Ikea furniture and kitchen utensils provide the scaffolding for those statement pieces. Indeed, she suggests that the majority of Swedes probably mix and match – there are few who rely on Ikea totally, although most depend on it to some degree. Home interiors should require some personal effort, she emphasised, in seeking out just the right thing. Ikea goods, such as storage cupboards and kitchen utensils, are classed by her as standard ware and provide a certain level of quality, inexpensive goods, she says. They contribute to the running of the home but meld into the background and quickly become part of the foundations underpinning everyday life.

> I believe that there are few who buy only Ikea. Most people probably mix. I think it's important to mix overall because otherwise it will be impersonal. I want more to look for a thing – 'Oh, I fell for that'; no, I do not think I would find everything in one place. And there's little excursions, and so it becomes a little bit, 'And I found that there' and so on.[7]

Two years after we first met, Siri and her partner had moved in together and had an infant daughter. In order to procure a new home, they advertised their apartment in housing magazines and web-based sites. After a year of searching, they secured a 'triangle trade', meaning they found two other households who wished to move, and all three were willing to swap apartments. Along all steps of this triangle trade (triangelbyte), the proposed move had to be acceptable to the various private landlords who own the blocks.[8] The new apartment needed work, and Siri was busy revamping the tired-looking interior during my visit. Ikea was the couple's first stop for wardrobes, a changing table and a cot, and Siri particularly stressed the immediate importance of storage, describing the shelving they planned to purchase. While Ikea was returned to as providing safe, reliable provision for a newborn, it was the flea-market goods that arose as problematic. The sofa, in particular, became the focus of negotiation.[9]

> Martin wouldn't like to get a sofa in the flea market (loppis). He likes to mix some things too. He likes to mix but not the sofa. I wouldn't mind. I think maybe not all Ikea furniture so much for my sake but solutions for storing things. Everything from Ikea would look sterile, like a newly built part of the city. I like some place that has grown over the years and you add something. But the sofa is a statement. But with the shelves, Martin says he doesn't want it to look like the 1980s, with the wine glass display cabinet. For storing solutions,

it doesn't really matter to have Ikea. I think that is the main thing. And then either the sofa or the dining table and the shelves from the flea market.

One could read these examples as underscoring a common distinction between alienable commercial products and inalienable second-hand goods. According to this axiology, Ikea products represent the dead hand of anonymous commerce in contrast to the personally infused biography of the heirloom. The high-street marketplace and the informal flea-market economy, separated spatially as well as financially, appear as distinct, operating on different sides of a modern/tradition polarity. However, such a reading would be mistaken because it is clear that both spheres – flea-market goods and Ikea products – exist in relation to each other. It is the contrast between both that is foregrounded in the dictum to mix and match. Instead of two distinct fashions, we find the creation of a composite that is formed of contrasting elements. Similarly, instead of flea markets as mere vendors of perceived 'traditional' material culture, they represent the sites for the exchange and circulation of classical Scandinavian furniture and 'authentically' modern style. More than traditional farming culture implements, my middle-class respondents in Stockholm particularly sought classic twentieth-century modern Scandinavian furniture at these sites, although they also acknowledged that original pieces are both prohibitively expensive and very difficult to find.

As far as Siri is concerned, Ikea provides her with 'safe options' that have withstood the test of time. Her storage provision purchased there is unmarked and ordinary but structural nevertheless. It is in the minutiae of ordinary stuff that helps her organise her life in the midst of sleep deprivation and caring for a young child. The humdrum quality is integral to the necessary routines of domestic life, but far from being incidental, such routines may be saturated with sentiment.

Shopping for inspiration

Sharply contrastive with the ordinariness by which Ikea goods come to be seen in domestic environments and practices, the international media reiterates metaphors of devotion, romance and religious transcendence when referring to global Ikea stores. As alluded to in the introduction to this book, these references tend to circulate on the Internet, proliferate through the broadsheet media, appear on art installations and YouTube clips and present a picture of Ikea as abstract and homogenous over vast geographical tracks. Romance is in focus for popular culture and personal meaning in the twenty-first century, and love is a 'privileged site for the experience of utopia' (Illouz 2007: 7; Wulff 2007). But this form of romantic expression, however aligned with consumerist practice, seems ill fitting for my examples here. Far from the spontaneity of the individual romantic encounter, Ikea provisioning is more closely associated by my respondents with the labour entailed in domestic construction. And that, usually, means company.

As an expression of sustained domestic activity, Ikea visitation most often is undertaken with significant others. Interviewees reiterated families, couples, school friends and work colleagues lunching together as typical scenarios. Interviewees thus described domestic acquisition as a non-solitary endeavour and emphasised the comfort of company over the loneliness of the solo visit. Such comments were interspersed with references to 'hanging out', browsing, day trips or family outings to the store. Numerous individuals pointed to a habit of families to make weekend day trips to Ikea. Niklas, a thirty-eight-year-old father of two, suggested he doesn't go alone: 'Ikea is a family thing, it's like an outing now'. And just as a day trip suggests both time and space given over to loved ones, respondents consistently point to the necessity of Ikea visitation with co-present others. Respondents reminisced on trips they made as young teenagers, when they would pop in with friends for lunch after (and possibly during) school. Indeed, in magazines and in newspapers, common cartoons that feature Ikea show individuals visiting the superstore in pairs, and families are emphasised in the store's 'homes' and catalogue images. Several mentioned, however, that it is only since they have acquired families that they started to enjoy a visit to Ikea.

Thrift, inspiration and gender

Maj was a mother of two teenagers in her mid-forties when we met and worked for a pharmaceutical company. At the time of our meeting, the boyfriend of her nineteen-year old daughter had moved into their family home, prompting several visits to Ikea in Kungens Kurva. When we spoke she continually referred to the number of people living in the family home and the consequent domestic disarray that followed, to which she responded with careful management of clutter and a dedicated pursuit of efficient storage. Vague about precisely what she needed yet confident that she would find solutions there, she described her most recent shopping trip in the following way:

> It was last weekend, and we needed to arrange the CDs and so on to make it look nice, tidy and arranged instead of just being . . . Ja, well, we had a Billy bookshelf, and we thought we needed another shelf beside it. We've had different Billys over the years. It is pine, I think – in the 1980s, a lot of people had pine. We went – my husband and I – and we weren't sure if we should buy one of those special shelves for CDs and DVDs or if we would buy an ordinary Billy which is . . . um . . . bigger . . . deeper, and then we thought, if we buy one of the ordinary ones that is deeper, then maybe the CDs will just, will be untidy anyway. CDs are not meant to be there, but we thought that maybe we should have books and CDs and so on, on them, but then we decided to buy a CD shelf made especially for CDs. We looked at both and discussed them when we were in Ikea.

During this meeting, Maj explains that all domestic projects are embarked upon in a spirit of collaboration with her architect husband, Thomas, who takes an active interest in household provisioning. Indeed, according to Maj, Thomas is often more emphatic than she in the expression of his views.

Maj: We make decisions together. He has very specific views. It is not my views that are … if he doesn't like it, then he says no (said emphatically). When I don't like them, I usually say no (said less emphatically). Sometimes it is not – I think we make the decisions together. I don't feel as if I have to start this discussion.
Pauline: Would you talk about things you need first or browse in Ikea?
Maj: Both. We go to buy one thing and then we start a new discussion: 'Oh, this might be good for hum-hum-hum', and then we don't decide that time but go home and think that might be good there. So maybe we come to look for a specific thing, and while we were there, we start to think about other things. Like I said at the beginning, we see things that we didn't know we needed. I suppose we are content, and also sometimes, we disagree and we walk away and say we don't need to decide this today, and we go home and think it over. I like … we are sort of buying something for our home together to make life easier, or so we think. I don't know if that is a good thing to say. To arrange things, to make it work.
Pauline: To make the home work?
Maj: Ja, to make the home work.
Pauline: Is ordering your things a priority?
Maj: Ja, when you have five people, you need to. Maybe I am that kind of person that I always, sort of, I like it to be tidy, but it usually never is. That is my aim, but I find pleasure in finding things that keep it tidy. This can be good to keep things tidy. There are different kinds of people, but I am that kind of person.
Pauline: Different from whom?
Maj: From members of my family and other people around.

From a position of general antagonism in the 1970s, the global furniture market has witnessed a reinvigorated 'return' to international modernism and design 'classics' (Leslie and Reimer 2003a: 294). Since the 1990s, modern design is increasingly visible in furniture outlets, lifestyle magazines, city bars and restaurants in Europe and the United States. In no way a singular or static movement, current avatars of international modern design generally depart from a strict twentieth-century adherence to machine aesthetics, strict functionalism and tubular materials but tend to comport well with the 'light and airy' ranges of Ikea products and its ever-growing global popularity. An abiding legacy of the twentieth-century modern movement is the gendering of design. Classic modern styles of furniture are still most often associated with famous male architects and male designers, bolstered by an elitist refusal to acknowledge practices in interior decoration that espoused ornamentation craft or sentiment – commonly maligned as both kitsch and feminine (Leslie and Reimer 2003a, Stratigakos 2001, Sparke 1995).

With the new millennium, a shift is evident in international furniture retail, whereby attention has turned to the male consumer as untapped potential. This shift in focus is relatively new but follows other commercial trends that valorise emotional expression in interiors, explicitly subsuming colour into the modern palette. Let's be clear, this trend does not herald a reconfiguration of male and female domestic roles in any straightforward manner, but does point to a more active role that men are adopting in interior planning (Leslie and Reimer 2003a). With men taking a greater role in decorative schemes, traditional models of femininity are explicitly challenged and rejected, Leslie and Reimer contend (2003a). This is demonstrated, they argue, in international Ikea advertising where its furnishings and interior arrangements were framed as vanguard of not only modern styles but also female emancipation. In the United Kingdom, the 1990s 'chuck out your chintz' advertisements depicted women flinging away flowery wallpaper and patterned textiles in favour of 'modern style featuring light furniture, natural materials, and functional layouts while exhorting others to fight "chintz oppression with bold self-expression"' and were compared to feminist exhortations to 'burn your bra' by members of Ikea's advertising team (Leslie and Reimer 2003a: 303). Departing from traditional female dominance of interior decoration then, men are increasingly targeted in turn-of-the-millennium European and North American marketing to take an interest in and open their wallets to their domestic interiors and layouts. Judging from this example, the result is more nuanced than might at first be apparent. On the one hand emphasising commonality in taste can be integral to a couple's ideas of compatibility, but on the other finding clear agreement in preferences is not necessarily straightforward, which Maj demonstrates through her somewhat subtle use of emphasis. Visiting Ikea allows the couple to negotiate their preferences and arrive at a decision acceptable to both. As Maj and Thomas consider their home, their needs and the requirements of their family, they do so through constant to and fro to the Ikea store, demonstrating that the showrooms are held as a third party to this discussion. Inspiration is found through browsing, apprehending a point of comparison for standard, dependable and popular goods. As a representation of what is 'out there' and has been adopted and endorsed in several homes in their vicinity, Maj and Thomas can contrast the specificity of their requirements to what is generally available. They follow a routine: on completing one decorative job, they are provoked to attend to others. This provocation tends to be followed by a trip to Ikea to see what is on offer, to find deals. They inspect the catalogue and peruse the in-store room sets. They scrutinise their own domestic arrangements and often find them lacking. The showrooms also provide a template of current designer and professional thinking, the latest in unobtrusive storage gadgets or light fittings against which Maj and Thomas compare their own arrangements and shortcomings. The current undertaking for them concerned storage, and the couple spoke of several journeys looking for 'solutions'.

Domestic projects described in this way are platforms for the mobilisation of further action, but strikingly, the object for this dedicated activity is the home – to 'make the home work'. Home used in this sense is the bedrock on which successful living is founded and sediments the dyad that constructs it, allowing minor conflicts to be subsumed into a higher purpose. Through their own labour and with a certain amount of skill and consideration, Maj and Thomas project their needs, desires and aspirations into an ongoing project. The Ikea store is certainly projected as an ally by Maj, acting as a bulwark against extraneous financial demands, but Thomas has the last word in their choices. In this household, thrift is identified through the benign term 'good deals' that facilitate domestic maintenance, curb clutter, save money and assist a comfortable life in nice surroundings. For her household, this is particularly necessary with the recent new addition to the household and the series of adjustments this requires. Good deals help maintain clutter, and in so doing, contain the social boundaries that are potentially transgressed with new bodies in the home.

Social isolation and loneliness

Whereas sociality and compatibility can find expression through shopping trips, a visit to Ikea can consequently highlight unwelcome isolation. Karin, for example, told me that her middle-aged and singleton sister often calls to collect one of her nieces when embarking on a shopping trip to Ikea. The reason given is not only that she enjoys their company but also going to Ikea alone heightens her feelings of solitariness, which she prefers to alleviate. Ikea is for everyone, Karin joked, but maybe not for the unhappy singletons. Again, a friend told me how visiting Ikea can be a particularly difficult exercise after a romantic break-up. This point was again made in a conversation I had with Jessica. Jessica was a woman in her midthirties who worked as a schoolteacher for many years but had recently returned to third-level education when I met her. It was during a discussion that she expressed an issue that I began to recognise as common. It is not so much the store itself, it was not the queues, the maze-like channelling of people that was important to understand Ikea consumption, she said, but rather, it was the potential to spotlight the quality of her own relationships. She described a friend who had divorced but still returned to Ikea with her ex-husband and his parents while he shopped for furniture for his new apartment. This situation is unusual, she acknowledged, and it was partly explained by the need to borrow her large car to transport the flat-pack boxes. It also became the point on which her own reflections hinged. The trip, she conceded, was difficult because he was there to buy furniture for a new life without her, and she, on the other hand, was divesting their apartment of all his possessions.

Jessica: He was feeling the same experience as I had of being single and not really enjoying it but having to get things that are only for one. But it can be a nice feeling too because you can get things that you really wanted for yourself. But you have to be in that state of mind to enjoy it, especially in Ikea, where people are holding hands and all lovey dovey and planning for their future together. So it can be a major blow, I mean, if you are

	not quite there in yourself. I have actually brought my gay best friend a couple times to hold my hand and walk around a little bit. Which sounds ridiculous, but it helps.
Pauline:	Would you avoid going there if you were single and not quite happy about that?
Jessica:	Definitely. It would be too difficult. I have never seen a single person walking around – I've probably seen single people – but you know a person walking around by themselves in Ikea. It is always two and two, or you see people my age with a parent, like a guy with his mother. Women with toddlers, always in pairs, it is a very social thing. It can be hard to go in there if you don't feel . . . prepared for it.

Similarly, as Kristin said, 'I don't have children and probably never will, and I am OK with that. It isn't an issue for me, but sometimes when I see parents in Ikea in the children's section buying cots and things, there is a moment, I do think . . . "yeah"'.

Two elderly respondents I spoke to claimed that they could not afford much Ikea furniture but frequented the store for food and company. One retired male lorry driver who lived in an apartment in a nearby block in the area of Bredäng describes Ikea merchandise as beyond his finances, but he said the store is worth visiting for the meatballs. Another seventy-eight-year-old widow, Inger, who I met one morning in Ikea, said she liked to visit because of her curiosity about the new items on show. I visited Inger at home some days later, and it emerged that she worked part time looking after a pair of Russian siblings aged eight and ten. Their mother worked nights in some unidentified shift work, Inger explained, and the children were newly arrived in Sweden and did not yet attend school. The elder girl could understand a little English, so Inger communicated with her, piecing together the little that each of them knew. Neither child spoke Swedish, and so the bored children squabbled for several hours while I was there. Standing in her dressing gown at noon, Inger seemed overwhelmed with two lively youngsters in a small one-bedroomed house in which their bickering borne out of tedium played havoc with her tightly furnished home. Possessions, books, papers and knick-knacks on tables and shelves were roughly pushed aside by the children as they played a wrestling game, incomprehensible to either of us. Inger, meanwhile, spoke to me of her future and asked me about work – she had been a teacher, she tells me, and she could teach still. She was a widow and lived alone, although she has middle-aged offspring who look in on her every once in a while. She was anxious to move on, she informed me, to get a better job maybe, accrue more financial resources and acquire new experiences. Ikea visits provide Inger with somewhere to go when the children's mother collected her energetic youngsters. She described her visits to Ikea to me in terms of curiosity, but she was not alone in visiting the store for a change of scene. On my first day distributing leaflets and approaching customers, one of the staff members who manned the information desk pointed out the arrival of the elderly man who comes to Ikea every day of the year without fail simply to connect with people.

Research respondents spoke of visits to Ikea in terms of changing contexts in order to induce an alternative subjective experience or to assuage loneliness through immersion in homemaking activities. Take Lucas, a fifty-nine-year-old man, an engineer by training but who had worked as a teacher for many years. He had had been resettled in his present apartment for six months when I met him, which was situated on the southern suburbs of Stockholm. Married for thirty-six years, Lucas had recently divorced and he emailed me after he saw one of my circulated flyers in Ikea Kungens Kurva, inviting me to visit his 'bachelor pad'. Adjusting to his new life as a divorcee, Lucas purchased an empty white-walled apartment, and because of his particular affection for birch wood, he furnished it from stores in his local area, avoiding Ikea except for cutlery and crockery. He particularly states a preference for bright neutral colours, such as his white walls, which allow him to furnish without worrying about clashing fabrics and colour schemes, and he talked at length of the beauty of real wood, showing me some of his own carpentry skills manifested in a coffee table he made several years before. He remembered Ikea when it was first established in Stockholm: 'I remember when Ikea was founded, right. I was a little kid then (jag var ju liten grabb då), but you could say I have been there through Ikea's whole history'. Throughout his adult life, he has returned there for specific purchases. His bed is from Ikea. 'I think Ikea has affordable and comfortable beds, so I've always bought beds from Ikea, and then we have a Billy bookshelf as well.'

Lucas bought his bed in the early years of marriage, when Ikea was somewhat new, and has always continued to make these purchases in the store: he would always sleep best in his Ikea bed, he asserted. In contrast to the transience to which Ikea goods are credited, the bed was a permanent fixture, although his adult daughter constantly urged him to replace it.

> Well, it's not only furniture that I have bought but quite a bit of household appliances as well. Yes, it was probably Ikea that sprung to mind immediately then, well, cos it's so familiar, and there isn't only furniture but a lot of other stuff as well. You can just pick out what you want for a reasonable price.

Lucas was still often finding himself bereft of small necessary items such as saucepans. On the day he was in Ikea, it was to purchase a whisk, which he only realised he was without when he went to use it.

> I live alone now, for the last six months, and that's my first time living on my own in my life. I got divorced early last autumn from a woman I had lived with for thirty-six years. She left me last summer, and we had really been living together since 1971. She fell in love with someone else. It took me a few months to get over that ... it's hard to live alone, you know. The practical part is no problem, but to be eating alone at night, to be cooking on your own, is no fun either. My restaurant visits are a lot more frequent now than they were before.

It is not loneliness in the abstract that Lucas identifies but the embodied routines of ordinary domestic living that he constantly encounters that are reminders of his social isolation. It is through these routines that he comments he has forgotten how to live alone and that he reverts to the cinema or Internet to secure social interaction. The cinema was not successful, he remarks, because it enhanced his feelings of isolation, and he has since replaced it with occasional visits to Ikea to eat or browse. It is in conversation of his everyday life that he notices the material and social absences in his new routine.

> And there are other shops there. It has happened that I have had to run errands to some of the other shops and then I go into Ikea just for fun. Yes, that's probably the only time that I've done that and that was now that I was alone and that was probably just to not have to come back here on my own but then I'm not there to buy anything but just to look, to get out amongst people.

During fieldwork, newspaper articles occasionally drew attention to the high proportion of single-occupied homes in Stockholm. Compared to 28 per cent in the United States, the average single-occupancy in Stockholm is closer to 60 per cent (Klinenberg 2013: 213). Although there was a shortage of housing during my time in Stockholm, traditionally, the city's housing is marked by an abundance of small apartments that facilitate single life. For middle-class Swedes who came of age after the Million Programme, moving into one's own place became an expectation, and thereafter, a norm. And it was common for parents to enlist their children on housing waiting lists from a young age, allowing individuals to live alone earlier than might be the case elsewhere. And indeed, contrary to expectations of social isolation that may follow the single life, it was more common to see articles dedicated to the positive potential of living alone, such as allowing independence and freedom, than negative aspects, such as social isolation. In Klinenberg's small-scale research, he found something similar, recounting that his informants told him that a high number of Scandinavian populations live alone 'because we can' (Klinenberg 2013: 216). This is not to say that individuals such as Lucas who live alone are not lonely. Lucas clearly is, and he assuages isolation by visiting populated parts of the city and also by spending time in Ikea.

The logic of loneliness encourages some respondents to find fora where one can comfortably escape the penetrating solitude of home. Instead of browsing as a voyeuristic exercise, Lucas describes travelling to Ikea to wander, to eat in tandem with his wishes to change an inner landscape. At the root of his difficulties was the surging feeling of aloneness that arose through basic intimate domestic routines. Ordinary domestic moments heightened the piquancy of his isolation: 'Going to bed alone, making food, I was alone, sitting at the table, I was alone'. But his choice of Ikea is not merely culinary. One of the mainstays of his domestic scaffolding was his particular attachment to Ikea beds, which he and his ex-wife had for the life of their marriage. At frequent intervals during the interview, Lucas discussed at length the comfort of his bed, the many years he had it, his daughter's remonstrations with him to purchase a new one and his claiming ownership of it with the break-up of his marriage. Although there were other features that he claimed he changed as soon as he was living independently – 'There will be no mat under that dining table!' – the Ikea bed was a source of permanence and pride in its longevity and comfort over many years.

Towards the end of our first meeting, Lucas told me about his new girlfriend, a woman he met on the Internet who lived in Bulgaria. After a number of visits to Sophia, he recounted that his girlfriend urgently needed a new bed. Every time he visited, her daughter was moved out of the room she shared with her mother and onto the living room sofa bed. She clearly needed a bed, Lucas surmised, and he was scouring the Internet to find a suitable item. Unfortunately, he emailed me later, there is no Ikea in Bulgaria, with the closest store being in Greece, which would require van rental and some organisation to travel between countries. Although his girlfriend could doubtless nominate a store in Sophia where an acceptable bed could be purchased, Lucas was adamant that no other solution could be countenanced and was planning the trip during our final email exchange. In his hope to rejoin the community of domestic coupledom, Ikea beds form a bedrock of memories and experiences with which he plans to build a future.

The domestic nexus

Although the commercial world of Ikea warehouses and the private sphere of the home are most usually considered by my respondents as oppositional, the oscillation from one to the other, evoking new practices, new purchases and new domestic arrangements pitches both spheres as relational. Exceeding the bounds of commercial workings an emotional register is evoked through the animation and liveliness of the Ikea tableau, whereby ideal versions of domestic arrangement with actual householders are coalesced through movement in and out of these spaces in which experiences and emotions are shared.

Ongoing activities create or configure new ways of thinking and living that may be saturated with sentiment. Research participants report that visiting Ikea Kungens Kurva assumes heightened emotional impact for those experiencing difficult transitions, whereby encountering couples in lifelike settings and the vibrant showrooms providing housing theatre was specifically highlighted. But if feelings are not merely isolated and isolating but rather can entwine people together, then this process is mobilised through the traversal of boundaries to actively create an emotional state, such as the assuagement of loneliness or boredom. In this respect, structures of feeling are evoked through the dynamic tension that arises from the oscillation between actual and extra-domestic spheres, such as Ikea Kungens Kurva that represents alternative homes replete with householders, animated with the lively hum of domestic acquisition. Other people vitalise these spaces in palpable ways. For some, these experiences are negative and work to magnify social isolation, or conversely, to assuage the piercing loneliness of solitary living. For others still, transience is viewed as a release whereby Ikea products are employed to realise one's own domestic arrangements as brief. Apart from the wider implications of these trends is the freedom that is afforded from circulation rather than from acquisition, the emotional impact acquired through crossing into animated environments and engaging with the effigy.

What is interesting is that these measures are presented as individual, singular and isolated, rather than as part of a much broader constituency of shoppers that I suspect are present in Ikea at any one time. Although the connection between feelings of loneliness or just plain boredom and its linkages to the store are never explicitly stated, the impact of Ikea consumption as aggregate practice, the animation of the showrooms, resounding echoes of the hum of activity that persists in and around the showrooms that 'strive for the familiar', is relevant. Of course, Ikea showrooms are not alone in alleviating isolation in providing the go-to place when nowhere else feels right. In addition to but apart from greater commercial attention given to vibrancy, diversity, colour and affect is the impact of mobility bridging market centres and domestic spaces. Standing in a nexus of activities and social relations, Ikea showrooms are animated through the engaged activities of people reimagining homes, rebounding on intimate routines in profound ways.

Notes

1 'Hejdaa! Kom snart tillbaka. Kom när det passer dig! Dröm i lugn och ro eller mingla runt med andra heminredningsälskare.'
2 Adam Tassle Gerschel-Clarke, '"Peak Stuff" Why IKEA Is Shifting Towards New Business Models', Sustainable Brands, February 17, 2016, accessed 07/02/17, www.sustainablebrands.com/news_and_views/brand_innovation/adam_gerschel-clarke/peak_stuff_why_ikea_shifting_towards_new_busine. To combat environmental concerns, Ikea has pledged to stock only extended lifespan LED lightbulbs in stores by 2016. Other initiatives include allowing consumers to earn store credit by bringing back old Ikea furnishings that are then resold within the store for the price they were purchased from the consumer.
3 'Circular Ikea' marks this awareness, which focuses on the circulation of things from store to home and back again. It involves the valorisation of recycling, up-styling and regenerating.
4 Its dimensions are 35 cm by 45 cm by 78 cm.
5 It was imagined to sell in the region of thirty thousand examples in total but it sells that much in a week. The Product Council represents the group of Ikea staff that decides what product lines will be produced.
6 In 2017, PS will focus on small-space products, such as collapsible tables and a 'quillow' – a duvet that can fold up to be used as a cushion. The website HowHousingMatters claims that the average size of a two-bedroom apartment built in 2015 in Sweden is 580 square feet, down from 670 in 2001 (see http://howhousingmatters.org/october-5-2015/).
7 'Jag tror att det är få som köper bara Ikea, blandar gör nog de flesta. Jag tycker det är viktigt att blanda överhuvudtaget, för att det blir opersonligt annars. Jag vill mer leta efter en grej "åh det där blev jag förtjust i". Nej jag tror inte att jag skulle hitta allt på ett ställe. och så blir det lite utflykter och så blir det lite, "och den hittade jag där" och så.'
8 I am indebted to Johan Nilsson for clarification of this term.
9 It is striking that concurrent with the increased popularity of storage to contain the minutiae of personal possessions is the lively circulation of singular objects with history. For respondents such as Siri, the designation of biographical objects belongs to

second-hand goods rather than to new Ikea furniture, which she perceives as culminating in a dead end of waste. The past lives of second-hand things trump the future trajectories that new things make possible, and she identifies 'personality' in her bright-orange wardrobe. Second-hand objects manifest histories, events and memories, but these histories are not only localised to individual trajectories but also expand to include householding and national imaginaries more generally, marking these objects as personal within a broader collective imagining. Instead of hiding previous owners, this history is increasingly made explicit and enhances the object's value (Appelgren and Bohlin 2015), while social relationships and individual choices are forged within a broader domestic project. But circulation as an object of value is central here too because flea markets keep things moving and aid Siri in containing her clutter while introducing novelty. As Siri says, 'We try – I try – to minimize my stuff. I try. You cannot have too much stuff, but you have to clear out a bit too. If I buy a thing at the flea market, then you have to throw out a little bit, and I think this is good about flea markets. There is a little circulation in the stuff.'

References

Appelgren, Staffan and Anna Bohlin. 2015. "Growing in Motion: The Circulation of Used Things on Second-Hand Markets." *Culture Unbound: Journal of Current Cultural Research* 7 (1): 143–168.
Buchli, Victor. 2013. *An Anthropology of Architecture*. London: Bloomsbury.
Clarke, Alison J. 2010. "The Second Hand Brand: Borrowed Goods and Liquid Assets." In *Cultures of Commodity Branding: Archaeological and Anthropological Perspectives*, edited by Andrew Bevan and David Wengrow, 235–254. Walnut Creek, CA: Left Coast Press.
Coppola, Vincent. 2002. "CP+B Wants to Change How Consumers Buy Home Furnishings." *VNU eMedia*, 23.
Crang, Mike, Alex Hughes, Nicky Gregson, Lucy Norris, and Farid Ahamed. 2013. "Rethinking Governance and Value in Commodity Chains Through Global Recycling Networks." *Transactions of the Institute of British Geographers* 38 (1): 12–24.
Crowley, David. 2012. "From Homelessness to Homelessness." In *Atomic Dwelling: Anxiety, Domesticity and Postwar Architecture*, edited by Robin Schuldenfrei, 277–289. Abingdon and Oxon: Routledge.
Garvey, Pauline 2001. 'Organised Disorder: Moving furniture in Norwegian Homes' in *Home Possessions: Material Culture Behind Closed Doors*, edited by Daniel Miller. Oxford: Berg
Garvey, Pauline. 2013. "'Ikea sofas are like H&M trousers': The Potential of Sensuous Signs." *Journal of Business Anthropology* 2 (1): 75–92.
Garvey, Pauline. Forthcoming. "Furniture and Furnishings: Material Culture and Making the Modern." In *A Cultural History of the Home in the Modern Age*, edited by Despina Stratigakos. London: Bloomsbury Academic Press.
Gregson, Nicky, Mike Crang, Jennifer Laws, Tamlynn Fleetwood, and Helen Holmes. 2013. "Moving Up the Waste Hierarchy: Car Boot Sales, Reuse Exchange and the Challenges of Consumer Culture to Waste Prevention." *Resources Conservation and Recycling* 77: 97–107.
Gregson, Nicky, Mike Crang, Sara Fuller, and Helen Holmes. 2015. "Interrogating the Circular Economy: The Moral Economy of Resource Recovery in the EU." *Economy and Society* 44 (2): 218–243.
Gregson, Nicky, Alan Metcalfe, and Louise Crewe. 2007. "Moving Things Along: The Conduits and Practices of Divestment in Consumption." *Transactions of the Institute of British Geographers* 32 (2): 187–200.
Illouz, Eva. 2007. *Cold Intimacies: The Making of Emotional Capitalism*. Cambridge: Polity.

Isenhour, Cindy. 2010a. "Building Sustainable Societies: A Swedish Case Study on the Limits of Reflexive Modernization." *American Ethnologist* 37 (3): 511–525.

Isenhour, Cindy. 2010b. "On Conflicted Swedish Consumers, the Effort to Stop Shopping and Neoliberal Environmental Governance." *Journal of Consumer Behaviour* 9 (6): 454–469.

Joyce, Rosemary A. and Susan D. Gillespie, eds. 2015. *Things in Motion: Object Itineraries in Anthropological Practice*. Santa Fe: SAR Press.

Klinenberg, Eric. 2013. *Going Solo: The Extraordinary Rise and Surprising Appeal of Living Alone*. London: Duckworth Overlook.

Kristoffersson, Sara. 2014. *Design by IKEA: A Cultural History*. London: Bloomsbury.

Leslie, Deborah and Suzanne Reimer. 2003a. "Gender, Modern Design, and Home Consumption." *Environment and Planning D: Society and Space* 21: 293–316.

Leslie, Deborah and Suzanne Reimer. 2003b. "Fashioning Furniture: Restructuring the Furniture Commodity Chain." *Area* 35 (4): 427–437.

Löfgren, Orvar. 1994. "Consuming Interests." *Consumption and Identity*, edited by Jonathan Friedman, 36–52. Chur, Switzerland: Harwood Academic.

Norris, Lucy. 2008. "Recycling and Reincarnation: The Journeys of Indian Saris." *Mobilities* 3 (3): 415–436.

Sparke, Penny. 1995. *As Long as It's Pink: The Sexual Politics of Taste*. London, San Francisco: Pandora Press/Harper Collins.

Stratigakos, Despina. 2001. "Architects in Skirts: The Public Image of Women Architects in Wilhelmine Germany." *Journal of Architectural Education* 55 (2): 90–100.

Weiner, Annette B. 1992. *Inalienable Possessions: The Paradox of Keeping-While-Giving*. Berkeley: University of California Press.

Wickman, Kirsten. 1995. "The Traditional Heritage: IKEA and the Swedish Home." In *Swedish Folk Art: All Tradition Is Change*, edited by Barbo Klein and Mats Widbom, 221–233. New York: Harry N. Abrams in Association with Kulturhuset, Stockholm.

Wulff, Helena, ed. 2007. *The Emotions: A Cultural Reader*. Oxford: Berg.

EPILOGUE

Ikea – design dispersed[1]

After only a couple of weeks of in Stockholm, I began to recognise the familiar scarlet glass lamps that routinely stood on windowsills, the scented candles, ceramic plant pots as well as the bulky Karlanda sofas or Billy bookcases in houses and apartments, hotels, offices and civic buildings. I noticed the same process in Dublin when, only a year after Ikea opened, a proliferation of small decorative items seemed to seep into the public spaces of high-street cafes and small businesses. Gradually, the most ordinary of things – Ikea plant pots or fake greenery, cushions with busy patterns and tea-light holders – added familiar splashes of colour to those places where people congregated and spent time. Such small flourishes were immediately identifiable to me and others in my company as 'Ikea', colouring in those spaces that were previously unadorned and presenting Ikea goods as both inexpensive, pervasive and fungible yet sufficiently homelike to provide a sheen of informal comfort to small businesses. By such means, the pervasiveness, the sheer ubiquity and the commonality of Ikea merchandise creates small manifestations of habitual domesticity to non-familiar public places. Over a year or two, small Ikea cushions, blinds and decorative candles saturate diverse, standard cafés that pitch themselves as catering to the middle-of-the road customer, forming a common aesthetic layer and connecting unconnected places through an unassuming but familiar material culture.

At first glance, and as a juggernaut of furniture retail, Ikea represents one kind of hegemonic force, exerting its presence on global households. It's not surprising, then, that the seeming infinite homogeneity of Ikea products is propagated within the international media as a series of abstractions, iconic of global furniture retail and current market economies.[2] As an abstract entity it is difficult to grasp. With 389 stores worldwide visited by 915 million people in 2016,[3] Ikea's diverse constituents are found in the labyrinthine web of foundations, designers, producers, distributers, marketers and consumers. Ikea is located in global factories, service offices in Sweden and the Netherlands and countless regional offices. Objects move from the factories, warehouses and shop floors to households – and occasionally back again – and then on to other houses, storage facilities, Internet sites and waste disposal locales or auctions. Clearly, looking at Ikea expansively implies recognising that it cannot be fixed to the financial entity or brand alone, not as long as stores, warehouses, designers, personnel and goods in public and private spaces are indiscriminately called 'Ikea' by householders. More than this, Ikea products are built to traverse commercial and cultural boundaries; they circulate within and between corporate, institutional, cultural, popular and everyday settings. Respondents refer to merchandise, to the warehouse and to the design process indiscriminately as 'Ikea', so that on some occasions, I am unsure exactly to what they are referring. 'I have more Ikea than I thought' was a common refrain. Equally, as an abstraction, Ikea encompasses unspecific notions of design and designers – 'Ikea designers are very clever', I was frequently told. 'Really?' I responded. 'Any favourite designers?' No was the common answer, just the people who are 'there'. 'There?' I probed on one occasion. 'Älmhult?' 'Yeah', one woman answered, 'probably'.

A salient contribution to this book derives from recognition that markets are not as stable as they seem but instead are part of a 'conflictual cultural dynamic' (Slater 2003: 98).[4] How commercial products are marked, branded, understood and used is subject to a constant process of adjudication, incorporating myriad actors. In the midst of a plurality of goods and retail categories, products may appear provisional, their social meaning insecure. Producers, retailers and consumers are aware of this shifting ground and consider its potential alongside their own interventions in disputing or stabilising things (Slater 2003). Therefore if goods appear less graspable or less secure, it is not because they are more abstract, less material or reduced to an immaterial brand but because of heightened reflexivity on the part of an array of actors, such as business and retail associations, expert opinion, governmental voices and consumers who intervene in the social categorisation of things (Slater 2003)

In negotiating these dynamics, Slater argues, we require a 'more adequate social ontology' to understand the distinction by which things (here, designed things) are separate from the world as objects, as 'durable, stable, external to individuals, with determinate properties and relations to other objects' (2003: 96). What he terms 'social thingness' stands apart from brute materiality as a battleground amongst producers, retailers and consumers who all play a part in their social framing (Slater 2003: 96). Instead of a focus on the dematerialisation of the brand, the salient issue pertains to the inherent contractions between the seeming stability of brands amid the constant renovations to product ranges, the plural voices and actors involved in the categorisation and stabilisation of things (Slater 2003: 111). By this measure, it is the dynamics that are harnessed in perceiving Ikea as somewhat stable, graspable and understandable that is a core concern. To capture this dynamic, we must delve into how such things are embedded in the messy contours of everyday life.

Understanding markets requires a 'historical and ethnographic study of entanglements' (Miller 2002: 228), and viewing Ikea purely in terms of its commercial practice masks the actual and rich ethnographic complexity that otherwise pertains to Ikea in Stockholm. When my respondents speak of Ikea, they are referring to practices as much as products, and one cannot disentangle the processes by which inspiration is acquired, stores visited and contrasted with home, questions of fit and finance considered and worries of proportion and singularity judged. Although it is not surprising that brand is pivotal in understanding corporate culture, actual practices in consuming Ikea goods encompass a broader social range that may too easily be downgraded to a lower key in commercial research.

Ikea stands as a significant participant in the story of national domestic history, a member of the coalition of actors who together constituted ordinary, middle-of-the road national modernity. The varieties of modern design that blossomed during the twentieth century are significant because they solidified and concretised social policy within an architectural movement and its choreographed interior arrangement. Housing emerges as the bedrock of social imaginaries. There is a long history in Sweden of placing the vernacular home and domestic material culture as centre stage as a public object of inspection (Arrhenius 2010). As a 'model for modern life' (Arrhenius 2010: 140), housing exhibitions and displays of domestic design, harnessed as a governmental tool and employed by commercial organisations, are often 'highly politicized acts' (Tigerman 2015: 280). Far more than an insignificant trend, therefore, the Swedish modern aesthetic stood at the vanguard of housing modernization in Sweden in which politicians, designers, architects, planners and housewives were pivotal. No mere metaphor, homes for the people was the salient mechanism through which the People's Home as idiom for the Social Democratic state was imagined and realised. Domestic living and their related aesthetic orders literally entwined individual households with large-scale national aspiration. Ordinary objects, such as domestic furnishings, provided tangible proof of economic affluence, corporate success and political strategy. Less evident in historical treaties is the emphasis on the unassuming quality of design that was advanced at this time, purportedly characteristic of the Scandinavian home (Hård 1961).

Considering the profound placement of the minutiae of domestic material culture in the constitution of national domesticity and modernity, it is not so surprising that design is integral to the mutual branding of the Ikea corporation and Swedish state (Kristoffersson 2014: 84). Whereas Kristoffersson notes a 'stripped-down, functional and even blond' aesthetic as best suited to represent the nation (Kristoffersson 2014: 84), the perceived benign qualities of design as an interventional practice are striking. Democratic design is advanced through insignificant thrifty, mass-produced and standardised goods, and these designed goods become indices of a national capacity, inflected with a moral position. Whereas the production of Ikea wares is global in scale, the design of the furnishings is *always* based in Älmhult, thus symbolically rooting design with a distinct provenance. Emerging strongly, therefore, is the place of design in the active constitution of domesticity rather than as supplementary to it.

And yet, quoting Roland Barthes, Ikea has a singular origin but plural effects (1957). Despite a remarkably homogenous brand and elusive centre of gravity, what attracted me to this project are the myriad contradictions that seem to characterise Ikea consumption. As an avatar of modernist design, Ikea aesthetics appear securely rooted in twentieth-century trends, even though domestic interiors and the housing market have never been so much in flux. Ideas of democratic design and standardised mass consumption may speak to equality on the one hand but simultaneously mediate ambivalences regarding fiscal resources and class on the other. An Ikea-sourced modern aesthetic may promise a relaxed, efficient lifestyle, but it is only acquired through ongoing effort, investments in time and money that not only call into question ideas of efficiency but also – through hired storage space – stretch the boundaries of home in unprecedented ways. The valorisation of diversity offers liberal inclusive values but is popularly translated into national frameworks of meaning. Finally, although the rationalised corporate environment appears to hold an inverse relationship to domestic ideologies, at times, Ikea showrooms permit a sense of companionship that cannot be found at home.

From the perspective of my informants, then, defining immutable boundaries of 'Ikea' is untenable. As a professional and vernacular practice, and as a material network that encompasses people and things, Ikea implies aggregate domestic practice. There are myriad ways 'Ikea' percolates into public and private spheres, as an indefinable brand and as a physical thing, as a group of individuals or as an architecture. For my respondents, 'Ikea' is minimally fixed within the financial and legal institution but is perceived as practiced, largely, in the home. Ikea as a brand, set of artefacts, design ideas and human practices is continually circulating throughout all these chains, of which the home is one link. These dynamics throw up their own ambiguities, such as in tensions between design's normative potential – what design 'should be' on the one hand – and actual goods that mediate such abstractions with sentient individuals on the other. Ikea is thus dispersed through the material capillaries and ongoing appropriations that compose all aspects of commercial and cultural life.

Notes

1 This title derives from our special edition of 'Design Dispersed' originally discussed with editors and contributors in 2013 but finally published in the *Journal of Design History* (2016).
2 Contingencies of practice destabilise the homogeneity with which the Ikea corporation is credited. Ikea policy might dictate that the individual stores should endorse only socially responsible or environmental policies, but it is much more difficult to police these guidelines over three hundred stores. One such example was evident in the Dublin store one day: under the sign that Ikea sells only fair-trade coffee was another handwritten on paper that the coffee machine was broken. It was replaced by individual-sized packets of Nescafé gold blend.
3 'IKEA Retailing Facts and Figures', Inter IKEA Systems BV, accessed 25/03/17, http://franchisor.ikea.com/ikea-retailing-facts-and-figures-new/.

4 Several studies demonstrate how social entities are black-boxed into physical form, meaning that everyday products operate as devices that incorporate the human and non-human, the social, the technical and the 'complex interwoven social systems of provision' (Slater 2003: 101; see also Callon 2002; Latour 2007; Miller 2002). From this perspective, a car is a car not because of its physicality but because it holds together systems of provision, and categories of things are 'materialised' in stable form (Slater 2003: 101). Focus on Ikea in the abstract facilitates one type of black-boxing, representing an ideology of the market and harnessing a sense of stability within a context that is constantly changing. Relevant here is Callon et al's (2002) argument that through a series of actions and evaluations, a product is transformed, moved, evaluated, transacted and evaluated. As it is produced, branded and bought and sold by economic agents, its characteristics are open to change. Therefore, Callon argues, any product is always a process, always under evaluation and open to transformation. When its potential is stabilised, for even a brief period, it can be considered a 'good'. See also Miller (2002) for critique.

References

Arrhenius, Thordis. 2010. "The Vernacular on Display: Skansen Open-Air Museum in 1930s Stockholm." In *Swedish Modernism: Architecture, Consumption, and the Welfare State*, edited by Helena Mattsson and Sven-Olov Wallenstein. London: Black Dog Publishing.
Attfield, Judy. 2000. *Wild Things: The Material Culture of Everyday Life*. Oxford: Berg.
Barthes, Roland. 1957. *Mythologies*. New York: The Noonday Press, Farrar, Straus and Giroux.
Callon, Michel, Cécile Méadel, and Vololona Rabeharisoa. 2002. "The Economy of Qualities." *Economy and Society* 31 (2): 194–217.
Ekström, Karin. 2010. "Design and Consumption." In *Consumer Behaviour: A Nordic Perspective,* edited by Karin Ekström. Lund: Studentlitteratur.
Hård af Segerstad, Ulf. 1961. *Scandinavian Design*. London: Studio.
Kristoffersson, Sara. 2014. *Design by IKEA: A Cultural History*. London: Bloomsbury.
Latour, Bruno. 2007. *Reassembling the Social*. Hampshire: Oxford University Press.
Miller, Daniel. 2002. "Turning Callon the Right Way Up." *Economy and Society* 31 (2): 218–233.
Slater, Don. 2003. "Markets, Materiality and the 'New Economy'." In *Market Relations and the Competitive Process*, edited by Stan Metcalfe and Alan Warde, 95–113. Manchester: Manchester University Press.
Tigerman, Bobbye. 2015. "Editor's Introduction." *Design and Culture* 7 (3): 277–282.

INDEX

Acceptera! (Accept!) 70, 72; social democracy and 60–2
advertisements, Wes Anderson-directed IKEA 27
aesthetics 4, 125
agents/agency 38–9
Agunnaryd 4
Ahl, Zandra 104, 124
Allmännytta 63
allmoge style 92
Älmhult 2, 7, 32, 76–8, 86, 104, 130, 132, 150–1; Democratic Design Day in 80
Anderson, Benedict 6–7
animated surfaces 119–23
anti-Ikea 93
Appelgren, Staffan 105, 133–4, 146
architectural inspiration 17
Arrhenius, Tordis 13, 52, 56, 108, 151
Art and Agency (Gell) 38–9
art objects 38–9
artworks 38–9
aspirations, shared 67
atmospherics 37

bad taste 94–5
Ballymun 43, 83, 132
Baltic exhibition 56
Barthes, Roland 152
Beauty for All 58
behaviour, natural 39
Billy bookcases 6, 79, 115, 149
blank canvas 120
Blocket 31

blue denim 95
Bohlin, Anna 105, 122, 133–4
Bohlin, Jonas 57–8, 122
boredom 145
brand/branding: icons of 10; Ikea-in-the-abstract 9; living the 14; as material culture 11–12; narrative for 4; recognition of 83
brand capital 34
brandscaping models of inspiration 37–8
Brandt, Lotta 121
British Arts and Crafts movement 58–9
Buchli, Victor 11, 120, 130
Bulgaria 144
Burbank, California 28

capital/capitalism 10, 34, 90
Carl and Karin Larsson exhibit 70–1
Casa Cor 51–2
catalogue for IKEA 54, 84, 105, 115
causal nexus 38
children's room 109
China 10
Chinese style 117–18
circular economies 132
circular IKEA 131–3
circular markets 133
circulating sketches 28
Clarke, Alison 133
classic design 138
Clean House 53
clutter, suppression of 107–8
co-branded 8

Coca-Cola 10
Coca Globalization 4
cold spots 41
colour, valorisation of 124
colour codes 41
colourful environments 119–23
commercial potential of exhibitions 68
commercial products *vs.* second-hand goods 136
Committee for the Home 64
common material culture 81–2
Common Store Planning group 32, 40
community, confidence of 7
complex coordination 114
concrete chair 122
confidence of community 7
consensus and democracy 78–9
construction of home, regulation on 63–4
Consumer Agency 64, 66
consumption 3–4, 109
consumptionscape, hegemonic 77
contextualised scenes 52
cool abstract 121–2
Cooperative Consumer 62
coordination, complex 114
corporate culture 86
corporate influence of IKEA 5
corporate oxymorons 3
corporate theme and management strategy, diversity as 85–6
corporate transparency 80
Coupledom 6
Course *(Corson)* 61
craftsmanship, smart 123
cultural capital 90
cultural identity 11
cultural imaginary 37
culture: common material 81–2; corporate 86; corporate, diversity and emphasis on 86; IKEA, influence of 5; material 11–12, 59–63, 81–2; Nordic democratic 78
cumulative identity 133–4
curious reality 9
Czarniawska, Barbara 105

Dagens Nyheter 84
Dahlvig, Anders 85, 96–7
Daniels, Inge 105–6
Deakin, Garry 34, 40
decluttering 104–6
deep emotion 121–2
deliberate development of types 61
democracy 78–9

democratic culture, Nordic 78
democratic design 76–7, 79–81; design philosophy and 77; in international publications 80–1; philosophy of 81; politics and, unshackling of 77–8; post-standardisation and 88–91; shop-floor strategy and 80; social cartography of 96–7; ubiquity and, impact of 91–4
Democratic Design Day 80
Denmark 104
design 94; classic 138; democratic 76–7; everyday 81–3; in every detail 123; good 94; *Good Housing* for establishing norms of 65–6; legacies of 69–72; opinions about 90, 92; philosophy of 77; Scandinavian modern 80–1; twentieth-century, simplicity of the 120; *see also* democratic design
designed environments 29–30, 82–3
designed objects 29–30, 38–9
Design House Stockholm 82
Deutscher Werkbund 59
devotion 136
digital folkhemmet 85
Dimbério, Roberto 51–2
dimensions, secondary 85
diversity: corporate culture and, emphasis on 86; as corporate theme and management strategy 85–6; ethnic 83; as global and local value 86; Ikea-in-the-abstract 10; launch of 83–8; long live 84, 88; possessions and 110; social and material distinction manifested with 84–5; 'we' and 85
Djurgården 55
domestic consumption 109; home staging and 53; Kungens Kurva 66–8
domesticity: conceptions of 104; global 132; mise-en-scène for 52; normative 1–2, 130
domestic materiality 59
domestic nexus 131, 144–5
domestic space, shrinkage of 109–10
domestic sphere 131
domestic style, modern 106
domestic utensils 95–6
dramatic nexus 39
Drazin, Adam 2, 13, 111
dual processes of objectification and appropriation theory 11
Dublin Ikea 13, 34, 40, 41–5, 111, 132

economies: circular 132; emotional 119–23
Economist 78

Index

Edmonton, London 5
effigy 52–3; spatial 54–6
Ekström 14
Ekström, Karin 14, 16, 53, 68, 124
Ektorp sofa 33–4
Elmtaryd 4
emotional economies 119–23
emotions: deep 121–2; impact of 144–5
emptiness, aesthetic of 108
environments: colourful 119–23; designed 29–30, 82–3
equality 83, 96
ethnic diversity 83
eureka moment 37
everyday design 81–3
exhibitions 29, 52, 68
experience: fractured 130; inspiration and 46
expressive forms 122

Fallan, Kjetil 14, 70, 81, 104
family 43
fashion 97–8; seasonal 95, 131
Fight Club 6
fin de siècle utopianism 58–9
Finland 104
500 Days of Summer 6, 28–9
flat-pack furniture trade 131–2
flea markets 133–6; circular markets and 133; furniture at 133–4; old furniture at 134–5; popularity of 133
fluidity 130–1
Folke Ohlsson Dux sofas 31
folkhemmet 62–3
Form 27
Forsgren, Veronica 71
Foster, Robert 2–4, 9–11
founding of IKEA 4
'14 Truths about Home Staging' 69
fractured experience 130
Frank, Josef 108
Frank Lloyd Wright's Guggenheim Museum 17–18
free-trade agreements, international 78
Frohlich, David 111
function/functionalism 33, 60
Funkis 60
furniture: flat-pack trade 131–2; at flea markets 133–4; follow the 20; global market for 138; international retail of 139; old 134–5

Geijer, Gustaf 56
Gell, Alfred 38–9

gender 138–7; equality in 83
Germany 59
Giddens, Anthony 86
global corporation, IKEA as 8–9
global domesticity 132
Global Furniture Forum 132
global furniture market 138
globalization, Western 10
good design 94
Good Housing (God Bostad) 65–6, 109; design, for establishing norms of 65–6; storage solutions and 109–10
goods: quality of 120; recycled 134; second-hand 136; vintage 133
good taste 94–5
Government Official Report 81, 90
grand restructuring of housing 89
Gravity 28
Greece 144
grey generation 109
Guardian 5
Guggenheim Museum in New York 72
Gustav, King 16

halo effect 69
hanging out 137
Hansson, Per Albin 59–60, 62
Hård, Ulf 108
Hazelius, Artur 54–6
heaviness of US rustic styles 118
hegemonic consumptionscape 77
Helsingborg 2, 8, 32, 68–9, 76, 83
Hernried, Ateljé 64
Hetherington, Kevin 119
H55 67
von Hijne, Hans 17
H&M 82, 90, 96
Hög på Hus 69
Holm, Lennart 67
homemaking activities 142
Home Research Institute *(Hemmens Forskningsinstitut)* 63–4, 64
homes/housing: construction and interior decoration of, regulation on 63–4; feel at 130; grand restructuring of 89; ideal 58; model 56, 69; norms of 63–4; ordinary 104; post war policy 63, 89; price of 89–90; Scandinavian 108; social reform in the 56–9; *see also* home staging
home staging 13, 68–9, 69–70; domestic consumption and 53; recruitment for participating in 53–4; of storage solutions 116–19; strategies for 54–5
hooks 111–12

Hoskins, Leoni 132
hotspots 41
'House of Colour' 51
housing *see* homes/housing
housing theatre 13, 71–2
how much is right perspective 96
HSB *see* National Association of Tenants Savings and Building (HSB)
Huddinge municipality 16

iconographies of the modern 124–5
icons of brand 10
ideal home 58
identity 11, 133–4
Ikano 77
IKEA: anti- 93; catalogue 54, 84, 105, 115; circular 131–3; consumption, dualities underpinning 3–4; corporate influence of 5; cultural influence of 5; domestic utensils 95–6; experience 13, 37; founding of 4; as global corporation 8–9; as hegemonic consumptionscape 77; IKEA brand and 8; inspiration at 37–8; international following of 5; Janus-faced 8; mass production and 6–7; minimalism, throwing out 85; myth 76; North American market research 131–2; public trust in 7–8; romance and 6; showrooms at, setting up 32–7; stock market and 7; symbolic production in 5–6; vision of 2; *see also* Ikea-in-the-abstract
IKEA consumption 20
IKEA Family 79
IKEA Foundation 78
IKEA Group 9
IKEA Heights 28
IKEA Heights 28
IKEA idiom 28–9
IKEA-in-the-abstract 9–12, 46–7; brand and concept of IKEA 9; diversity 10; suppliers 9–10
Ikeaization 4
IKEA Museum 1
IKEA of Sweden AB 32
imagination/imaginary 37, 56
imitation 42
index of solidarity 114
informal markets 131–3
Ingka Holding 9
innovation and inspiration 37
inspiration: brandscaping and 37–8; evoking 29; experience and 46; at IKEA 37–8; innovation and 37; shopping for 136–7
intention, originating 39

Inter IKEA Systems BV 5, 9, 46–7, 121
interior decoration, regulation on 63–4
interiors, white-painted 120–1
international following of IKEA 5
international free-trade agreements 78
international furniture retail 139
internationally circulating sketches 28
international modernism 138
international publications 80–1
international spatial analyses 19
Internet 9, 41, 133
Interogo 9
Ireland 111
Irish Research Council for Humanities and Social Sciences 20
isolation, social 140–4

Janus-faced IKEA 8

Kamprad, Ingvar 2, 4, 7–8, 59, 80, 91
Kamprad family 9
Karlanda sofas 149
Karlstad sofas 33
Keane, Webb 11–12
Key, Ellen 58, 69–70
Keynesian economic policy 59–60
KF *see* Swedish Co-Operative Union (KF)
kitchen worktop (diskbänk) 93
Kleberg, Anna 104, 124
Klippan sofas 33, 79
Knutsson, Claes 17
Konsumentbladet 62
Kotler 37
Krause-Jensen, Jakob 86
Kristoffersson, Sara 8
Kumpulainen, Lea 32, 77, 80, 107
Kungens Kurva (King's Curve) 16–20, 27, 31, 33, 35–6, 47, 66–7, 72, 79, 86, 93, 95, 105, 131, 135, 137, 142; architectural inspiration for 17; domestic consumption and 66–8; emotional impact of visiting 144–5; IKEA consumption 20; international spatial analyses 19; location of 16; Million Programme 16–17; showrooms 19; upper floors 20

Lack table 122–3
lagom 95
Larsson, Carl 56–8
Larsson, Nils 8, 69, 76, 83–5, 120–1
Latin America 51
layer cake approach 105
lazy spaces 105
Le Corbusier 107

Index

legacies of design 69–72
Leslie, Deborah 37, 81, 95, 107, 131–2, 138–9
Liechtenstein foundation 9
lightness of Swedish style 118
Lijevalchs art gallery 56
Liljevalch Konsthall 5
Lindqvist 84, 86
Live 121
lived experience in model homes 69
living the brand 14
LO *see* trade union movement (LO)
Löfgren, Orvar 67, 105, 108, 121–2, 130
long live diversity 84, 88
Long Live Diversity campaign 82, 87
lonliness 140–4
Lot, Maíra 51
Lundgren 33–4
Luxembourg 9

Malaysia 4
Malefyt, Timothy Dwight de Waal 37, 49
Malmö 32, 40, 56
Malmsten, Carl 108
manifestly standard 94
Marius 30
market: neoliberal reforms 78; Nordic 51–2; North American research 131–2; stock 7; *see also* specific types of
mass production and IKEA 6–7
material culture: brand as 11–12; common 81–2; of social democracy 59–63
material distinction manifested with diversity 84–5
material forms 11
materialisation, social 12
material minutlae of storage solutions 110–16
Mathsson, Bruno 82, 108
Mattsson, Helena 53, 60, 63, 66, 68
McDonalisation 4
meaning over matter 10
meatballs, Swedish 8
metasymbol 10
Middle East 117
Milan 9, 80
milestone events 70
Miller, Daniel 11
Miller, Daniel 2, 10–11, 38, 105, 151, 153
Million Programme 16–17, 63, 143
mimetic capacity 41–2
minimalism, throwing out 85
mise-en-scène for domesticity 52

mixing and matching 121, 133–6
mobility and transition 131–2
model homes 56, 69
modern design, Scandinavian 80–1
modern domestic style 106
modernism, international 138
modern living 67
modern theme in showrooms 33
monolithic tyranny of aesthetics 4
More Beautiful Everyday Things (Vackare Vardagsvara) 59
Morning Breeze (Morgonbris) 62
Moscow 4
Mouffe, Chantal 79
Murphy, Keith 14
Museum of Modern Art 5
myth 76, 124

narrative for brand 4
National Association of Tenants Savings and Building (HSB) 64, 109
National Design Organisation 109
National Housing Board 65
National Institute for Consumer Affairs 64
National Museum and Moderna Museet 5
National Museum of Stockholm 57–8, 122–3
natural behaviour, imprint and parody of 39
neofunctionalism 123
neoliberal market reforms 78
neominimalism 123
Netherlands 150
New Star of Swedish modernity 70
New York 5, 17–18
New Yorker 5
Nike 4
1957 Without Borders exhibition 67–8
no-exit strategy 19
no junk mail sticker 83
Nordic democratic culture 78
Nordic display 27
Nordic market 51–2
Nordic Museum 55
Nordiska Galleriet 82
Norén, Alexander 69
normative domesticity 1–2, 130
North American market research 131–2
Norton, Edward 6

object institutions 52
objects: art 38–9; designed 29–30, 38–9
old furniture 134–5
Olsson, Emma 104, 124
ombildning 92

opinions about design 90, 92
options, safe 136
ordinary homes 104
originating intention 39
'Ornament and Crime' 107
Our Residence (Vår Bostad) 109
'Our Roots,' 'Our Story' and 'Your Stories' theme 1
own space 109

Paradise *(Paradiset)* 61
Paulsson, Gregor 58–9, 69–70
peak stuff 132
Penn, Alan 19
People's Home 60, 63, 70–1, 151; social democracy and 60
'Pick a Colour: The Ones That Make You Happy Are Always in Style!' 121
piggybacking 8
Pinakothek der Moderne in Munich 5
Poland 10
politics, unshackling of 77–8
possessions 110
post-politics 79
post-standardisation 88–91
post war housing policy 63, 89
price of housing 89–90
primary agency 38–9
Product Council 32, 132
prop room 28
publications, international 80–1
public trust in IKEA 7–8

quality 120, 123
quasi-utopian vision of the social democratic tradition 88

range 32–3, 90
Råskog 132
recognition of brand 83
recommendations 40
recruitment for participating in home staging 53–4
recycled goods 134
regulation on construction of home 63–4
Reilly, Gill 40
Reimer, Suzanne 37, 81, 95, 107, 131–2, 138–9
religious transcendence 136
Rent Hus 53
representational order 105
romance 6, 136
room for children 109

routines of decluttering 104–5
Royal Board of Residential Housing 109

safe options 136
Sandberg, Mark 27
satellite-based sketches 28
Saudi Arabia 9
Scandinavian-Ethnographic Collection 55
Scandinavian home 108
Scandinavian modern design 80–1
seasonal fashion 95, 131
secondary dimensions 85
second-hand goods 136
self-expression 121, 130, 139
service offices 2
setting up showrooms 32–43
shared aspiration 67
shelving 112–14
shop-floor strategy 80
shopping for inspiration 136–7
showrooms 28; brand capital in 34; housing theater in 72; at IKEA, setting up 32–7; Kungens Kurva (King's Curve) 19; modern theme in 33; range in 32–3; setting up 32–43; theme names in 33–4; as traps 39–43
simplicity of the twentieth-century design 120
Skansen 54–6, 62, 72; founding of 55–6; imagination, display of 56
Skärholmen 17, 88
sketches 28
Småland 7
Smålänning 91
small spaces 133
smart craftsmanship 123
social cartography of democratic design 96–7
social democracy: Acceptera! (Accept!) and 60–2; material culture of 59–63; 'People's Home' and 60; quasi-utopian vision of 88; twentieth-century housing provision and 60
Social Democrats 16, 59, 151
social distinction manifested with diversity 84–5
social isolation 140–4
social materialisation 12
social reform 56–9
sofas 33, 79, 149
solidarity, index of 114
space 109–10, 133
spatial effigy 54–6
standard fare 135

standard/standardisation: equality and 94–7; manifestly 94
Stockholm Association of Building Engineers 56
stock market 7
storage cupboards 112–14
storage solutions 103–25; animated surfaces and 119–23; benefits of 105; clutter, suppression of 107–8; *Good Housing* and 109–10; home staging of 116–19; material minutlae of 110–16; Swedish style and 123–35
study circles 64
stuga 62
Stureplan 91
styles: heaviness of US rustic 118; modern domestic 106; Swedish 106, 118, 123–5
suppliers 9–10
surfaces 110–11; animated 119–23; tired 121; unadorned 108
Sustainable Brand Insights 8
Svedberg, Elias 90
Svenska Slöjdföreningen 13
Svensk Byggtjänst 16–17, 71
Svensk Form 13, 27, 58–9
Svensk Tenn 82
swapping 133, 135
SWEA *see* Swedish Women's Educational Association (SWEA)
Sweden 8, 10, 13, 40, 150
Swedish-Brazilian Chamber of Commerce 51
Swedish Building Service (Byggtjänst) 16–17, 71, 109
Swedish Cooperative Movement 68
Swedish Co-Operative Union (KF) 64
Swedish equality 96
Swedish Form 13
Swedish Institute 8, 20
Swedish meatballs 8
Swedish model 63
Swedish modern 14, 70, 120, 151
Swedishness 8, 14, 32, 40
Swedish Social Democrats 59
Swedish Society for Art, Craft and Design 13, 64, 109
Swedish Society of Applied Arts 56
Swedish Society of Industrial Design 68
Swedish style 106; lightness of 118; storage solutions and 123–35
Swedish Women's Educational Association (SWEA) 71
symbolic production 5–6, 71

tableaux vivant 46–7
tactics 30
taste 94–5
Taussig, Michael 42, 107–8, 121
T-Bana train 85
'The 1900s – The Century of Design!' 122
theme names in showrooms 33–4
30 Rock 29
T-house at Engelbrektsplan 51
Tiden 62
tired surfaces 121
trade union movement (LO) 64
transition and mobility 131–2
transnational corporations 78–9
transparency in corporations 80
traps, showrooms as 39–43
triangle trade 135
Trivia range 90
trust in IKEA 7–8
TV4 53
twentieth-century design, simplicity of the 120
twentieth-century housing provision 60

ubiquity 94; democratic design and, impact of 91–4; managing 92–4
unadorned surface 108
United Kingdom 13, 40, 139
universal provision, ideals and benefits of 88–9
University College London 19
University of Gothenburg 7
upper floors of Kungens Kurva 20
Uppsala 53
urban myth 76
utensils, domestic 95–6
utopianism 58–9

Vackare Vardagsvara 59
valorisation of colour 124
values 86
Vaxholm sof 19
Victoria and Albert Museum 70
Vienna's Imperial Furniture Collection 5
vintage goods 133
Virtual Reality Centre for the Built Environment 19
vision of IKEA 2

Wallenstein, Sven-Olov 53, 60, 66
'we' 85
Wennerhag, Henrik 79
Werkbund, Deutscher 59

Wes Anderson-directed IKEA
  advertisements 27
Western capitalism 10
Western globalization 10
white-painted interiors 120–1
Without Borders exhibition 67–8
Woodward, Sophie 95–6
World Health Organisation 78

worldly things 8–9
World War II 59
Wørts, Erik 90

Young, Diana 120
YouTube 136

Zetterlund, Christina 60, 70, 81